GILBERT MURRAY'S
EURIPIDES

James Morwood is Dean of Wadham College, Oxford, translator of eleven of Euripides' plays in the Oxford World's Classics series, author of numerous Greek and Latin language books, and co-editor, with David Crane, of *Sheridan Studies* (1995).

Edyth Olive as Medea

GILBERT MURRAY'S

EURIPIDES

The Trojan Women and Other Plays

Introduction by
JAMES MORWOOD

BRISTOL
PHOENIX
PRESS

First published as individual volumes by Allen and Unwin:
Hippolytus 1902; *The Bacchae* 1904;
The Trojan Women 1905; *Electra* 1905;
Medea 1910

This new edition published by
Bristol Phoenix Press
an imprint of The Exeter Press
Reed Hall, Streatham Drive
Exeter, Devon, EX4 4QR

www.exeterpress.co.uk

British Library Cataloguing in Publication Data
A catalogue record for this book is available
from the British Library.

Paperback ISBN 1 904675 35 2
Hardback ISBN 1 904675 45 X

Printed in Great Britain by Antony Rowe, Chippenham

CONTENTS

PUBLISHER'S NOTE

For this new edition, the publisher has paginated the volume throughout at the foot of each page, in one consecutive sequence. A prominent open-face typeface has been used and it is to these page numbers that the Contents page and James Morwood's new introduction refer.

The much smaller original page numbers of the five original volumes from which the book has been reprinted have also been retained because Murray's notes at the end of each play refer to these.

INTRODUCTION

Gilbert Murray's translations of Greek tragedy, above all those of Euripides, met with considerable success in London and throughout England at the outset of the twentieth century. They also made a significant impact in the USA. They found favour with such distinguished theatre managers as Granville Barker and John Vedrenne, and appealed to actors of the calibre of Sybil Thorndike who was to write a moving and informative memoir of the translator.[1] They were praised by eminent judges, most notably George Bernard Shaw and William Archer, the famous critic and translator of Ibsen. By the 1920s, over a quarter of a million copies of Murray's translations of Euripides had been sold.[2] And they had a renewed life on the radio, which lasted well into the nineteen-fifties.[3]

The aim of this volume is to present five of the translations, together with Murray's introductions to them and notes on them, to a new generation. I have placed *Trojan Women* first because it strikes me as the translation that has lasted best, still possessed of real immediacy and power. The other plays follow in their probable order of composition by Euripides, i.e. *Medea*, *Hippolytus*, *Electra* and *Bacchae*. (The order of the first performances of Murray's translations goes *Hippolytus* [1904], *Trojan Women* [1905], *Electra* [1906], *Medea* [1907] and *Bacchae*

[1908].) The introductions and notes have been included because, while the style of the translations themselves does not vary much from play to play, Murray lays out a distinctive view of each tragedy in the prefatory material and then drives home the evidence for it in his notes. In addition, the notes give with a fine clarity and economy the necessary background to points in the translations that need elucidating.[4] They are ideally suited to the general reader and reflect Murray's passionate desire to popularise these great works of Greek culture.[5]

While it is clear that Murray's translations could prove highly effective in the theatre, their status as literature remains open to question. Murray certainly saw them as poetry in their own right and viewed himself as a poet.[6] A letter to his daughter Rosalind shows him as the poet-translator at work:

> I have done a chorus this morning bang through in one go. I began about 7, in bed, and did not get up but just lay working, and had it done by about 11.30. Then I got up, walked to the post; altered the last six lines, and wrote it out. When I looked at my watch and found it was 12.30, I had expected it to be about 10.[7]

Murray's friend Bernard Shaw always valued the translations highly, declaring as late as 1940 that they alone were likely to survive from the revolutionary burst of London playwriting through which he had lived.[8] In 1966, Murray's former student and academic friend Maurice Bowra wrote, in a rather less starry-eyed manner, that in the first decade of the twentieth century 'Murray's translations were almost the only new verse in English to command a large sale'.[9]

Bowra's assessment of them is in fact penetrating and not unsympathetic. At the same time, it is shot through with an ironic playfulness which reaches its apogee in the satire on the translations printed in the appendix to this introduction (xxxi–xxxv below).[10] 'Murray's success,' he writes, 'came the more easily because he presented Greek poetry to the English-speaking public in an idiom in which it felt at home. The high Victorian manner, mellifluously romantic and consciously archaic, was still regarded as the right way to write poetry . . . . If Murray had been a truly creative poet, he would not have been content with mere translations. It was because his poetic talent was essentially derivative that he never altered his style . . . . [T]o the last he kept astonishingly close to the Greek text, which was all the more remarkable since he used rhyme throughout.'[11] Murray himself wrote that, in order to achieve his aim of catching the 'spirit' of Euripides, 'the first thing needed was a work of painstaking scholarship, a work in which there should be no neglect of the letter in an attempt to snatch at the spirit, but, on the contrary, close study of the letter and careful tracking of the spirit by means of its subtleties'.[12] This is an admirable ambition.

Everyone who feels well-disposed towards Murray's translations has to take on board T.S. Eliot's 1920 denunciation of them ('Euripides and Professor Murray'), an essay which the poet-playwright preserved, as Mick Morris has pointed out,[13] in successive editions of his essays. 'Greek poetry,' writes Eliot, 'will never have the slightest vitalizing effect upon English poetry if it can only appear masquerading as a vulgar debasement of the eminently personal idiom of Swinburne .... [I]t is because Professor Murray has no creative instinct that he leaves Euripides quite dead.'[14] Devotees of Murray have unsurprisingly reacted with hostility to this condemnation. Bowra, for instance, refers to 'T.S.Eliot's sharp little judgement that "as a poet Mr Murray is merely a very insignificant follower of the pre-Raphaelite movement"'.[15] But it surely makes sense to view Eliot's broadside less as an attack on Murray than as the personal manifesto of a poet who some twenty years later was himself to try to bring Greek tragedy to the West End stage. In *The Family Reunion* (1939) and *The Elder Statesmen* (1958) (versions of Aeschylus' *Choephori* and Sophocles' *Oedipus at Colonus* respectively), for example, Eliot wanted to communicate the sacred through the familiar, the Furies outside the drawing room window, the 'incense in the latrine'.[16] Murray's translation of *Choephori* begins: 'O Warder Hermes of the world beneath, / Son of the Father who is lord of Death'. Eliot's version, by contrast, opens:

'[DENMAN *enters to draw the curtains.*] AMY. Not yet! I will ring for you. It is still quite light'.

There could be no meeting of minds here.

Eliot quotes three lines from Murray's *Medea* translation:

This thing undreamed of, sudden from on high,
Hath sapped my soul: I dazzle where I stand,
The cup of all life shattered in my hand . . .

they ever come to me, ever again' from his *Bacchae* (p. 431, lines 862–76), and the third to more or less any section of Murray's dialogue.

From Swinburne's *Atalanta in Calydon*:

1. When the hounds of spring are on winter's traces,
     The mother of months in meadow or plain
   Fills the shadows and windy places
     With lisp of leaves and ripple of rain;
   And the brown bright nightingale amorous
     Is half assuaged for Itylus,
   For the Thracian ships and the foreign faces,
     The tongueless vigil and all the pain.

2. And Pan by noon and Bacchus by night,
     Fleeter of foot than the fleet-foot kid,
   Follows with dancing and fills with delight
     The Maenad and the Bassarid;
   And soft as lips that laugh and hide
     The laughing leaves of the tree divide,
   And screen from seeing and leave in sight
     The god pursuing, the maiden hid.

From William Morris' *The Earthly Paradise* (1868–70), the start of *The Love of Alcestis*:

3. Midst sunny grass-clad meads that slope adown
   To lake Bœbius stands an ancient town,
   Where dwelt of old a lord of Thessaly,
   The son of Pheres and fair Clymene,
   Who had the name Admetus: long ago
   The dwellers by the lake have ceased to know

His name, because the world grows old, but then
He was accounted great among great men;
Young, strong, and godlike, lacking naught at all
Of gifts that unto royal men might fall
In those old simple days, before men went
To gather unseen harm and discontent,
Along with all the alien merchandize
That rich folk need, too restless to be wise.

One more point should be made before we move on to the individual plays. Murray's true instinct for the theatre comes across very clearly in his stage directions. Throughout the translations, they are models of their kind. There are, of course, notoriously few stage directions in Greek tragedy. Mainly they have to be inferred from what the characters say. Murray is a master of this, above all insisting on one of the great sound effects of tragedy when the Greek trumpet blows at line 1327 of *The Trojan Women* (p. 74). This is the cue, announced by Talthybius (p. 70, lines 1266–8), for Hecuba and the Trojan women to get to their feet and trudge off to the ships and their future. Modern editors ignore the trumpet call but Murray, the man of the theatre as well as the first Oxford Classical Texts editor of Euripides, knew that it was there.[26] It rings out to harrowing effect on the tape of a 1946 Val Gielgud production for the BBC (with Thorndike as Hecuba).[27] Indeed, the stage directions for the whole conclusion of this play are superbly responsive to Euripides' text and repay close attention (from p. 65 on).

*   *   *

The Trojan Women

Murray's *Trojan Women* was first performed at the Court Theatre in 1905. Though the translation soon established itself, the production was not a complete success. Murray himself commented that it was too painful and the critic of the *Times Literary Supplement* (14 April 1905), making use of the same word, pronounced the play 'too monotonously painful, and in the scenes of the child, positively heart-breaking'. Much the same had been said about Euripides' play by A.W. von Schlegel in 1808: 'the accumulation of helpless suffering . . . at last wearies us, and exhausts our compassion'.[28] We may feel that both Schlegel and the *TLS* critic were mistaken in their view and that it is indeed in its remorseless concentration on horror that the greatness of Euripides' tragedy lies.[29] Murray's translation was – and in my view continues to be – profoundly true to the spirit of the original. Edith Hall and Fiona Macintosh demonstrate that it implicitly reflects on the Boer War (1899–1902) and embodies Murray's pro-Boer sympathies.[30] In an essay in *The International Journal of Ethics* (1901) Murray had maintained that powerful nations inevitably sink into subhuman, barbaric treatment of their enemies and rivals. He was opposed to the war because he was convinced that the Boers had justice on their side. In addition, the appalling plight of the Boer women and children, dying in the concentration camps which the British had built to house them after destroying their homes and property, had been the subject of a famous speech by Henry Campbell-Bannerman, the leader of the Liberal opposition to the

Conservative government, on 14 June 1901.[31] The Boer subtext in Murray's translation howled forth its message, above all no doubt at line 764 (p. 45) where the point is rammed home by his addition of the word 'gentle': 'O, ye have found an anguish that outstrips / All tortures of the East, you gentle Greeks.'[32]

Hall and Macintosh go on to observe that Murray was the first modern scholar to see the play in a historical light and to relate its horrors to the Athenians' treatment of the inhabitants of the island of Melos in 416 BC, the year before Euripides' play was first performed.[33] They trawled pretty exhaustively through the relevant pre-1900 literature before reaching this conclusion and, even in the unlikely event that someone discovers that others had made the connection before Murray, the strong probability will remain that he was the first to make something significant out of it. In the introduction to his translation he says that the historian Thucydides selected the Melos episode, in which the Athenians had killed the male population of the island and sold the women and children into slavery, as 'the great crucial crime' of the Peloponnesian War. 'Not, of course,' says Murray, 'that we have in the *Troades* a case of political allusion. Far from it. Euripides does not mean Melos when he says Troy ... but he writes under the influence of a year which to him, as to Thucydides, had been filled full of indignant pity and dire foreboding.' The qualification is judicious. And Murray's historical and political linking of *The Trojan Women* to Melos has proved impossible to ignore in subsequent Euripidean literary scholarship.

Medea

Gilbert Murray had supported the women's suffrage movement since 1889 and Hall and Macintosh show convincingly
how his translation of *Medea*, staged at the Savoy Theatre
in 1907, 'was deliberately performed against the upsurge of
public interest in the movement'.[34] Murray was later to
challenge 'the universal assumption of our authorities that
Euripides was a notorious castigator of the female sex and
that the women of Athens naturally hated him'. He remarks,
'To us he seems an aggressive champion of women; more
aggressive, and certainly far more appreciative, than Plato.
Songs and speeches from the *Medea* are recited to-day at
suffragist meetings.'[35] However, the complete presentation
of the heroine, a mother who kills her children to take
vengeance upon her husband, surely makes this play a
disturbing manifesto for women's rights. Great libertarian
though Murray undoubtedly was, his view seems to have
been that the inheritance of Liberal Victorian England
should lead the world to enlightenment. This stance is not
without its problems. At his first Assembly meeting at the
League of Nations in 1921, he wrote that he 'was
conscious of many weaknesses in the Assembly: some
intrigue, some loquacity, a rather large proportion of small
dark Latin nations and so on'.[36] The spirit of Hellenism
was a guiding beacon for him too. After World War II he
told Arnold Toynbee, echoing Jason's words at *Medea*
536–41:

> I begin to feel that we should aim not at a peaceful law-
> abiding world but at some form of unity of Christian or

Hellenic civilisation, based of course on the Commonwealth, the United States and Western Europe but embracing India and Ceylon and whoever else may be willing to co-operate. I get the horrors when I think of enormous numbers of Russians, Chinese and possibly Arabs and of coloured people – a vast sea of barbarism round an island of Hellenism. I try to allow for prejudice, but somehow feel that our Hellenic or Christian standards and moral values are enormously precious approximations to truth.[37]

In his introduction to his translation of *Iphigenia in Tauris*, he remarks that the Greeks Orestes and Pylades 'stand out like heroes against the mob of cowardly little Taurians [Crimeans] in the Herdsman's speech'. It may sound a decidedly dubious compliment, but Murray's views on race surely made him the ideal translator to bring out the sinister barbaric side of a woman who comes from the far shores of the Black Sea. In his introduction to *Medea*, he remarks, 'An ordered and law-abiding Greek state was scarcely the place for the untamed Colchian'.[38] Murray's libertarian feminism combines with his ethnic stereotyping in a way which many may feel reflects the ambivalence of Euripides' original rather effectively.

Hippolytus

Hippolytus was one of the first three of Murray's translations to be published (as a single collection in 1902

– the others were *Bacchae* and Aristophanes' *Frogs*). It was the first to be staged, by Granville Barker at the Lyric Theatre in May 1904. Together with performances by Greek actors of Sophocles' *Electra* at the Court Theatre at the same time,[39] it launched a remarkable flowering of Greek drama on the stages of England and America.

But Murray's *Hippolytus* is of more than historical importance. It contains poetry that he never managed to surpass. There is, for example, a fine scope and power in his version of the Nurse's great tribute to Aphrodite (the Cyprian), the goddess of love, somewhat expanded from Euripides' original (p. 227, lines 447–50).

> She ranges with the stars of eve and morn,
> She wanders in the heaving of the sea,
> And all life lives from her. – Aye, this is she
> That sows Love's seed and brings Love's fruit to birth;
> And great Love's brethren are all we on earth!

The wonderful chorus 'Could I take me to some cavern for mine hiding' (pp. 240–41, lines 732–75) – which contains the famous line, 'The Apple-tree, the singing and the gold'[40] – is deservedly the best-known of his lyrics: he responds with poignant emotion to the Trozenian women's longing to escape. The comments on this song in his notes are well worth reading. And Granville Barker himself clearly made the messenger speech a real *tour de force*, declaiming it 'in a wildly exciting fashion'.[41] No wonder that the play was revived later in 1904 and again in 1906. It clearly worked most effectively as theatre.

Electra

Murray's *Electra* was first staged at the Court in 1906 and attracted encouraging audiences.[42] The translator was clearly fascinated by the psychology of the characters in this play, repeatedly returning to the subject in his introduction and notes. Invoking the name of Ibsen, he writes that Euripides 'seeks real people. And few attentive readers of this play can doubt that he has found them' (p. 289). Of Electra herself, he declares, 'There is, perhaps, no woman's character in the range of Greek tragedy so profoundly studied. Not Aeschylus' Clytemnestra, not Phaedra nor Medea.' (p. 290) The relationships between the play's characters have never been better analysed than by Murray. In his note on lines 998 ff. he also writes penetratingly of Euripides' Clytemnestra: it is 'a piteous and most real character that we have here, in this sad middle-aged woman, whose first words are an apology; controlling quickly her old fires, anxious to be as little hated as possible' (p. 378).

In the introduction his judicious and insightful comparison of the three Electra plays (the two eponymous works by Sophocles and Euripides and Aeschylus' *Choephori*) is a model of its kind. He writes chillingly – and surely rightly – of the role played by the unseen Apollo: 'He is no god of light; he is only a demon of old superstition, acting, among other influences, upon a sore-beset man [i.e. Orestes], and driving him towards a miscalled duty, the horror of which, when done, will unseat his reason'. (p. 289)

Murray certainly stuck a chord with the public with this translation. Writing in *The Nation* in 1910, Shaw observed that its popularity meant that 'we know the poem as if it were an English one'.[43] The playscript in fact proved his best seller: by the end of World War II it had sold 54,000 copies in the English edition alone.[44]

The Bacchae

Murray's *Bacchae* first reached the stage in 1908, though it had been published six years earlier as part of the trio of Murray's first translations of Greek drama. Bernard Shaw, impressed in particular by the way in which Murray's reading 'explored religious experiences and questions of moral identity' in terms remarkably similar to his own,[45] was bowled over by it. In the epigraph to his play *Major Barbara* (1905) he writes that Murray's 'English version of The Bacchae came into our dramatic literature with all the impulsive power of an original work'. Murray in fact has a starring role in Shaw's comedy as the Greek professor Cusins, while the Bacchae themselves also feature there too as the Salvation Army, described by Shaw in his preface as 'always in the wildest spirits, laughing, joking, singing, rejoicing, and tambourining'. The debt Shaw's play owes to Murray's 1902 volume of translations is illuminatingly analysed by Hall and Macintosh.[46]

Murray's introductory note insists on a religious, ritualistic and anthropological reading of the play. As Hall and Macintosh observe, much of what he has to say about Dionysus is 'new and very close to the discussions of the

Cambridge Ritualists and Jane Harrison's work in particular'.[47] And Murray acknowledges his debt: 'On points of ancient religion I have had the great advantage of frequent consultation with Miss J.E. Harrison'.[48] Murray's *Bacchae* translation was an excitingly innovatory project; and, interestingly enough, it is not only decidedly more accurate but also far more instinct with Dionysiac feeling than, for example, Colin Teevan's translation (2002) written for the National Theatre exactly a hundred years on.

* * *

In the story of the reception of Greek tragedy in the English-speaking world, Murray is a figure of immense importance. He unlocked the gates of the commercial theatre to its performance – and its performance in verse – on both sides of the Atlantic.[49] He brought immense personal prestige to the cause, especially after he became Regius Professor of Greek at Oxford in 1908. His Oxford text of all the complete plays of Euripides lent a huge scholarly weight to the enterprise;[50] for, passionate though he was about communicating Greek culture to the widest possible public, it was impossible to write him off as a mere popularizer. Most significantly of all, in the opening years of the twentieth century he laid down the terms on which scholars and public alike have viewed Greek drama throughout its duration and into the twenty-first. It was he who insisted, from the pulpit of the popular stage, on their political nature, their historical resonances, their social urgency, the religious and anthropological assumptions that permeate them, and the remarkable psychological truth in their delineation of character. And he insisted on all that as a man with a real instinct for the theatre who was deferred to by actors and directors alike.[51] His was the voice which had something wonderful and important to communicate and which could not be ignored.

WORKS CITED

Ackerman, Robert (1986) 'Euripides and Professor Murray', *The Classical Journal* 81 (April-May, 1986) 329–36.

Bierl, Anton, Calder, William M and Fowler, Robert L. (1991) *The Prussian and The Poet: The Letters of Ulrich von Wilamovitz-Moellendorff to Gilbert Murray (1894–1930)* (Hildesheim).

Blakeney, E.H. (1904), 'Murray's *Euripides*', *Classical Review* 18 (1984) 463–4.

Bowra, C.M. (1996) *Memories 1898–1939* (London).

Burian, Peter (2000) Olive Classe, *Encyclopedia of Literary Translation into English*, (London & Chicago) 981–3.

Calder, William M. [ed.] (1991) 'The Cambridge Ritualists Reconsidered', *Illinois Classical Studies*: Supplement Volume 2 (= *Illinois Studies in the History of Classical Scholarship*).

Easterling, P.E. (1997) 'Gilbert Murray's Reading of Euripides', *Colby Quarterly* XXXIII.2 (1997) 113–27.

Edwards, Paul A. (1987) *The World's Greatest Peace Play: The Chicago Little Theater Production of* The Trojan Women *1915, "Putting on the Greeks": Euripidean Tragedy and the Twentieth Century American Theatre* (Diss. Colorado)

Eliot, T.S. (1951) 'Euripides and Professor Murray' in *Selected Essays* (London) 59–64.

Goldhill, Simon (2002) *Who needs Greek? Contests in the Cultural History of Hellenism* (Cambridge)

Gregory, Justina (1999–2000) 'Comic Elements in Euripides', *Illinois Classical Studies* 24–25 (1999–2000) 59–74.

Hall, Edith and Macintosh, Fiona (2005) 'The Shavian Euripides and the New Euripidean Shaw: Greek Tragedy and the New Drama' (= ch.17) in their *Greek Tragedy and the British Theatre, 1660–1914* (Oxford).

Kennedy, Dennis (1985) *Granville Barker and the Dream of Theatre* (Cambridge).

INTRODUCTION

Lloyd-Jones, Hugh (1982) *Blood for the Ghosts: Classical Influences in the Nineteenth and Twentieth Centuries* (London).

Macintosh, Fiona (1997) 'Tragedy in performance: nineteenth- and twentieth-century productions' in P.E.Easterling [ed.] *The Cambridge Companion to Greek Tragedy*, 284–323 (Cambridge).

Morwood, James (2002) *The Plays of Euripides* (Bristol).

Murray, Gilbert (1933) *Aristophanes: A Study* (Oxford).

___ (1902) *Euripides Translated into English Rhyming Verse* (London).

___ (1913) *Euripides and His Age* (London & New York).

Schlegel, A.W. von (1846), tr. John Black, *A Course of Lectures on Dramatic Art and Literature* (London).

Sidwell, Keith (2001), 'Melos and the *Trojan Women*' in *Essays on Trojan Women*, David Stuttard and Tamsin Sasha [eds] (York).

Stray, Christopher (1998) *Classics Transformed: Schools, Universities, and Society in England, 1830–1960* (Oxford).

Thorndike, Sybil (1960) with Lewis Casson, 'The Theatre and Gilbert Murray' in Jane Smith and Arnold Toynbee [eds] *Gilbert Murray: An Unfinished Autobiography* (London).

West, Francis (1984) *Gilbert Murray, A Life* (London, Canberra & New York).

Wilson, Duncan (1987) *Gilbert Murray OM, 1866–1957* (Oxford).

ENDNOTES

I am grateful to John Betts, William M.Calder III, Christopher Collard, Edith Hall, Ian McAuslan, Fiona Macintosh, C.W. Marshall, David Raeburn, Christopher Stray, John Taylor, Christopher Tyerman and Chris Vervain for their valuable help with this introduction. Any defects that remain are my responsibility, not theirs.

1. Thorndike acted Artemis in the first Manchester production of *Hippolytus* in 1908. To her inquiry as to how to play the part, Murray responded, 'I want you to be like an opalescent dawn'; 'enlightening,' the actress later commented, 'but exceedingly difficult in performance.' (Thorndike [1960] 158).
2. 'By 1954, nearly half a million copies of [all] the translations had been sold worldwide.' (Burian [2000] 982).
3. 'Between 1936 and 1956 there were 26 broadcast performances of 11 plays.' (Burian, note 2 above; and see also Wilson [1987] 454). West (1984) ch. 5 and Wilson (1987) chs 9 and 13 both give excellent accounts of the performance history of Murray's translations. In March 2003 a showcase production of Murray's translation of Sophocles' *Antigone* was successfully staged at the Royal Academy of Dramatic Art in London, directed by Nona Shepphard.
4. In his *Bacchae*, the introductory note launches the notes.
5. In his review of the first collection of translations to be published, Blakeney (1904) 463 gives due praise, writing, 'Some notes, slight in texture but always useful, and occasionally packed with suggestive criticism, have been added; and an Introduction has been prefixed of which, perhaps, it is not too much to say that it would be difficult to find anything at once saner, more illuminating, or more sympathetic.'
6. West (1984) 98.
7. MS Gilbert Murray 455 86, 9 July 1900, quoted in Wilson (1987) 107.
8. West (1984) 100.
9. Bowra (1966) 216.

10. For a less sympathetic though still ambivalent estimate, see Lloyd-Jones (1982) 204–8.
11. Bowra (1966) 216–7.
12. Murray (1902) vii-viii. He adds, 'I am bound to confess that, the groundwork of careful translation once laid, I have thought no more about anything but the poetry. I have often laboured long to express a slight shade of meaning or of beauty which I felt lurking in some particular word or cadence; and, on the other hand, I have often changed metaphors, altered the shapes of sentences, and the like' (viii-ix).
13. In a paper entitled '"He leaves Euripides quite dead": Gilbert Murray and the Art of Translation' given at the Classical Association conference at Warwick in 2003; see also Ackermann (1986).
14. Eliot (1951) 61 and 64.
15. Bowra (1966) 217; Eliot (1951) 62.
16. The last quotation is from Eliot's verse play *Murder in the Cathedral* (1935).
17. Eliot (1951) 61.
18. The 'cold white thing' may be from Murray's translation of *Hippolytus* 786 (the Greek simply means 'wretched corpse'). If so, the emotive cries referred to in the story are conspicuous by their absence! Christopher Stray's unpublished version of this deathless line is: 'Drunk! And a cold white wine within the fridge!'
19. Bowra (1966) 218.
20. Burian sums up the matter thus: 'In the preface to Murray's first volume of translations, the stated aim is "to put before English readers a translation of some very beautiful poetry", and poetry remains his chief concern: "the groundwork of careful translation once laid, I have thought no more of anything but the poetry." Murray's emphasis on "poetic beauties" reflects a sincere desire to convey, as well as the meaning of the words, the emotive power of the Greek text to a wide audience. For Murray this meant freeing his translations from the constraints of the strictly literal in favour of his own conception of the "spirit" of the orginal ...' (Burian [2000] 982).
21. Bowra (1966) 218 and 217.
22. Thorndike (1969) 153. Murray, it may be noted, had a famously beautiful speaking voice. (Wilson [1987] 105).
23. West (1984) 98.
24. Thorndike (1960) 163. For Granville Barker's uncertainty about how to stage the chorus, see Kennedy (1985) 42–4.
25. Murray (1913) 202–3

26. Patricia E. Easterling (Easterling [1997] 115) helpfully quotes a passage from Murray's Latin preface to volume I of his Oxford text, in which he sums up the qualities the interpreter of Euripides needs: he will not succeed unless (among other things) '*artis scaenicae aliquid sapiat*' (he knows something of the art of theatre).

27. The tape is held by the Archive of Performance of Greek and Roman Drama at Oxford University. The Archive possesses a copy of Murray's *Electra* (donated by David Harvey) annotated by the translator's own hand. Beside Electra's name at line 682 he has written, 'beating the ground'. It is clear from line 678 of the original play that this is what she should be doing; but Murray has arrestingly delayed the effect until Electra demands of her father's spirit beneath the earth, 'Dost hear us yet . . .?'

28. Schlegel (1846) 136.

29. Morwood (2002) 45–7.

30. Hall and Macintosh (2005). The rest of this paragraph is based on their account.

31. He became prime minister in 1905.

32. The play has remained highly political. A production of Murray's translation at the Chicago Little Theater in 1915 was financed by the English to try to end American sympathy with the Germans and reluctance to enter World War I. It was performed before 33,000 people in thirty-one cities over a fifteen week period. In 1941 the Experimental Theater under the direction of Margaret Webster opened their production of *The Trojan Women* at the Cort Theatre with Dame May Whitty as Hecuba, Walter Slezak as Menelaus and Margaret Webster as Andromache. Murray's translation was used but the Poseidon/Athena prologue was replaced with a modern one by Robert Turney. Modern clothes were worn. The Greek soldiers were dressed in Nazi uniforms and the women were refugees stuck on a road in northern France. It received mixed reviews but popular reaction was generally favourable.

At the time of the Vietnam War, in December 1963 the play was staged by the Greek director Michael Cacoyannis at the Circle in the Square in New York. The production used the Edith Hamilton translation, with Mildred Dunnock as Hecuba, Carrie Nye as Cassandra and Joyce Ebert as Andromache. The National Repertory Theatre under the direction of Eva La Gallienne and Margaret Webster included *Trojan Women* in its repertory for 1966. (I am indebted to William M. Calder III for the information in this note.)

33. For the case against relating the Melos episode to *The Trojan Women*, see Sidwell (2001) 30–44.
34. Hall and Macintosh (2005) ch. 17.
35. Murray (1913) 32.
36. West (1984) 190 and 229.
37. West (1984) 235.
38. In the first production, Edyth Olive, the actress playing Medea, was dressed in a beautifully simple Greek peplos decorated with the Greek key pattern (see frontispiece). Was this intended to suggest that her assimilation to Greek culture was only costume deep?
39. Hall and Macintosh (2005) ch. 17. It was also being performed in Greek by schoolboys at Bradfield College as part of a tradition of the open-air staging of Greek plays in the original which has lasted till this day.
40. It constitutes both the epigraph and the final sentence of John Galsworthy's 1916 'tale' *The Apple Tree*.
41. West (1984) 89. Barker's performance 'sent "a lady in the pit into hysterics" (*Pall Mall Gazette* 19 Oct. 1904:11), requiring her "to be conducted sobbing from the house" (*Daily Graphic* same date: 266)'. (Kennedy [1985] 44). Murray calls the messenger a henchman, and the henchman calls himself a 'thrall', a word some may feel that the translator decidedly overworks.
42. In February six performances earned almost £588, of which Murray received just over £44. (West [1984] 90). These are healthy figures. Kennedy comments that 'the Greek plays never could achieve the popularity of Shaw or some of the realist pieces at the Court. Yet they achieved a sizable matinee audience, and a persistent one' (Kennedy [1985] 50).
43. VI.25, 19 March 1910: 969, quoted in Goldhill (2002) 169.
44. Burian (2000) 982
45. Hall and Macintosh (2005) ch. 17.
46. Note 45 above.
47. Note 45 above. For the work of the Cambridge Ritualists, among whom Murray is numbered, see Calder (1991). A brief summary can be found at Stray (1998) 161–2. Harrison was the pre-eminent member of the group.
48. Murray (1902) vii. Harrison had designed the statues of the goddesses for the 1904 *Hippolytus*, the only aspect of that production which won A.E. Housman's whole-hearted approval (Wilson [1987] 105).

49. In 1915 Granville Barker took *The Trojan Women* and *Iphigenia in Tauris* on a tour to America, performing the latter in the open air at Harvard, Princeton, the University of Pennsylvania and at the College of the City of New York. Fiona Macintosh remarks that 'it became the first professional production of a Greek play in America to be critically acclaimed', quoting the *New York Mirror* as considering that the work emerged 'living, with the glory of a drama that has never, at any time, been dead'. (Macintosh [1997] 303–4). See also note 32 above for the 1915 Chicago Little Theater production. Of the initial productions, Kennedy remarks that 'in three years the Vedrenne-Barker seasons had reclaimed a great playwright for the stage, and by extension rescued an entire literature from theatrical oblivion'. (Kennedy [1985] 49).

50. The public was of course then unaware of how enormously the great German scholar Wilamowitz had contributed to the success of the enterprise. (Bierl, Calder and Fowler [1991] *passim*).

51. He was not regarded as a professional dramatist. He did not need the income from this aspect of his work. He was seen as the 'scholar-poet' (West [1984] 105).

APPENDIX

If parody is the most sincere of tributes, it seems appropriate to conclude, in place of a satyr play, with an excerpt from an unpublished poem of 1941 by Maurice Bowra.[1] Bowra had a genuine admiration for Murray as a teacher, a scholar and a proponent of Hellenism. His memoir of him concludes with the sentence, 'It was impossible to know him without loving him, or to see him without being revived and encouraged and inspired'.[2] We may wonder whether he would have felt so warmly towards him had he known how Murray had sabotaged his chances when he was a candidate for the Oxford professorship of Greek in 1936. Murray, the outgoing holder of the Chair, wrote to the Prime Minister Stanley Baldwin, 'I have been to a paper of Bowra's at the Philological and to an open lecture of his, and I have come reluctantly to the conclusion that his would not be a good appointment. It is not so much that he sometimes makes mistakes or rash statements. It is a certain lack of quality, precision, and reality in his scholarship as a whole.'[3] After the appointment had been made, Murray wrote to another unsuccessful candidate, 'I did my best to put before Baldwin the case for each'[4] – a somewhat disingenuous comment.

The poem is entitled *Gilbert and Mary: an eclogue*. The lubricious nature of the lyrics is an entertainingly malicious touch on Bowra's part, since Murray abhorred obscenity.

When he was translating the comedies of Aristophanes (three of them, *The Birds*, *Clouds* and *The Frogs*) and found himself faced with what his friend J.W. Mackail called the 'magnificent indecency'[5] of the comic poet, he simply cut it out.[6] In Bowra's poem, Murray's wife, Lady Mary, upbraids him for having visited a lady of low repute. Gilbert gives three different explanations. The third is that he went to find

> Wild honey and the East and loveliness.
> She was reciting in a satin dress
> Some version that I wrote for her, a thing
> Full of sharp anguish and old suffering.

This 'thing' Gilbert goes on to recite:

> Few and far, far and few,
>   Words of a whirling daughter,
> A wet wild sheet and a flowing sea,
> And a blossom of virgin modesty
> That opes its lips when the blade strikes true
>   And flows with the flowing water.
> Few and far, far and few,
>   A stroke from a spear-shaft falling
> Brings back the dreams of the days that were,
> The languid lips and the flowerlike hair,
> The limbs that gleam like the falling dew
>   And a voice in the midnight calling.

Awake, O my feet, awake,
    With glitter of trembling toes.
        Let the lithe long fingers rove
        On the bosky Mount of Love,
    Where the wild wan insect goes
And the fur is soft in the brake.
Hymen, O Hymen pale,
    Yield to the bold attack.
        Let the taut bow-string snap
        To the roar of a thunder-clap
    When the beast lies down on its back
And the bites and the wrestlings fail.[7]

MARY.
  Your melody recalls the days of old,
  The apple-juice, the peanuts and the cold,
  And that so nameless and so shining thing
  That made us sick for love and love-making.
  You would hold speeches upon women's rights
  And bid the children gather round at nights
  For tenants' pudding and warm lemonade.
  Good Dr Zavitz often with us stayed
  And lectured to the Meeting of the Friends.
  Then you translated 'Where the Rainbow Ends'
  Into Greek verse. They often acted it,
  And good Jane Harrison watched it from the pit.
  Oh far-off happy days of minstrelsy!
  Greek for the Greekless, O abide with me!

Come, let us see if we cannot restore
Some blissful moment of the days of yore.
You shall not find, for all that you have said,
Death and a cold white thing within the bed.
O tender twining arms, and O the sweet
Falling asleep together in the heat!
Our fate is calling — let us follow quick.

GILBERT.
Mary, you've mixed the Horlicks[8] much too thick.

NOTES

1. An edition of Maurice Bowra's satirical verse is in preparation, edited by Henry Hardy, to be published by Robert Dugdale.
2. Bowra (1966) 229.
3. Public Record Office <MP 77/138-40: CC TS>.
4. Wilson (1987) 328.
5. West (1984) 219.
6. Yet he was certainly alive to it. Modern productions of *Lysistrata*, he says in 1933, achieve little because they 'lack the two things which make [it] not merely a tolerable but an inspiring work of art. They lack utterly the background of traditional ritual; a ritual to which fertility was the main object of desire, and the phallus the recognized symbol of fertility. Without that background the play becomes consciously obscene instead of simply taking the indecency in its stride' (Murray [1933] 176).

   It is interesting too that he eliminates the one obvious joke in Greek tragedy (*The Trojan Women*, 1049-50). Hecuba here asks Menelaus not to let Helen travel back to Greece on the same boat as himself, to which he replies, 'Why? Has she put on weight since I saw her last?'. Murray, surely mistakenly, moralizes the idea: 'How? Shall the ship go heavier for her sin?'. (Gregory [1999-2000] 69-72) argues that it isn't a joke.) Unsurprisingly Murray did not translate Euripides' at times obscene satyr play, *Cyclops*. See Bowra (1966) 229.

7. The last five lines seem to be based on the following passage from Murray's 1947 translation of Sophocles' *Women of Trachis* (he called it *The Wife of Heracles*) in which the Chorus describe the fight between Heracles and a monstrous river god over the virgin Deianeira (517ff.):

> All was a thud of fists, a deadly whirr
> Of arrows, clash of wild-beast horn on horn,
> Grapple of writhing trunks, brows battle-torn
> And one overmastering groan.

I am grateful to C.W. Marshall for making this connection. If it is right, Bowra must have known at least this part of Murray's translation some time before it was published.

8. An English hot drink with relaxing properties.

EURIPIDES

THE TROJAN WOMEN

Translated into English rhyming verse
with Explanatory Notes

by
GILBERT MURRAY

London
GEORGE ALLEN & UNWIN LTD
Museum Street

INTRODUCTORY NOTE

JUDGED by common standards, the *Troädes* is far from a perfect play; it is scarcely even a good play. It is an intense study of one great situation, with little plot, little construction, little or no relief or variety. The only movement of the drama is a gradual extinguishing of all the familiar lights of human life, with, perhaps, at the end, a suggestion that in the utterness of night, when all fears of a possible worse thing are passed, there is in some sense peace and even glory. But the situation itself has at least this dramatic value, that it is different from what it seems.

The consummation of a great conquest, a thing celebrated in paeans and thanksgivings, the very height of the day-dreams of unregenerate man—it seems to be a great joy, and it is in truth a great misery. It is conquest seen when the thrill of battle is over, and nothing remains but to wait and think. We feel in the background the presence of the conquerors, sinister and disappointed phantoms; of the conquered men, after long torment, now resting in death. But the living drama for Euripides lay in the conquered women. It is from them that he has named his play and built up his scheme of parts: four figures clearly lit and heroic, the others in varying grades of characterisation, nameless and barely articulate, mere half-heard voices of an eternal sorrow.

Indeed, the most usual condemnation of the play is not that it is dull, but that it is too harrowing; that scene after scene passes beyond the due limits of tragic art. There are points to be pleaded against this criticism. The very beauty of the most fearful scenes, in spite of their fearfulness, is one; the quick comfort of the lyrics is another, falling like a spell of peace when the strain is too hard to bear (cf. p. 89). But the main defence is that, like many of the greatest works of art, the *Troädes* is something more than art. It is also a prophecy, a bearing of witness. And the prophet, bound to deliver his message, walks outside the regular ways of the artist.

For some time before the *Troädes* was produced, Athens, now entirely in the hands of the War Party, had been engaged in an enterprise which, though on military grounds defensible, was bitterly resented by the more humane minority, and has been selected by Thucydides as the great crucial crime of the war. She had succeeded in compelling the neutral Dorian island of Mêlos to take up arms against her, and after a long seige had conquered the quiet and immemorially ancient town, massacred the men and sold the women and children into slavery. Mêlos fell in the autumn of 416 B.C. The *Troädes* was produced in the following spring. And while the gods of the prologue were prophesying destruction at sea for the sackers of Troy, the fleet of the sackers of Mêlos, flushed with conquest and marked by a slight but unforgettable taint of sacrilege, was actually preparing to set sail for its fatal enterprise against Sicily.

Not, of course, that we have in the *Troädes* a case of political allusion. Far from it. Euripides does not mean Mêlos when he says Troy, nor mean Alcibiades' fleet when he speaks of Agamemnon's. But he writes under the influence of a year which to him, as to Thucydides, had been filled full of indignant pity and of dire foreboding. This tragedy is perhaps, in European literature, the first great expression of the spirit of pity for mankind exalted into a moving principle; a principle which has made the most precious, and possibly the most destructive, elements of innumerable rebellions, revolutions, and martyrdoms, and of at least two great religions.

Pity is a rebel passion. Its hand is against the strong, against the organised force of society, against conventional sanctions and accepted Gods. It is the Kingdom of Heaven within us fighting against the brute powers of the world; and it is apt to have those qualities of unreason, of contempt for the counting of costs and the balancing of sacrifices, of recklessness, and even, in the last resort, of ruthlessness, which so often mark the paths of heavenly things and the doings of the children of light. It brings not peace, but a sword.

So it was with Euripides. The *Troädes* itself has indeed almost no fierceness and singularly little thought of revenge. It is only the crying of one of the great wrongs of the world wrought into music, as it were, and made beautiful by " the most tragic of the poets." But its author lived ever after in a deepening atmosphere of strife and even of hatred, down to the day when, " because almost all in Athens rejoiced at his suffering," he took his way to the remote valleys of Macedon to write the *Bacchae* and to die.

CHARACTERS IN THE PLAY

THE GOD POSEIDON.
THE GODDESS PALLAS ATHENA.

HECUBA, *Queen of Troy, wife of Priam, mother of Hector and Paris.*
CASSANDRA, *daughter of Hecuba, a prophetess.*
ANDROMACHE, *wife of Hector, Prince of Troy.*
HELEN, *wife of Menelaus, King of Sparta; carried off by Paris, Prince of Troy.*

TALTHYBIUS, *Herald of the Greeks.*
MENELAUS, *King of Sparta, and, together with his brother Agamemnon, General of the Greeks.*

SOLDIERS ATTENDANT ON TALTHYBIUS AND MENELAUS.
CHORUS OF CAPTIVE TROJAN WOMEN, YOUNG AND OLD
MAIDEN AND MARRIED.

The Troädes was first acted in the year 415 B.C. *"The firs prize was won by Xenocles, whoever he may have been, with the four plays Oedipus, Lycaön, Bacchae and Athamas, a Satyr-play The second by Euripides with the Alexander, Palamēdēs, Troädes and Sisyphus, a Satyr-play."*—AELIAN, *Varia Historia,* ii. 8.

THE TROJAN WOMEN

The scene represents a battlefield, a few days after the battle. At the back are the walls of Troy, partially ruined. In front of them, to right and left, are some huts, containing those of the Captive Women who have been specially set apart for the chief Greek leaders. At one side some dead bodies of armed men are visible. In front a tall woman with white hair is lying on the ground asleep.

It is the dusk of early dawn, before sunrise. The figure of the god POSEIDON *is dimly seen before the walls.*

POSEIDON.

Up from Aegean caverns, pool by pool
Of blue salt sea, where feet most beautiful
Of Nereïd maidens weave beneath the foam
Their long sea-dances, I, their lord, am come,
Poseidon of the Sea.   'Twas I whose power,
With great Apollo, builded tower by tower
These walls of Troy; and still my care doth stand
True to the ancient People of my hand;
Which now as smoke is perished, in the shock
Of Argive spears.   Down from Parnassus' rock
The Greek Epeios came, of Phocian seed,
And wrought by Pallas' mysteries a Steed
Marvellous, big with arms; and through my wall
It passed, a death-fraught image magical.

7

The groves are empty and the sanctuaries
Run red with blood. Unburied Priam lies
By his own hearth, on God's high altar-stair,
And Phrygian gold goes forth and raiment rare
To the Argive ships; and weary soldiers roam
Waiting the wind that blows at last for home,
For wives and children, left long years away,
Beyond the seed's tenth fullness and decay,
To work this land's undoing.

                          And for me,
Since Argive Hera conquereth, and she
Who wrought with Hera to the Phrygians' woe,
Pallas, behold, I bow mine head and go
Forth from great Ilion and mine altars old.
When a still city lieth in the hold
Of Desolation, all God's spirit there
Is sick and turns from worship.—Hearken where
The ancient River waileth with a voice
Of many women, portioned by the choice
Of war amid new lords, as the lots leap
For Thessaly, or Argos, or the steep
Of Theseus' Rock. And others yet there are,
High women, chosen from the waste of war
For the great kings, behind these portals hid;
And with them that Laconian Tyndarid,
Helen, like them a prisoner and a prize.

    And this unhappy one—would any eyes
Gaze now on Hecuba? Here at the Gates
She lies 'mid many tears for many fates
Of wrong. One child beside Achilles' grave
In secret slain, Polyxena the brave,
Lies bleeding. Priam and his sons are gone
And, lo, Cassandra, she the Chosen One,

Whom Lord Apollo spared to walk her way
A swift and virgin spirit, on this day
Lust hath her, and she goeth garlanded
A bride of wrath to Agamemnon's bed.

> [*He turns to go; and another divine Presence
> becomes visible in the dusk.* It is the
> goddess PALLAS ATHENA.

O happy long ago, farewell, farewell,
Ye shining towers and mine own citadel;
Broken by Pallas, Child of God, or still
Thy roots had held thee true.

PALLAS.

Is it the will
Of God's high Brother, to whose hand is given
Great power of old, and worship of all Heaven,
To suffer speech from one whose enmities
This day are cast aside?

POSEIDON.

His will it is:
Kindred and long companionship withal,
Most high Athena, are things magical.

PALLAS.

Blest be thy gentle mood!—Methinks I see
A road of comfort here, for thee and me.

POSEIDON.

Thou hast some counsel of the Gods, or word
Spoken of Zeus? Or is it tidings heard
From some far Spirit?

PALLAS.

For this Ilion's sake,
Whereon we tread, I seek thee, and would make
My hand as thine.

POSEIDON.

Hath that old hate and deep
Failed, where she lieth in her ashen sleep?
Thou pitiest her?

PALLAS.

Speak first; wilt thou be one
In heart with me and hand till all be done?

POSEIDON.

Yea; but lay bare thy heart.   For this land's sake
Thou comest, not for Hellas?

PALLAS.

I would make
Mine ancient enemies laugh for joy, and bring
On these Greek ships a bitter homecoming.

POSEIDON.

Swift is thy spirit's path, and strange withal,
And hot thy love and hate, where'er they fall.

PALLAS.

A deadly wrong they did me, yea within
Mine holy place: thou knowest?

POSEIDON.

I know the sin
Of Ajax, when he cast Cassandra down . . .

PALLAS.

And no man rose and smote him; not a frown
Nor word from all the Greeks!

POSEIDON.

And 'twas thine hand
That gave them Troy!

PALLAS.

Therefore with thee I stand
To smite them.

POSEIDON.

All thou cravest, even now
Is ready in mine heart.   What seekest thou?

PALLAS.

An homecoming that striveth ever more
And cometh to no home.

POSEIDON.

Here on the shore
Wouldst hold them or amid mine own salt foam?

PALLAS.

When the last ship hath bared her sail for home!
    Zeus shall send rain, long rain and flaw of driven
Hail, and a whirling darkness blown from heaven;

To me his leven-light he promiseth
O'er ships and men, for scourging and hot death:
Do thou make wild the roads of the sea, and steep
With war of waves and yawning of the deep,
Till dead men choke Euboea's curling bay.
So Greece shall dread even in an after day
My house, nor scorn the Watchers of strange lands!

POSEIDON.

I give thy boon unbartered. These mine hands
Shall stir the waste Aegean; reefs that cross
The Delian pathways, jag-torn Myconos,
Scyros and Lemnos, yea, and storm-driven
Caphêreus with the bones of drownèd men
Shall glut him.—Go thy ways, and bid the Sire
Yield to thine hand the arrows of his fire.
Then wait thine hour, when the last ship shall wind
Her cable coil for home!   [*Exit* PALLAS.
                How are ye blind,
Ye treaders down of cities, ye that cast
Temples to desolation, and lay waste
Tombs, the untrodden sanctuaries where lie
The ancient dead; yourselves so soon to die!
                        [*Exit* POSEIDON.

The day slowly dawns: HECUBA *wakes.*

HECUBA.

Up from the earth, O weary head!
This is not Troy, about, above—
Not Troy, nor we the lords thereof.
Thou breaking neck, be strengthenèd!

Endure and chafe not.   The winds rave
  And falter.   Down the world's wide road,
  Float, float where streams the breath of God;
Nor turn thy prow to breast the wave.

Ah woe! . . . For what woe lacketh here?
  My children lost, my land, my lord.
  O thou great wealth of glory, stored
Of old in Ilion, year by year

We watched . . . and wert thou nothingness?
  What is there that I fear to say?
  And yet, what help? . . . Ah, well-a-day,
This ache of lying, comfortless

And haunted!   Ah, my side, my brow
  And temples!   All with changeful pain
  My body rocketh, and would fain
Move to the tune of tears that flow:
For tears are music too, and keep
A song unheard in hearts that weep.
    [*She rises and gazes towards the Greek ships
        far off on the shore.*

        O ships, O crowding faces
          Of ships, O hurrying beat
          Of oars as of crawling feet,
        How found ye our holy places?
        Threading the narrows through,
          Out from the gulfs of the Greek,
        Out to the clear dark blue,
          With hate ye came and with joy,
        And the noise of your music flew,
          Clarion and pipe did shriek,

13

As the coilèd cords ye threw,
  Held in the heart of Troy!

What sought ye then that ye came?
  A woman, a thing abhorred:
  A King's wife that her lord
Hateth: and Castor's shame
  Is hot for her sake, and the reeds
Of old Eurôtas stir
With the noise of the name of her.
  She slew mine ancient King,
  The Sower of fifty Seeds,
    And cast forth mine and me,
  As shipwrecked men, that cling
    To a reef in an empty sea.

Who am I that I sit
  Here at a Greek king's door,
Yea, in the dust of it?
  A slave that men drive before,
A woman that hath no home,
  Weeping alone for her dead;
  A low and bruisèd head,
And the glory struck therefrom.
[*She starts up from her solitary brooding, and
  calls to the other Trojan Women in the huts.*

O Mothers of the Brazen Spear,
  And maidens, maidens, brides of shame,
  Troy is a smoke, a dying flame;
Together we will weep for her:
  I call ye as a wide-wing'd bird
    Calleth the children of her fold,

14 ──────────────────────────────

To cry, ah, not the cry men heard
In Ilion, not the songs of old,
That echoed when my hand was true
On Priam's sceptre, and my feet
Touched on the stone one signal beat,
And out the Dardan music rolled;
And Troy's great Gods gave ear thereto.
[*The door of one of the huts on the right opens,
and the Women steal out severally, startled
and afraid.*

FIRST WOMAN.   [*Strophe* 1.
How say'st thou?   Whither moves thy cry,
Thy bitter cry?   Behind our door
We heard thy heavy heart outpour
Its sorrow: and there shivered by
Fear and a quick sob shaken
From prisoned hearts that shall be free no more!
HERCUBA.
Child, 'tis the ships that stir upon the shore . . .
SECOND WOMAN.
The ships, the ships awaken!
THIRD WOMAN.
Dear God, what would they?   Overseas
Bear me afar to strange cities?
HECUBA.
Nay, child, I know not.   Dreams are these,
Fears of the hope-forsaken.

FIRST WOMAN.
Awake, O daughters of affliction, wake
And learn your lots!   Even now the Argives break
Their camp for sailing!

HECUBA.

Ah, not Cassandra! Wake not her
    Whom God hath maddened, lest the foe
Mock at her dreaming. Leave me clear
    From that one edge of woe.
O Troy, my Troy, thou diest here
    Most lonely; and most lonely we
The living wander forth from thee,
    And the dead leave thee wailing!
    [*One of the huts on the left is now open, and the
    rest of the* CHORUS *comes out severally. Their
    number eventually amounts to fifteen.*

FOURTH WOMAN.
                                    [*Antistrophe* 1.
Out of the tent of the Greek king
    I steal, my Queen, with trembling breath:
What means thy call? Not death; not death!
    They would not slay so low a thing!
FIFTH WOMAN.
            O,'tis the ship-folk crying
To deck the galleys: and we part, we part!
HECUBA.
Nay, daughter: take the morning to thine heart.
FIFTH WOMAN.
            My heart with dread is dying!
SIXTH WOMAN.
An herald from the Greek hath come!
FIFTH WOMAN.
How have they cast me, and to whom
    A bondmaid?
HECUBA.   Peace, child: wait thy doom.
    Our lots are near the trying.

FOURTH WOMAN.

Argos, belike, or Phthia shall it be,
Or some lone island of the tossing sea,
    Far, far from Troy?

HECUBA.

And I the agèd, where go I,
    A winter-frozen bee, a slave
Death-shapen, as the stones that lie
    Hewn on a dead man's grave:
The children of mine enemy
    To foster, or keep watch before
    The threshold of a master's door,
I that was Queen in Troy!

A WOMAN TO ANOTHER.
                                    [*Strophe* 2.
And thou, what tears can tell thy doom?
THE OTHER.
    The shuttle still shall flit and change
    Beneath my fingers, but the loom,
        Sister, be strange.
ANOTHER (*wildly*).
    Look, my dead child!   My child, my love,
    The last look. . . .
ANOTHER.   Oh, there cometh worse.
    A Greek's bed in the dark. . . .
ANOTHER.   God curse
    That night and all the powers thereof!

17

ANOTHER.

> Or pitchers to and fro to bear
> To some Pirênê on the hill,
> Where the proud water craveth still
> Its broken-hearted minister.

ANOTHER.

> God guide me yet to Theseus' land,
> The gentle land, the famed afar . . .

ANOTHER.

> But not the hungry foam—Ah, never!—
> Of fierce Eurotas, Helen's river,
> To bow to Menelaus' hand,
> That wasted Troy with war!

A WOMAN.

[Antistrophe 2.

> They told us of a land high-born,
> Where glimmers round Olympus' roots
> A lordly river, red with corn
> And burdened fruits.

ANOTHER.

> Aye, that were next in my desire
> To Athens, where good spirits dwell . . .

ANOTHER.

> Or Aetna's breast, the deeps of fire
> That front the Tyrian's Citadel:
> First mother, she, of Sicily
> And mighty mountains: fame hath told
> Their crowns of goodness manifold. . . .

ANOTHER.

> And, close beyond the narrowing sea,
> A sister land, where float enchanted
> Ionian summits, wave on wave,

And Crathis of the burning tresses
Makes red the happy vale, and blesses
With gold of fountains spirit-haunted
Homes of true men and brave!

LEADER.

But lo, who cometh: and his lips
    Grave with the weight of dooms unknown
A Herald from the Grecian ships.
    Swift comes he, hot-foot to be done
And finished.   Ah, what bringeth he
Of news or judgment?   Slaves are we,
    Spoils that the Greek hath won!
        [TALTHYBIUS, *followed by some Soldiers, enters*
        from the left.

TALTHYBIUS.

Thou know'st me, Hecuba.   Often have I crossed
Thy plain with tidings from the Hellene host.
'Tis I, Talthybius. . . . Nay, of ancient use
Thou know'st me.   And I come to bear the news.

HECUBA.

Ah me, 'tis here, 'tis here,
Women of Troy, our long embosomed fear!

TALTHYBIUS.

The lots are cast, if that it was ye feared.

HECUBA.

What lord, what land. . . .   Ah, me,
Phthia or Thebes, or sea-worn Thessaly?

TALTHYBIUS.

Each hath her own.   Ye go not in one herd.

19

HECUBA.

Say then what lot hath any?   What of joy
Falls, or can fall on any child of Troy?

TALTHYBIUS.

I know: but make thy questions severally.

HECUBA.

My stricken one must be
Still first.   Say how Cassandra's portion lies.

TALTHYBIUS.

Chosen from all for Agamemnon's prize!

HECUBA

How, for his Spartan pride
A tirewoman?   For Helen's sister's pride?

TALTHYBIUS.

Nay, nay: a bride herself, for the King's bed.

HECUBA.

The sainted of Apollo?   And her own
Prize that God promisèd
Out of the golden clouds, her virgin crown? . . .

TALTHYBIUS.

He loved her for that same strange holiness.

HECUBA.

Daughter, away, away
Cast all away,
The haunted Keys, the lonely stole's array
That kept thy body like a sacred place

TALTHYBIUS.

Is't not rare fortune that the King hath smiled
On such a maid?

HECUBA.

What of that other child
Ye reft from me but now?

TALTHYBIUS (*speaking with some constraint*).
Polyxena?   Or what child meanest thou?

HECUBA.

The same.   What man now hath her, or what doom?

TALTHYBIUS.

She rests apart, to watch Achilles' tomb.

HECUBA.

To watch a tomb?   My daughter?   What is this? . . .
Speak, Friend!   What fashion of the laws of Greece?

TALTHYBIUS.

Count thy maid happy!   She hath naught of ill
To fear . . .

HECUBA.

What meanest thou?   She liveth still?

TALTHYBIUS.

I mean, she hath one toil that holds her free
From all toil else.

HECUBA.

What of Andromache,
Wife of mine iron-hearted Hector, where
Journeyeth she?

TALTHYBIUS.

Pyrrhus, Achilles' son, hath taken her.

HECUBA.

And I, whose slave am I,
The shaken head, the arm that creepeth by,
Staff-crutchèd, like to fall?

TALTHYBIUS.

Odysseus, Ithaca's king, hath thee for thrall.

HECUBA.

Beat, beat the crownless head:
Rend the cheek till the tears run red!
A lying man and a pitiless
Shall be lord of me, a heart full-flown
    With scorn of righteousness:
O heart of a beast where law is none,
Where all things change so that lust be fed,
The oath and the deed, the right and the wrong,
Even the hate of the forkèd tongue:
Even the hate turns and is cold,
False as the love that was false of old!

O Women of Troy, weep for me!
Yea, I am gone: I am gone my ways.
Mine is the crown of misery,
The bitterest day of all our days.

LEADER.

Thy fate thou knowest, Queen: but I know not
What lord of South or North has won my lot.

22

TALTHYBIUS.

Go, seek Cassandra, men! Make your best speed,
That I may leave her with the King, and lead
These others to their divers lords. . . . Ha, there!
What means that sudden light? Is it the flare
Of torches?

      [*Light is seen shining through the crevices of the
         second hut on the right. He moves towards it.*

           Would they fire their prison rooms,
Or how, these dames of Troy?—'Fore God, the dooms
Are known, and now they burn themselves and die
Rather than sail with us! How savagely
In days like these a free neck chafes beneath
Its burdens! . . . Open! Open quick! Such death
Were bliss to them, it may be: but 'twill bring
Much wrath, and leave me shamed before the King!

HECUBA.

There is no fire, no peril: 'tis my child,
Cassandra, by the breath of God made wild.

      [*The door opens from within and* CASSANDRA
         *enters, white-robed and wreathed like a
         Priestess, a great torch in her hand. She
         is singing softly to herself and does not see the
         Herald or the scene before her.*

CASSANDRA.

Lift, lift it high: [*Strophe.*
    Give it to mine hand!
      Lo, I bear a flame
      Unto God! I praise his name.
    I light with a burning brand
This sanctuary.

Blessèd is he that shall wed,
  And blessèd, blessèd am I
  In Argos: a bride to lie
With a king in a king's bed.

  Hail, O Hymen red,
  O Torch that makest one!
Weepest thou, Mother mine own?
Surely thy cheek is pale
With tears, tears that wail
For a land and a father dead.

But I go garlanded:
I am the Bride of Desire:
  Therefore my torch is borne—
  Lo, the lifting of morn,
Lo, the leaping of fire!—

  For thee, O Hymen bright,
  For thee, O Moon of the Deep,
So Law hath charged, for the light
  Of a maid's last sleep.

Awake, O my feet, awake: [*Antistrophe.*
  Our father's hope is won!
    Dance as the dancing skies
    Over him, where he lies
  Happy beneath the sun! . . .
Lo, the Ring that I make . . .
  [*She makes a circle round her with the torch,
    and visions appear to her.*

Apollo! . . . Ah, is it thou?
  O shrine in the laurels cold,
  I bear thee still, as of old,
Mine incense!   Be near to me now.
  [*She waves the torch as though bearing incense.*

24

O Hymen, Hymen fleet:
 Quick torch that makest one!..
How?   Am I still alone?
Laugh as I laugh, and twine
In the dance, O Mother mine:
 Dear feet, be near my feet!

Come, greet ye Hymen, greet
 Hymen with songs of pride:
Sing to him loud and long,
Cry, cry, when the song
 Faileth, for joy of the bride!

O Damsels girt in the gold
 Of Ilion, cry, cry ye,
For him that is doomed of old
 To be lord of me!

Leader.

O hold the damsel, lest her trancèd feet
Lift her afar, Queen, toward the Hellene fleet!

Hecuba.

O Fire, Fire, where men make marriages
Surely thou hast thy lot; but what are these
Thou bringest flashing?   Torches savage-wild
And far from mine old dreams.—Alas, my child,
How little dreamed I then of wars or red
Spears of the Greek to lay thy bridal bed!
Give me thy brand; it hath no holy blaze
Thus in thy frenzy flung.   Nor all thy days
Nor all thy griefs have changed them yet, nor learned
Wisdom.—Ye women, bear the pine half burned

To the chamber back; and let your drownèd eyes
Answer the music of these bridal cries!
            [*She takes the torch and gives it to one of
            the women.*

CASSANDRA.

O Mother, fill mine hair with happy flowers,
And speed me forth.   Yea, if my spirit cowers,
Drive me with wrath!   So liveth Loxias,
A bloodier bride than ever Helen was
Go I to Agamemnon, Lord most high
Of Hellas!... I shall kill him, mother; I
Shall kill him, and lay waste his house with fire
As he laid ours.   My brethren and my sire
Shall win again...
            (*Checking herself*) But part I must let be,
And speak not.   Not the axe that craveth me,
And more than me; not the dark wanderings
Of mother-murder that my bridal brings,
And all the House of Atreus down, down, down...

    Nay, I will show thee.   Even now this town
Is happier than the Greeks.   I know the power
Of God is on me: but this little hour,
Wilt thou but listen, I will hold him back!
    One love, one woman's beauty, o'er the track
Of hunted Helen, made their myriads fall.
And this their King so wise, who ruleth all,
What wrought he?   Cast out Love that Hate might
            feed:
Gave to his brother his own child, his seed

Of gladness, that a woman fled, and fain
To fly for ever, should be turned again!
  So the days waned, and armies on the shore
Of Simois stood and strove and died.   Wherefore?
No man had moved their landmarks; none had
    shook
Their wallèd towns.—And they whom Ares took,
Had never seen their children: no wife came
With gentle arms to shroud the limbs of them
For burial, in a strange and angry earth
Laid dead.   And there at home, the same long
    dearth:
Women that lonely died, and aged men
Waiting for sons that ne'er should turn again,
Nor know their graves, nor pour drink-offerings,
To still the unslakèd dust.   These be the things
The conquering Greek hath won!
                  But we—what pride,
What praise of men were sweeter?—fighting died
To save our people.   And when war was red
Around us, friends upbore the gentle dead
Home, and dear women's hands about them wound
White shrouds, and here they sleep in the old
    ground
Belovèd.   And the rest long days fought on,
Dwelling with wives and children, not alone
And joyless, like these Greeks.
               And Hector's woe,
What is it?   He is gone, and all men know
His glory, and how true a heart he bore.
It is the gift the Greek hath brought!   Of yore
Men saw him not, nor knew him.   Yea, and even
Paris hath loved withal a child of heaven:

Else had his love but been as others are.

Would ye be wise, ye Cities, fly from war!
Yet if war come, there is a crown in death
For her that striveth well and perisheth   ɔ
Unstained: to die in evil were the stain!
Therefore, O Mother, pity not thy slain,
Nor Troy, nor me, the bride.   Thy direst foe
And mine by this my wooing is brought low.

TALTHYBIUS (*at last breaking through the spell
that has held him*).

I swear, had not Apollo made thee mad,
Not lightly hadst thou flung this shower of bad
Bodings, to speed my General o'er the seas!
'Fore God, the wisdoms and the greatnesses
Of seeming, are they hollow all, as things
Of naught?   This son of Atreus, of all kings
Most mighty, hath so bowed him to the love
Of this mad maid, and chooseth her above
All women!   By the Gods, rude though I be,
I would not touch her hand!

                Look thou; I see
Thy lips are blind, and whatso words they speak,
Praises of Troy or shamings of the Greek,
I cast to the four winds!   Walk at my side
In peace! . . . And heaven content him of his
     bride!   [*He moves as though to go, but turns to*
                HECUBA, *and speaks more gently.*
And thou shalt follow to Odysseus' host
When the word comes.   'Tis a wise queen thou go'st
To serve, and gentle: so the Ithacans say.

CASSANDRA (*seeing for the first time the Herald and
all the scene*).

How fierce a slave! . . . O Heralds, Heralds! Yea,
Voices of Death; and mists are over them
Of dead men's anguish, like a diadem,
These weak abhorrèd things that serve the hate
Of kings and peoples! . . .
                    To Odysseus' gate
My mother goeth, say'st thou? Is God's word
As naught, to me in silence ministered,
That in this place she dies? . . . (*To herself*) No
    more; no more!
Why should I speak the shame of them, before
They come? . . . Little he knows, that hard-beset
Spirit, what deeps of woe await him yet;
Till all these tears of ours and harrowings
Of Troy, by his, shall be as golden things.
Ten years behind ten years athwart his way
Waiting: and home, lost and unfriended . . .
                          Nay:
Why should Odysseus' labours vex my breath?
On; hasten; guide me to the house of Death,
To lie beside my bridegroom! . . .
                    Thou Greek King,
Who deem'st thy fortune now so high a thing,
Thou dust of the earth, a lowlier bed I see,
In darkness, not in light, awaiting thee:
And with thee, with thee . . . there, where yawneth
    plain
A rift of the hills, raging with winter rain,

Dead . . . and out-cast . . . and naked . . . It is I
Beside my bridegroom: and the wild beasts cry,
And ravin on God's chosen!

> [*She clasps her hands to her brow and feels the
> wreaths.*

O, ye wreaths!
Ye garlands of my God, whose love yet breathes
About me; shapes of joyance mystical;
Begone! I have forgot the festival,
Forgot the joy. Begone! I tear ye, so,
From off me! . . . Out on the swift winds they go.
With flesh still clean I give them back to thee,
Still white, O God, O light that leadest me!

> [*Turning upon the Herald.*

Where lies the galley? Whither shall I tread?
See that your watch be set, your sail be spread.
The wind comes quick! . . . Three Powers—mark
   me, thou!—
There be in Hell, and one walks with thee now!
  Mother, farewell, and weep not! O my sweet
City, my earth-clad brethren, and thou great
Sire that begat us; but a space, ye Dead,
And I am with you: yea, with crownèd head
I come, and shining from the fires that feed
On these that slay us now, and all their seed!

> [*She goes out, followed by* TALTHYBIUS *and the
> Soldiers:* HECUBA, *after waiting for an in-
> stant motionless, falls to the ground.*

LEADER OF CHORUS.

The Queen, ye Watchers! See, she falls, she falls,
Rigid without a word! O sorry thralls,

Too late! And will ye leave her downstricken,
A woman, and so old?   Raise her again!
  [Some women go to HECUBA, *but she refuses their
        aid and speaks without rising.*

HECUBA.

Let lie . . . the love we seek not is no love . . .
This ruined body!   Is the fall thereof
Too deep for all that now is over me
Of anguish, and hath been, and yet shall be?
Ye Gods . . . Alas!   Why call on things so weak
For aid?   Yet there is something that doth seek,
Crying, for God, when one of us hath woe.
O, I will think of things gone long ago
And weave them to a song, like one more tear
In the heart of misery. . . .   All kings we were;
And I must wed a king.   And sons I brought
My lord King, many sons . . . nay, that were naught
But high strong princes, of all Troy the best.
Hellas nor Troäs nor the garnered East
Held such a mother!   And all these things beneath
The Argive spear I saw cast down in death,
And shore these tresses at the dead men's feet.
  Yea, and the gardener of my garden great,
It was not any noise of him nor tale
I wept for; these eyes saw him, when the pale
Was broke, and there at the altar Priam fell
Murdered, and round him all his citadel
Sacked.   And my daughters, virgins of the fold,
Meet to be brides of mighty kings, behold,
'Twas for the Greek I bred them!   All are gone;
And no hope left, that I shall look upon
Their faces any more, nor they on mine.

And now my feet tread on the utmost line:
An old, old slave-woman, I pass below
Mine enemies' gates; and whatso task they know
For this age basest, shall be mine; the door,
Bowing, to shut and open. . . . I that bore
Hector! . . . and meal to grind, and this racked head
Bend to the stones after a royal bed;
Torn rags about me, aye, and under them
Torn flesh; 'twill make a woman sick for shame!
Woe's me; and all that one man's arms might hold
One woman, what long seas have o'er me rolled
And roll for ever! . . . O my child, whose white
Soul laughed amid the laughter of God's light,
Cassandra, what hands and how strange a day
Have loosed thy zone! And thou, Polyxena,
Where art thou? And my sons? Not any seed
Of man nor woman now shall help my need.

Why raise me any more? What hope have I
To hold me? Take this slave that once trod high
In Ilion; cast her on her bed of clay
Rock-pillowed, to lie down, and pass away
Wasted with tears. And whatso man thay call
Happy, believe not ere the last day fall!

Chorus.

[*Strophe.*

O Muse, be near me now, and make
A strange song for Ilion's sake,
Till a tone of tears be about mine ears
And out of my lips a music break
For Troy, Troy, and the end of the years:
When the wheels of the Greek above me pressed,
And the mighty horse-hoofs beat my breast;
And all around were the Argive spears

A towering Steed of golden rein—
  O gold without, dark steel within!—
Ramped in our gates; and all the plain
  Lay silent where the Greeks had been.
And a cry broke from all the folk
Gathered above on Ilion's rock:
"Up, up, O fear is over now!
  To Pallas, who hath saved us living,
To Pallas bear this victory-vow!"
Then rose the old man from his room,
The merry damsel left her loom,
And each bound death about his brow
  With minstrelsy and high thanksgiving!

                                [*Antistrophe.*

O, swift were all in Troy that day,
  And girt them to the portal-way,
Marvelling at that mountain Thing
  Smooth-carven, where the Argives lay,
And wrath, and Ilion's vanquishing:
  Meet gift for her that spareth not,
  Heaven's yokeless Rider. Up they brought
Through the steep gates her offering:
Like some dark ship that climbs the shore
  On straining cables, up, where stood
Her marble throne, her hallowed floor,
  Who lusted for her people's blood.

A very weariness of joy
Fell with the evening over Troy:
And lutes of Afric mingled there
  With Phrygian songs: and many a maiden,
With white feet glancing light as air,

Made happy music through the gloom:
And fires on many an inward room
All night broad-flashing, flung their glare
    On laughing eyes and slumber-laden.

A Maiden.

I was among the dancers there
    To Artemis, and glorying sang
Her of the Hills, the Maid most fair,
    Daughter of Zeus: and, lo, there rang
A shout out of the dark, and fell
    Deathlike from street to street, and made
A silence in the citadel:
    And a child cried, as if afraid,
And hid him in his mother's veil.
    Then stalked the Slayer from his den,
The hand of Pallas served her well!
    O blood, blood of Troy was deep
About the streets and altars then:
And in the wedded rooms of sleep,
    Lo, the desolate dark alone,
    And headless things, men stumbled on.

And forth, lo, the women go,
The crown of War, the crown of Woe,
To bear the children of the foe
    And weep, weep, for Ilion!

_[As the song ceases a chariot is seen approaching
    from the town, laden with spoils. On it sits
    a mourning Woman with a child in her
    arms._

LEADER.

Lo, yonder on the heapèd crest
  Of a Greek wain, Andromachê,
  As one that o'er an unknown sea
Tosseth; and on her wave-borne breast
Her loved one clingeth, Hector's child,
  Astyanax . . . O most forlorn
  Of women, whither go'st thou, borne
'Mid Hector's brozen arms, and piled
Spoils of the dead, and pageantry
  Of them that hunted Ilion down?
  Aye, richly thy new lord shall crown
The mountain shrines of Thessaly!

ANDROMACHE.   [*Strophe* 1.
  Forth to the Greek I go,
    Driven as a beast is driven.
HEC. Woe, woe!
AND.   Nay, mine is woe:
  Woe to none other given,
  And the song and the crown therefor!
HEC. O Zeus!
AND.   He hates thee sore!
HEC. Children!
AND.   No more, no more
  To aid thee: their strife is striven!

HECUBA.   [*Antistrophe* 1.
  Troy, Troy is gone!
AND.   Yea, and her treasure parted.
HEC. Gone, gone, mine own
    Children, the noble-hearted!

AND.   Sing sorrow. . . .

HEC.   For me, for me!

AND.   Sing for the Great City,
That falleth, falleth to be
A shadow, a fire departed.

ANDROMACHE.

[Strophe 2.

Come to me, O my lover!

HEC.   The dark stroudeth him over,
My flesh, woman, not thine, not thine!

AND.   Make of thine arms my cover!

HECUBA.

[Antistrophe 2.

O thou whose wound was deepest,
Thou that my children keepest,
Priam, Priam, O age-worn King,
Gather me where thou sleepest.

ANDROMACHE (*her hands upon her heart*).

[Strophe 3.

O here is the deep of desire,

HEC.   (How? And is this not woe?)

AND.   For a city burned with fire;

HEC.   (It beateth, blow on blow.)

AND.   God's wrath for Paris, thy son, that he died not
long ago:

Who sold for his evil love
Troy and the towers thereof:
Therefore the dead men lie
Naked, beneath the eye

Of Pallas, and vultures croak
And flap for joy:
So Love hath laid his yoke
On the neck of Troy!

HECUBA.

O mine own land, my home, [*Antistrophe* 3.

AND.   (I weep for thee, left forlorn,)
HEC.   See'st thou what end is come?
AND.   (And the house where my babes were born.)
HEC.   A desolate Mother we leave, O children, a
City of scorn:

Even as the sound of a song
Left by the way, but long
Remembered, a tune of tears
Falling where no man hears,
In the old house, as rain,
For things loved of yore:
But the dead hath lost his pain
And weeps no more.

LEADER.

How sweet are tears to them in bitter stress,
And sorrow, and all the songs of heaviness.

ANDROMACHE.

Mother of him of old, whose mighty spear
Smote Greeks like chaff, see'st thou what things are
here?

HECUBA.

I see God's hand, that buildeth a great crown
For littleness, and hath cast the mighty down.

37

ANDROMACHE.

I and my babe are driven among the droves
Of plundered cattle.   O, when fortune moves
So swift, the high heart like a slave beats low.

HECUBA.

'Tis fearful to be helpful.   Men but now
Have taken Cassandra, and I strove in vain.

ANDROMACHE.

Ah, woe is me; hath Ajax come again?
But other evil yet is at thy gate.

HECUBA.

Nay, Daughter, beyond number, beyond weight
My evils are!   Doom raceth against doom.

ANDROMACHE.

Polyxena across Achilles' tomb
Lies slain, a gift flung to the dreamless dead.

HECUBA.

My sorrow! . . . 'Tis but what Talthybius said:
So plain a riddle, and I read it not.

ANDROMACHE.

I saw her lie, and stayed this chariot;
And raiment wrapt on her dead limbs, and beat
My breast for her.

HECUBA (to herself).

O the foul sin of it!
The wickedness!   My child.   My child!   Again
I cry to thee.   How cruelly art thou slain!

ANDROMACHE.

She hath died her death, and howso dark it be,
Her death is sweeter than my misery.

HECUBA.

Death cannot be what Life is, Child; the cup
Of Death is empty, and Life hath always hope.

ANDROMACHE.

O Mother, having ears, hear thou this word
Fear-conquering, till thy heart as mine be stirred
With joy.   To die is only not to be;
And better to be dead than grievously
Living.   They have no pain, they ponder not
Their own wrong.   But the living that is
      brought
From joy to heaviness, his soul doth roam,
As in a desert, lost, from its old home.
Thy daughter lieth now as one unborn,
Dead, and naught knowing of the lust and scorn
That slew her.   And I . . . long since I drew
      my bow
Straight at the heart of good fame; and I know
My shaft hit; and for that am I the more
Fallen from peace.   All that men praise us for,
I loved for Hector's sake, and sought to win.
I knew that alway, be there hurt therein
Or utter innocence, to roam abroad
Hath ill report for women; so I trod
Down the desire thereof, and walked my way
In mine own garden.   And light words and gay

Parley of women never passed my door.
The thoughts of mine own heart . . . I craved no
    more . . .
Spoke with me, and I was happy. Constantly
I brought fair silence and a tranquil eye
For Hector's greeting, and watched well the way
Of living, where to guide and where obey.
    And, lo! some rumour of this peace, being gone
Forth to the Greek, hath cursed me. Achilles' son,
So soon as I was taken, for his thrall
Chose me. I shall do service in the hall
Of them that slew . . . How? Shall I thrust aside
Hector's belovèd face, and open wide
My heart to this new lord? Oh, I should stand
A traitor to the dead! And if my hand
And flesh shrink from him . . . lo, wrath and despite
O'er all the house, and I a slave!
                      One night,
One night . . . aye, men have said it . . . maketh tame
A woman in a man's arms. . . . O shame, shame!
What woman's lips can so forswear her dead,
And give strange kisses in another's bed?
Why, not a dumb beast, not a colt will run
In the yoke untroubled, when her mate is gone—
A thing not in God's image, dull, unmoved
Of reason. O my Hector! best beloved,
That, being mine, wast all in all to me,
My prince, my wise one, O my majesty
Of valiance! No man's touch had ever come
Near me, when thou from out my father's home
Didst lead me and make me thine. . . . And thou art
    dead,
And I war-flung to slavery and the bread

Of shame in Hellas, over bitter seas!
    What knoweth she of evils like to these,
That dead Polyxena, thou weepest for?
There liveth not in my life any more
The hope that others have.   Nor will I tell
The lie to mine own heart, that aught is well
Or shall be well. . . . Yet, O, to dream were sweet!

LEADER.

Thy feet have trod the pathway of my feet,
And thy clear sorrow teacheth me mine own.

HECUBA.

Lo, yonder ships: I ne'er set foot on one,
But tales and pictures tell, when over them
Breaketh a storm not all too strong to stem,
Each man strives hard, the tiller gripped, the mast
Manned, the hull baled, to face it: till at last
Too strong breaks the o'erwhelming sea: lo, then
They cease, and yield them up as broken men
To fate and the wild waters.   Even so
I in my many sorrows bear me low,
Nor curse, nor strive that other things may be.
The great wave rolled from God hath conquered me
    But, O, let Hector and the fates that fell
On Hector, sleep.   Weep for him ne'er so well,
Thy weeping shall not wake him.   Honour thou
The new lord that is set above thee now,
And make of thine own gentle piety
A prize to lure his heart.   So shalt thou be
A strength to them that love us, and—God knows,
It may be—rear this babe among his foes,

My Hector's child, to manhood and great aid
For Ilion.   So her stones may yet be laid
One on another, if God will, and wrought
Again to a city!   Ah, how thought to thought
Still beckons! . . . But what minion of the Greek
Is this that cometh, with new words to speak?
          [*Enter* TALTHYBIUS *with a band of Soldiers.   He
          comes forward slowly and with evident disquiet.*

TALTHYBIUS.
Spouse of the noblest heart that beat in Troy,
Andromache, hate me not!   'Tis not in joy
I tell thee.   But the people and the Kings
Have with one voice . . .

ANDROMACHE.
                    What is it?   Evil things
Are on thy lips!
                    TALTHYBIUS.
                    'Tis ordered, this child . . . Oh,
How can I tell her of it?

ANDROMACHE.
                    Doth he not go
With me, to the same master?

TALTHYBIUS.
                         There is none
In Greece, shall e'er be master of thy son.

ANDROMACHE.
How?   Will they leave him here to build again
The wreck? . .

TALTHYBIUS.

I know not how to tell thee plain!

ANDROMACHE.

Thou hast a gentle heart . . . if it be ill,
And not good, news thou hidest!

TALTHYBIUS.

'Tis their will
Thy son shall die. . . . The whole vile thing is said
Now!

ANDROMACHE.

Oh, I could have borne mine enemy's bed!

TALTHYBIUS.

And speaking in the council of the host
Odysseus hath prevailed—

ANDROMACHE.

O lost! lost! lost! . . .
Forgive me! It is not easy . . .

TALTHYBIUS.

. . . That the son
Of one so perilous be not fostered on
To manhood—

ANDROMACHE.

God; may his own counsel fall
On his own sons!

TALTHYBIUS.

        . . . But from this crested wall
Of Troy be dashed, and die. . . . Nay, let the thing
Be done. Thou shalt be wiser so. Nor cling
So fiercely to him. Suffer as a brave
Woman in bitter pain; nor think to have
Strength which thou hast not. Look about thee here!
Canst thou see help, or refuge anywhere?
Thy land is fallen and thy lord, and thou
A prisoner and alone, one woman; how
Canst battle against us? For thine own good
I would not have thee strive, nor make ill blood
And shame about thee. . . . Ah, nor move thy lips
In silence there, to cast upon the ships
Thy curse! One word of evil to the host,
This babe shall have no burial, but be tossed
Naked. . . . Ah, peace! And bear as best thou may,
War's fortune. So thou shalt not go thy way
Leaving this child unburied; nor the Greek
Be stern against thee, if thy heart be meek!

ANDROMACHE (*to the child*).

Go, die, my best-beloved, my cherished one,
In fierce men's hands, leaving me here alone.
Thy father was too valiant; that is why
They slay thee! Other children, like to die,
Might have been spared for that. But on thy head
His good is turned to evil

                         O thou bed
And bridal; O the joining of the hand,
That led me long ago to Hector's land

To bear, O not a lamb for Grecian swords
To slaughter, but a Prince o'er all the hordes
Enthroned of wide-flung Asia. . . . Weepest thou?
Nay, why, my little one?   Thou canst not know.
And Father will not come; he will not come;
Not once, the great spear flashing, and the tomb
Riven to set thee free!   Not one of all
His brethren, nor the might of Ilion's wall.
    How shall it be?   One horrible spring . . . deep,
      deep
Down.   And thy neck . . . Ah God, so cometh
      sleep! . . .
And none to pity thee! . . . Thou little thing
That curlest in my arms, what sweet scents cling
All round thy neck!   Belovèd; can it be
All nothing, that this bosom cradled thee
And fostered; all the weary nights, wherethrough
I watched upon thy sickness, till I grew
Wasted with watching?   Kiss me.   This one time;
Not ever again.   Put up thine arms, and climb
About my neck: now, kiss me, lips to lips. . . .
    O, ye have found an anguish that outstrips
All tortures of the East, ye gentle Greeks!
Why will ye slay this innocent, that seeks
No wrong? . . . O Helen, Helen, thou ill tree
That Tyndareus planted, who shall deem of thee
As child of Zeus?   O, thou hast drawn thy breath
From many fathers, Madness, Hate, red Death,
And every rotting poison of the sky!
Zeus knows thee not, thou vampire, draining dry
Greece and the world!   God hate thee and destroy,
That with those beautiful eyes hast blasted Troy,
And made the far-famed plains a waste withal.

45

Quick! take him: drag him: cast him from the wall,
If cast ye will! Tear him, ye beasts, be swift!
God hath undone me, and I cannot lift
One hand, one hand, to save my child from death . . .
O, hide my head for shame: fling me beneath
Your galleys' benches! . . .

> [*She swoons: then half-rising.*
> Quick: I must begone
To the bridal. . . . I have lost my child, my own!
> [*The Soldiers close round her.*

LEADER.

O Troy ill-starred; for one strange women, one
Abhorrèd kiss, how are thine hosts undone!

TALTHYBIUS (*bending over* ANDROMACHE *and gradually
taking the Child from her*).

Come, Child: let be that clasp of love
    Outwearied! Walk thy ways with me,
Up to the crested tower, above
    Thy father's wall . . . where they decree
Thy soul shall perish.—Hold him: hold!—
    Would God some other man might ply
These charges, one of duller mould,
    And nearer to the iron than I!

HECUBA.

O Child, they rob us of our own,
    Child of my Mighty One outworn:
Ours, ours thou art!—Can aught be done
    Of deeds, can aught of pain be borne,

To aid thee?—Lo, this beaten head,
This bleeding bosom! These I spread
As gifts to thee. I can thus much.
Woe, woe for Troy, and woe for thee!
What fall yet lacketh, ere we touch
The last dead deep of misery?

[*The Child, who has started back from* TALTHY-
BIUS, *is taken up by one of the Soldiers and
borne back towards the city, while* ANDRO-
MACHE *is set again on the Chariot and driven
off towards the ships.* TALTHYBIUS *goes with
the Child.*

CHORUS.

[*Strophe* 1.

In Salamis, filled with the foaming
    Of billows and murmur of bees,
Old Telamon stayed from his roaming,
    Long ago, on a throne of the seas;
Looking out on the hills olive-laden,
    Enchanted, where first from the earth
The grey-gleaming fruit of the Maiden
    Athena had birth;
A soft grey crown for a city
    Belovèd, a City of Light:
Yet he rested not there, nor had pity,
    But went forth in his might,
Where Heracles wandered, the lonely
    Bow-bearer, and lent him his hands
For the wrecking of one land only,
Of Ilion, Ilion only,
    Most hated of lands!

[*Antistrophe* 1.

Of the bravest of Hellas he made him
A ship-folk, in wrath for the Steeds,
And sailed the wide waters, and stayed him
At last amid Simoïs' reeds;
And the oars beat slow in the river,
And the long ropes held in the strand,
And he felt for his bow and his quiver,
The wrath of his hand.
And the old king died; and the towers
That Phoebus had builded did fall,
And his wrath, as a flame that devours,
Ran red over all;
And the fields and the woodlands lay blasted,
Long ago. Yea, twice hath the Sire
Uplifted his hand and downcast it
On the wall of the Dardan, downcast it
As a sword and as fire.

[*Strophe* 2.

In vain, all in vain,
O thou 'mid the wine-jars golden
That movest in delicate joy,
Ganymêdês, child of Troy,
The lips of the Highest drain
The cup in thine hand upholden:
And thy mother, thy mother that bore thee,
Is wasted with fire and torn;
And the voice of her shores is heard,
Wild, as the voice of a bird,
For lovers and children before thee
Crying, and mothers outworn.
And the pools of thy bathing are perished,
And the wind-strewn ways of thy feet;

Yet thy face as aforetime is cherished
   Of Zeus, and the breath of it sweet;
Yea, the beauty of Calm is upon it
   In houses at rest and afar.
But thy land, He hath wrecked and o'erthrown it
   In the wailing of war.

                        [*Antistrophe* 2.

O Love, ancient Love,
   Of old to the Dardan given;
      Love of the Lords of the Sky;
      How didst thou lift us high
In Ilion, yea, and above
   All cities, as wed with heaven!
For Zeus—O leave it unspoken:
   But alas for the love of the Morn;
      Morn of the milk-white wing,
      The gentle, the earth-loving,
That shineth on battlements broken
   In Troy, and a people forlorn!
And, lo, in her bowers Tithônus,
   Our brother, yet sleeps as of old:
O, she too hath loved us and known us,
   And the Steeds of her star, flashing gold,
Stooped hither and bore him above us;
   Then blessed we the Gods in our joy.
But all that made them to love us
   Hath perished from Troy.

[*As the song ceases, the King* MENELAUS *enters,
   richly armed and followed by a bodyguard of
   Soldiers. He is a prey to violent and con-
   flicting emotions.*

MENELAUS.

How bright the face of heaven, and how sweet
The air this day, that layeth at my feet
The woman that I . . . Nay: 'twas not for her
I came. 'Twas for the man, the cozener
And thief, that ate with me and stole away
My bride. But Paris lieth, this long day,
By God's grace, under the horse-hoofs of the Greek,
And round him all his land. And now I seek . . .
Curse her! I scarce can speak the name she bears,
That was my wife. Here with the prisoners
They keep her, in these huts, among the hordes
Of numbered slaves.—The host whose labouring swords
Won her, have given her up to me, to fill
My pleasure; perchance kill her, or not kill,
But lead her home.—Methinks I have foregone
The slaying of Helen here in Ilion . . .
Over the long seas I will bear her back,
And there, there, cast her out to whatso wrack
Of angry death they may devise, who know
Their dearest dead for her in Ilion.—Ho!
Ye soldiers! Up into the chambers where
She croucheth! Grip the long blood-reeking hair,
And drag her to mine eyes . . . [Controlling himself.
                              And when there come
Fair breezes, my long ships shall bear her home.
      [The Soldiers go to force open the door of the second
      hut on the left.

HECUBA.

Thou deep Base of the World, and thou high Throne
Above the World, whoe'er thou art, unknown

And hard of surmise, Chain of Things that be,
Or Reason of our Reason; God, to thee
I lift my praise, seeing the silent road
That bringeth justice ere the end be trod
To all that breathes and dies.

MENELAUS (*turning*).
Ha! who is there

That prayeth heaven, and in so strange a prayer?

HECUBA.

I bless thee, Menelaus, I bless thee,
If thou wilt slay her!   Only fear to see
Her visage, lest she snare thee and thou fall!
She snareth strong men's eyes; she snareth tall
Cities; and fire from out her eateth up
Houses.   Such magic hath she, as a cup
Of death! . . . Do I not know her? Yea, and thou,
And these that lie around, do they not know?

> [*The Soldiers return from the hut and stand aside
> to let* HELEN *pass between them.   She comes
> through them, gentle and unafraid: there is
> no disorder in her raiment.*

HELEN.

King Menelaus, thy first deed might make
A woman fear.   Into my chamber brake
Thine armèd men, and lead me wrathfully.
  Methinks, almost, I know thou hatest me.
Yet I would ask thee, what decree is gone
Forth for my life or death?

MENELAUS (*struggling with his emotion*).
There was not one

That scrupled for thee.   All, all with one will
Gave thee to me, whom thou hast wronged, to kill!

HELEN.

And is it granted that I speak, or no,
In answer to them ere I die, to show
I die most wronged and innocent?

MENELAUS.

I seek
To kill thee, woman; not to hear thee speak!

HECUBA.

O hear her!   She must never die unheard,
King Menelaus!   And give me the word
To speak in answer!   All the wrong she wrought
Away from thee, in Troy, thou knowest not.
The whole tale set together is a death
Too sure; she shall not 'scape thee!

MENELAUS.

'Tis but breath
And time.   For thy sake, Hecuba, if she need
To grant, I grant the prayer.   I have no heed
Nor mercy—let her know it well—for her!

HELEN.

It may be that, how false or true soe'er
Thou deem me, I shall win no word from thee.
So sore thou holdest me thine enemy.
Yet I will take what words I think thy heart
Holdeth of anger: and in even part
Set my wrong and thy wrong, and all that fell.
[*Pointing to* HECUBA.

She cometh first, who bare the seed and well
Of springing sorrow, when to life she brought
Paris: and that old King, who quenchèd not
Quick in the spark, ere yet he woke to slay,
The firebrand's image.—But enough: a day
Came, and this Paris judged beneath the trees
Three Crowns of Life, three diverse Goddesses.
The gift of Pallas was of War, to lead
His East in conquering battles, and make bleed
The hearths of Hellas.　Hera held a Throne—
If Majesties he craved—to reign alone
From Phrygia to the last realm of the West.
And Cypris, if he deemed her loveliest,
Beyond all heaven, made dreams about my face
And for her grace gave me.　And, lo! her grace
Was judged the fairest, and she stood above
Those twain.—Thus was I loved, and thus my
　　love
Hath holpen Hellas.　No fierce Eastern crown
Is o'er your lands, no spear hath cast them down.
O, it was well for Hellas!　But for me
Most ill; caught up and sold across the sea
For this my beauty; yea, dishonourèd
For that which else had been about my head
A crown of honour. . . . Ah, I see thy thought;
The first plain deed, 'tis that I answer not,
How in the dark out of thy house I fled . . .
There came the Seed of Fire, this woman's seed;
Came—O, a Goddess great walked with him then—
This Alexander, Breaker-down-of-Men,
This Paris, Strength - is - with - him; whom thou,
　　whom—
O false and light of heart—thou in thy room

Dɪdst leave, and spreadest sail for Cretan seas,
Far, far from me!... And yet, how strange it is!
I ask not thee; I ask my own sad thought,
What was there in my heart, that I forgot
My home and land and all I loved, to fly
With a strange man?   Surely it was not I,
But Cypris, there!   Lay thou thy rod on her,
And be more high than Zeus and bitterer,
Who o'er all other spirits hath his throne,
But knows her chain must bind him.   My wrong done
Hath its own pardon....
                    One word yet thou hast,
Methinks, of righteous seeming.   When at last
The earth for Paris oped and all was o'er,
And her strange magic bound my feet no more,
Why kept I still his house, why fled not I
To the Argive ships?... Ah, how I strove to fly!
The old Gate-Warden could have told thee all,
My husband, and the watchers from the wall;
It was not once they took me, with the rope
Tied, and this body swung in the air, to grope
Its way toward t h e e, from that dim battlement.
    Ah, husband still, how shall thy hand be bent
To slay me?   Nay, if Right be come at last,
What shalt thou bring but comfort for pains past,
And harbour for a woman storm-driven:
A woman borne away by violent men:
And this one birthright of my beauty, this
That might have been my glory, lo, it is
A stamp that God hath burned, of slavery.
    Alas! and if thou cravest still to be
As one set above gods, inviolate,
'Tis but a fruitless longing holds thee yet.

LEADER.

O Queen, think of thy children and thy land,
And break her spell! The sweet soft speech, the
    hand
And heart so fell: it maketh me afraid.

HECUBA.

Meseems her goddesses first cry mine aid
Against these lying lips! . . . Not Hera, nay,
Nor virgin Pallas deem I such low clay,
To barter their own folk, Argos and brave
Athens, to be trod down, the Phrygian's slave,
All for vain glory and a shepherd's prize
On Ida! Wherefore should great Hera's eyes
So hunger to be fair? S h e doth not use
To seek for other loves, being wed with Zeus.
And maiden Pallas . . . did some strange god's face
Beguile her, that she craved for loveliness,
Who chose from God one virgin gift above
All gifts, and fleëth from the lips of love?
    Ah, deck not out thine own heart's evil springs
By making spirits of heaven as brutish things
And cruel. The wise may hear thee, and guess all!
    And Cypris must take ship—fantastical!
Sail with my son and enter at the gate
To seek thee! Had she willed it, she had sate
At peace in heaven, and wafted thee, and all
Amyclae with thee, under Ilion's wall.
    My son was passing beautiful, beyond
His peers; and thine own heart, that saw and conned
His face, became a spirit enchanting thee.
For all wild things that in mortality

55

Have being, are Aphroditê; and the name
She bears in heaven is born and writ of them.
  Thou sawest him in gold and orient vest
Shining, and lo, a fire about thy breast
Leapt! Thou hadst fed upon such little things,
Pacing thy ways in Argos. But now wings
Were come! Once free from Sparta, and there rolled
The Ilian glory, like broad streams of gold,
To steep thine arms and splash the towers! How
  small,
How cold that day was Menelaus' hall!
  Enough of that. It was by force my son
Took thee, thou sayest, and striving. . . . Yet not one
In Sparta knew! No cry, no sudden prayer
Rang from thy rooms that night. . . . Castor was there
To hear thee, and his brother: both true men,
Not yet among the stars! And after, when
Thou camest here to Troy, and in thy track
Argos and all its anguish and the rack
Of war—Ah God!—perchance men told thee ' Now
The Greek prevails in battle ': then wouldst thou
Praise Menelaus, that my son might smart,
Striving with that old image in a heart
Uncertain still. Then Troy had victories:
And this Greek was as naught! Alway thine eyes
Watched Fortune's eyes, to follow hot where she
Led first. Thou wouldst not follow Honesty.
  Thy secret ropes, thy body swung to fall
Far, like a desperate prisoner, from the wall!
Who found thee so? When wast thou taken? Nay,
Hadst thou no surer rope, no sudden way
Of the sword, that any woman honest-souled
Had sought long since, loving her lord of old?

Often and often did I charge thee; ' Go,
My daughter; go thy ways.   My sons will know
New loves.   I will give aid, and steal thee past
The Argive watch.   O give us peace at last,
Us and our foes! '   But out thy spirit cried
As at a bitter word.   Thou hadst thy pride
In Alexander's house, and O, 'twas sweet
To hold proud Easterns bowing at thy feet.
They were great things to thee! . . . And comest
        thou now
Forth, and hast decked thy bosom and thy brow,
And breathest with thy lord the same blue air,
Thou evil heart?   Low, low, with ravaged hair,
Rent raiment, and flesh shuddering, and within—
O shame at last, not glory for thy sin;
So face him if thou canst! . . . Lo, I have done.
Be true, O King; let Hellas bear her crown
Of Justice.   Slay this woman, and upraise
The law for evermore: she that betrays
Her husband's bed, let her be judged and die.

LEADER.

Be strong, O King; give judgment worthily
For thee and thy great house.   Shake off thy long
Reproach; not weak, but iron against the wrong!

MENELAUS.

Thy thought doth walk with mine in one intent.
'Tis sure; her heart was willing, when she went
Forth to a stranger's bed.   And all her fair
Tale of enchantment, 'tis a thing of air! . . .
                    [*Turning furiously upon* HELEN.

Out, woman!   There be those that seek thee yet
With stones!   Go, meet them.   So shall thy long
  debt
Be paid at last.   And ere this night is o'er
Thy dead face shall dishonour me no more!

HELEN (*kneeling before him and embracing him*).
Behold, mine arms are wreathed about thy knees;
Lay not upon my head the phantasies
Of Heaven.   Remember all, and slay me not!

HECUBA.
Remember them she murdered, them that fought
Beside thee, and their children!   Hear that prayer!

MENELAUS.
Peace, agèd woman, peace!   'Tis not for her;
She is as naught to me.
    (*To the Soldiers*) . . . March on before,
Ye ministers, and tend her to the shore . . .
And have some chambered galley set for her,
Where she may sail the seas.

HECUBA.
                If thou be there,
I charge thee, let not her set foot therein!

MENELAUS.
How?   Shall the ship go heavier for her sin?

HECUBA.
A lover once, will alway love again.

MENELAUS.

If that he loved be evil, he will fain
Hate it! . . . Howbeit, thy pleasure shall be done.
Some other ship shall bear her, not mine own. . . .
Thou counsellest very well . . . And when we come
To Argos, then . . . O then some pitiless doom
Well-earned, black as her heart! One that shall bind
Once for all time the law on womankind
Of faithfulness! . . . 'Twill be no easy thing,
God knoweth. But the thought thereof shall fling
A chill on the dreams of women, though they be
Wilder of wing and loathèd more than she!

> [*Exit, following* HELEN, *who is escorted by the
> Soldiers.*

CHORUS.
Some Women.

[*Strophe* 1.

And hast thou turned from the Altar of frankin-
    cense,
  And given to the Greek thy temple of Ilion?
The flame of the cakes of corn, is it gone from
    hence,
    The myrrh on the air and the wreathèd towers
      gone?
And Ida, dark Ida, where the wild ivy grows,
The glens that run as rivers from the summer-broken
    snows,
And the Rock, is it forgotten, where the first sunbeam
    glows,
    The lit house most holy of the Dawn?

Others.

[*Antistrophe* 1.

The sacrifice is gone and the sound of joy,
   The dancing under the stars and the night-long
      prayer:
The Golden Images and the Moons of Troy,
   The Twelve Moons and the mighty names they
      bear:
My heart, my heart crieth, O Lord Zeus on high,
Were they all to thee as nothing, thou thronèd in the
      sky,
Thronèd in the fire-cloud, where a City, near to die,
   Passeth in the wind and the flare?

A Woman.

[*Strophe* 2.

Dear one, O husband mine,
   Thou in the dim dominions
Driftest with waterless lips,
Unburied; and me the ships
Shall bear o'er the bitter brine,
   Storm-birds upon angry pinions,
Where the towers of the Giants shine
O'er Argos cloudily,
And the riders ride by the sea.

Others.

And children still in the Gate
   Crowd and cry,
A multitude desolate,
Voices that float and wait
   As the tears run dry:

' Mother, alone on the shore
   They drive me, far from thee:
Lo, the dip of the oar,
   The black hull on the sea!
Is it the Isle Immortal,
   Salamis, waits for me?
Is it the Rock that broods
Over the sundered floods
Of Corinth, the ancient portal
   Of Pelops' sovranty?'

A Woman.   *[Antistrophe 2.*

Out in the waste of foam,
   Where rideth dark Menelaus,
Come to us there, O white
And jagged, with wild sea-light
And crashing of oar-blades, come,
   O thunder of God, and slay us:
While our tears are wet for home,
While out in the storm go we,
Slaves of our enemy!

Others.

And, God, may Helen be there,
   With mirror of gold,
Decking her face so fair,
Girl-like; and hear, and stare,
   And turn death-cold:
Never, ah, never more
   The hearth of her home to see,
Nor sand of the Spartan shore,
   Nor tombs where her fathers be,

Nor Athena's bronzen Dwelling,
Nor the towers of Pitanê;
For her face was a dark desire
Upon Greece, and shame like fire,
And her dead are welling, welling,
From red Simoïs to the sea!

[TALTHYBIUS, *followed by one or two Soldiers
and bearing the child* ASTYANAX *dead, is
seen approaching.*

LEADER.

Ah, change on change! Yet each one racks
This land with evil manifold;
Unhappy wives of Troy, behold,
They bear the dead Astyanax,
Our prince, whom bitter Greeks this hour
Have hurled to death from Ilion's tower.

TALTHYBIUS.

One galley, Hecuba, there lingereth yet,
Lapping the wave, to gather the last freight
Of Pyrrhus' spoils for Thessaly. The chief
Himself long since hath parted, much in grief
For Pêleus' sake, his grandsire, whom, men say,
Acastus, Pelias' son, in war array
Hath driven to exile. Loath enough before
Was he to linger, and now goes the more
In haste, bearing Andromache, his prize.
'Tis she hath charmed these tears into mine eyes,
Weeping her fatherland, as o'er the wave
She gazed, and speaking words to Hector's grave.

Howbeit, she prayed us that due rites be done
For burial of this babe, thine Hector's son,
That now from Ilion's tower is fallen and dead.
And, lo! this great bronze-fronted shield, the dread
Of many a Greek, that Hector held in fray,
O never in God's name—so did she pray—
Be this borne forth to hang in Pêleus' hall
Or that dark bridal chamber, that the wall
May hurt her eyes; but here, in Troy o'erthrown,
Instead of cedar wood and vaulted stone,
Be this her child's last house. . . . And in thine hands
She bade me lay him, to be swathed in bands
Of death and garments, such as rest to thee
In these thy fallen fortunes; seeing that she
Hath gone her ways, and, for her master's haste,
May no more fold the babe unto his rest.
   Howbeit, so soon as he is garlanded
And robed, we will heap earth above his head
And lift our sails. . . . See all be swiftly done,
As thou art bidden.   I have saved thee one
Labour.   For as I passed Scamander's stream
Hard by, I let the waters run on him,
And cleansed his wounds.—See, I will go forth now
And break the hard earth for his grave: so thou
And I will haste together, to set free
Our oars at last to beat the homeward sea!
        [*He goes out with his Soldiers, leaving the body of
            the Child in* Hecuba's *arms*

HECUBA.

Set the great orb of Hector's shield to lie
Here on the ground.   'Tis bitter that mine eye

Should see it. . . . O ye Argives, was your spear
Keen, and your hearts so low and cold, to fear
This babe? 'Twas a strange murder for brave
    men!
For fear this babe some day might raise again
His fallen land! Had ye so little pride?
While Hector fought, and thousands at his side,
Ye smote us, and we perished; and now, now,
When all are dead and Ilion lieth low,
Ye dread this innocent! I deem it not
Wisdom, that rage of fear that hath no thought. . . .
    Ah, what a death hath found thee, little one!
Hadst thou but fallen fighting, hadst thou known
Strong youth and love and all the majesty
Of godlike kings, then had we spoken of thee
As of one blessèd . . . could in any wise
These days know blessedness. But now thine eyes
Have seen, thy lips have tasted, but thy soul
No knowledge had nor usage of the whole
Rich life that lapt thee round. . . . Poor little child!
Was it our ancient wall, the circuit piled
By loving Gods, so savagely hath rent
Thy curls, these little flowers innocent
That were thy mother's garden, where she laid
Her kisses; here, just where the bone-edge frayed
Grins white above—Ah heaven, I will not see!
    Ye tender arms, the same dear mould have ye
As his; how from the shoulder loose ye drop
And weak! And dear proud lips, so full of hope
And closed for ever! What false words ye said
At daybreak, when he crept into my bed,
Called me kind names, and promised: 'Grandmother,
When thou art dead, I will cut close my hair,

And lead out all the captains to ride by
Thy tomb.' Why didst thou cheat me so? 'Tis I,
Old, homeless, childless, that for thee must shed
Cold tears, so young, so miserably dead.
   Dear God, the pattering welcomes of thy feet,
The nursing in my lap; and O, the sweet
Falling asleep together! All is gone.
How should a poet carve the funeral stone
To tell thy story true? ' There lieth here
A babe whom the Greeks feared, and in their fear
Slew him.' Aye, Greece will bless the tale it
   tells!
   Child, they have left thee beggared of all else
In Hector's house; but one thing shalt thou keep,
This war-shield bronzen-barred, wherein to sleep.
Alas, thou guardian true of Hector's fair
Left arm, how art thou masterless! And there
I see his handgrip printed on thy hold;
And deep stains of the precious sweat, that rolled
In battle from the brows and beard of him,
Drop after drop, are writ about thy rim.
   Go, bring them—such poor garments hazardous
As these days leave. God hath not granted us
Wherewith to make much pride. But all I can,
I give thee, Child of Troy.—O vain is man,
Who glorieth in his joy and hath no fears:
While to and fro the chances if the years
Dance like an idiot in the wind! And none
By any strength hath his own fortune won.

> [During these lines several Women are seen ap-
>   proaching with garlands and raiment in
>   their hands.

LEADER.

Lo these, who bear thee raiment harvested
From Ilion's slain, to fold upon the dead.

> [*During the following scene* HECUBA *gradually
> takes the garments and wraps them about the
> Child.*

HECUBA.

O not in pride for speeding of the car
Beyond thy peers, not for the shaft of war
True aimed, as Phrygians use; not any prize
Of joy for thee, nor splendour in men's eyes,
Thy father's mother lays these offerings
About thee, from the many fragrant things
That were all thine of old.   But now no more.
One woman, loathed of God, hath broke the door
And robbed thy treasure-house, and thy warm breath
Made cold, and trod thy people down to death!

CHORUS.
Some Women.

Deep in the heart of me
    I feel thine hand,
  Mother: and is it he
Dead here, our prince to be,
   And lord of the land?

HECUBA.

Glory of Phrygian raiment, which my thought
Kept for thy bridal day with some far-sought
Queen of the East, folds thee for evermore.
   And thou, grey Mother, Mother-Shield that bore

A thousand days of glory, thy last crown
Is here. . . . Dear Hector's shield! Thou shalt lie
    down
Undying with the dead, and lordlier there
Than all the gold Odysseus' breast can bear
The evil and the strong!

CHORUS.

Some Women.

Child of the Shield-bearer,
    Alas, Hector's child!
Great Earth, the All-mother,
Taketh thee unto her
    With wailing wild!

Others.

Mother of misery,
    Give Death his song!

(HEC. WOE!) Aye and bitterly
(HEC. WOE!) We too weep for thee,
    And the infinite wrong!
    [*During these lines* HECUBA, *kneeling by the body,
    has been performing a funeral rite, symboli-
    cally staunching the dead Child's wounds.*

HECUBA.

    I make thee whole;
I bind thy wounds, O little vanished soul.
This wound and this I heal with linen white·
O emptiness of aid! . . . Yet let the rite
Be spoken. This and . . . Nay, not I, but he,
Thy father far away shall comfort thee!
    [*She bows her head to the ground and remains
    motionless and unseeing.*

CHORUS.

Beat, beat thine head:
    Beat with the wailing chime
    Of hands lifted in time:
Beat and bleed for the dead.
Woe is me for the dead!

HECUBA.

O Women! Ye, mine own . . .
        [*She rises bewildered, as though she had seen a
            vision.*

LEADER.

                Hecuba, speak!
Thine are we all.   Oh, ere thy bosom break . . .

HECUBA.

Lo, I have seen the open hand of God;
And in it nothing, nothing, save the rod
Of mine affliction, and the eternal hate,
Beyond all lands, chosen and lifted great
For Troy!   Vain, vain were prayer and incense-swell
And bull's blood on the altars! . . . All is well.
Had He not turned us in His hand, and thrust
Our high things low and shook our hills as dust,
We had not been this splendour, and our wrong
An everlasting music for the song
Of earth and heaven!
                Go, women: lay our dead
In his low sepulchre.   He hath his meed
Of robing.   And, methinks, but little care
Toucheth the tomb, if they that moulder there

Have rich encerëment. 'Tis we, 'tis we,
That dream, we living and our vanity!

> [*The Women bear out the dead Child upon the
> shield, singing, when presently flames of fire
> and dim forms are seen among the ruins of the
> City.*

CHORUS.

Some Women.

Woe for the mother that bare thee, child,
    Thread so frail of a hope so high,
That Time hath broken: and all men smiled
    About thy cradle, and, passing by,
    Spoke of thy father's majesty.
        Low, low, thou liest!

Others.

Ha! Who be these on the crested rock?
Fiery hands in the dusk, and a shock
Of torches flung! What lingereth still
O wounded City, of unknown ill,
        Ere yet thou diest?

TALTHYBIUS (*coming out through the ruined Wall*).

Ye Captains that have charge to wreck this keep
Of Priam's City, let your torches sleep
No more! Up, fling the fire into her heart!
Then have we done with Ilion, and may part
In joy to Hellas from this evil land.
    And ye—so hath one word two faces—stand,

Daughters of Troy, till on your ruined wall
The echo of my master's trumpet call
In signal breaks: then, forward to the sea,
Where the long ships lie waiting.

                     And for thee,
O ancient woman most unfortunate,
Follow: Odysseus' men be here, and wait
To guide thee. . . . 'Tis to him thou go'st for thrall.

HECUBA.

Ah, me! and is it come, the end of all,
The very crest and summit of my days?
I go forth from my land, and all its ways
Are filled with fire! Bear me, O aged feet,
A little nearer: I must gaze, and greet
My poor town ere she fall.

                Farewell, farewell!
O thou whose breath was mighty on the swell
Of orient winds, my Troy! Even thy name
Shall soon be taken from thee. Lo, the flame
Hath thee, and we, thy children, pass away
To slavery . . . God! O God of mercy! . . . Nay:
Why call I on the Gods? They know, they know,
My prayers, and would not hear them long ago.
  Quick, to the flames! O, in thine agony,
My Troy, mine own, take me to die with thee!

    [*She springs toward the flames, but is seized and
      held by the Soldiers.*

TALTHYBIUS.

Back! Thou art drunken with thy miseries,
Poor woman!—Hold her fast, men, till it please

Odysseus that she come. She was his lot
Chosen from all and portioned. Lose her not!
  [*He goes to watch over the burning of the City*
    The dusk deepens.

CHORUS.
Divers Women.
Woe, woe, woe!
Thou of the Ages, O wherefore fleëst thou,
  Lord of the Phrygian, Father that made us?
'Tis we, thy children; shall no man aid us?
'Tis we, thy children! Seëst thou, seëst thou?

Others.
He seëth, only his heart is pitiless;
  And the land dies: yea, she,
She of the Mighty Cities perisheth citiless!
  Troy shall no more be!

Others.
Woe, woe, woe!
  Ilion shineth afar!
  Fire in the deeps thereof,
  Fire in the heights above,
    And crested walls of War!

Others.
As smoke on the wing of heaven
  Climbeth and scattereth.
Torn of the spear and driven,
  The land crieth for death:
O stormy battlements that red fire hath riven,
  And the sword's angry breath!
  [*A new thought comes to* HECUBA; *she kneels and*
    beats the earth with her hands.

HECUBA.   [*Strophe.*

O Earth, Earth of my children; hearken! and O
     mine own,
    Y e have hearts and forget not, y e in the darkness
     lying!

LEADER.

Now hast thou found thy prayer, crying to them that
     are gone.

HECUBA.

Surely my knees are weary, but I kneel above your
     head;
Hearken, O ye so silent!   My hands beat your bed!

LEADER.

I, I am near thee;
I kneel to thy dead to hear thee,
Kneel to mine own in the darkness; O husband, hear
     my crying!

HECUBA.

Even as the beasts they drive, even as the loads they
     bear,

LEADER.

(Pain; O pain!)

HECUBA.

We go to the house of bondage. Hear, ye dead, O hear!

LEADER.

(Go, and come not again!)

HECUBA.

Priam, mine own Priam,
    Lying so lowly,
Thou in thy nothingness,
Shelterless, comfortless,
See'st thou the thing I am?
Know'st thou my bitter stress?

LEADER.

Nay, thou art naught to him!
Out of the strife there came,
Out of the noise and shame,
Making his eyelids dim,
    Death, the Most Holy!
    [*The fire and smoke rise constantly higher.*

HECUBA.

                    [*Antistrophe.*
O high houses of Gods, belovèd streets of my birth,
    Ye have found the way of the sword, the fiery and
        blood-red river!

LEADER.

Fall, and men shall forget you! Ye shall lie in the
    gentle earth.

HECUBA.

The dust as smoke riseth; it spreadeth wide its wing;
It maketh me as a shadow, and my City a vanished
    thing!

LEADER.

Out on the smoke she goeth,
And her name no man knoweth;
And the cloud is northward, southward; Troy is
gone for ever!
*[A great crash is heard, and the Wall is lost in
smoke and darkness.*

HECUBA.

Ha! Marked ye? Heard ye? The crash of the
towers that fall!

LEADER.

All is gone!

HECUBA.

Wrath in the earth and quaking and a flood that
sweepeth all,

LEADER.

And passeth on!
[The Greek trumpet sounds.

HECUBA.

Farewell!—O spirit grey,
Whatso is coming,
Fail not from under me.
Weak limbs, why tremble ye?
Forth where the new long day
Dawneth to slavery!

74

CHORUS.

Farewell from parting lips,
Farewell!—Come, I and thou,
Whatso may wait us now,
Forth to the long Greek ships
And the sea's foaming.
[*The trumpet sounds again, and the Women go out
in the darkness.*

NOTES ON THE TROJAN WOMEN

P. 11, l. 5, Poseidon.]—In the *Iliad* Poseidon is the enemy of Troy, here the friend. This sort of confusion comes from the fact that the Trojans and their Greek enemies were largely of the same blood, with the same tribal gods. To the Trojans, Athena the War-Goddess was, of course, *their* War-Goddess, the protectress of their citadel. Poseidon, god of the sea and its merchandise, and Apollo (possibly a local shepherd god?), were their natural friends and had actually built their city wall for love of the good old king, Laomedon. Zeus, the great father, had Mount Ida for his holy hill and Troy for his peculiar city. (Cf. on p. 63.)

To suit the Greek point of view all this had to be changed or explained away. In the *Iliad* generally Athena is the proper War-Goddess of the Greeks. Poseidon had indeed built the wall for Laomedon, but Laomedon had cheated him of his reward—as after wards he cheated Heracles, and the Argonauts and everybody else! So Poseidon hated Troy. Troy is chiefly defended by the barbarian Ares, the oriental Aphrodite, by its own rivers Scamander and Simoïs and suchlike inferior or unprincipled gods.

Yet traces of the other tradition remain. Homer knows that Athena is specially worshipped in Troy. He knows that Apollo, who had built the wall with Poseidon, and had the same experience of Laomedon, still loves the Trojans. Zeus himself, though eventually in obedience to destiny he permits the fall of the city, nevertheless has a great tenderness towards it.

P. 11, l. 11, A steed marvellous.]—See below, on p. 36.

P. 12, l. 25, I go forth from great Ilion, &c.]—
The correct ancient doctrine. When your gods forsook you, there was no more hope. Conversely, when
your state became desperate, evidently your gods were
forsaking you. From another point of view, also,
when the city was desolate and unable to worship its
gods, the gods of that city were no more.

P. 12, l. 34, Laconian Tyndarid.]—Helen was the
child of Zeus and Leda, and sister of Castor and Polydeuces; but her human father was Tyndareus, an old
Spartan king. She is treated as "a prisoner and a
prize," *i.e.*, as a captured enemy, not as a Greek
princess delivered from the Trojans.

P. 12, l. 40, In secret slain.]—Because the Greeks
were ashamed of the bloody deed. See below, p. 42,
and the scene on this subject in the *Hecuba*.

P. 12, l. 42, Cassandra.]—In the *Agamemnon* the
story is more clearly told, that Cassandra was loved by
Apollo and endowed by him with the power of
prophecy; then in some way she rejected or betrayed
him, and he set upon her the curse that though
seeing the truth she should never be believed. The
figure of Cassandra in this play is not inconsistent with
that version, but it makes a different impression. She
is here a dedicated virgin, and her mystic love for
Apollo does not seem to have suffered any breach.

P. 13, l. 47, Pallas.]—(See above.) The historical
explanation of the Trojan Pallas and the Greek Pallas
is simple enough, but as soon as the two are mytho-
logically personified and made one, there emerges just
such a bitter and ruthless goddess as Euripides, in his
revolt against the current mythology, loved to depict.
But it is not only the mythology that he is attacking.
He seems really to feel that if there are conscious gods
ruling the world, they are cruel or "inhuman"
beings.

P. 15, l. 70.]—Ajax the Less, son of Oïleus, either ravished or attempted to ravish Cassandra (the story occurs in both forms) while she was clinging to the Palladium or image of Pallas. It is one of the great typical sins of the Sack of Troy, often depicted on vases.

P. 17, l. 123, Faces of ships.]—Homeric ships had prows shaped and painted to look like birds' or beasts' heads. A ship was always a wonderfully live and vivid thing to the Greek poets. (Cf. p. 64.)

P. 18, l. 132, Castor.]—Helen's brother: the Eurôtas, the river of her home, Sparta.

P. 18, l. 135, Fifty seeds.]—Priam had fifty children, nineteen of them children of Hecuba (*Il.* vi. 451, &c.).

P. 22, l. 205, Pirênê.]—The celebrated spring on the hill of Corinth. Drawing water was a typical employment of slaves.

P. 22, l. 211 ff., Theseus' land, &c.]—Theseus' land is Attica. The poet, in the midst of his bitterness over the present conduct of his city, clings the more to its old fame for humanity. The "land high-born" where the Penêüs flows round the base of Mount Olympus in northern Thessaly is one of the haunts of Euripides' dreams in many plays. Cf. *Bacchae*, 410 (p. 97 in my translation). Mount Aetna fronts the "Tyrians' citadel," *i.e.*, Carthage, built by the Phoenicians. The "sister land" is the district of Sybaris in South Italy, where the river Crathis has, or had, a red-gold colour, which makes golden the hair of men and the fleeces of sheep; and the water never lost its freshness.

P. 23, l. 235.]—Talthybius is a loyal soldier with every wish to be kind. But he is naturally in good spirits over the satisfactory end of the war, and his tact is not sufficient to enable him to understand the Trojan Women's feelings. Yet in the end, since he has to see and do the cruelties which his Chiefs only order from a distance, the real nature of his work forces itself upon him, and he feels and speaks at times almost like a Trojan. It is worth noticing how the Trojan Women generally avoid addressing him. (Cf. pp. 48, 67, 74.)

P. 24, l. 256, The haunted keys (literally, "with God through them, penetrating them ").]—Cassandra was his Key-bearer, holding the door of his Holy Place. (Cf. *Hip.* 540, p. 30.)

P. 25, l. 270, She hath a toil, &c.]—There is something true and pathetic about this curious blindness which prevents Hecuba from understanding "so plain a riddle." (Cf. below, p. 42.) She takes the watching of a Tomb to be some strange Greek custom, and does not seek to have it explained further.

P. 26, l. 277, Odysseus.]—In Euripides generally Odysseus is the type of the successful unscrupulous man, as soldier and politician—the incarnation of what the poet most hated. In Homer of course he is totally different.

P. 27, l. 301, Burn themselves and die.]—Women under these circumstances did commit suicide in Euripides' day, as they have ever since. It is rather curious that none of the characters of the play, not even Andromache, kills herself. The explanation must be that no such suicide was recorded in the tradition (though cf. below, on p. 33); a significant fact, suggesting that in the Homeric age, when this kind of treatment of women captives was regular, the victims did not suffer quite so terribly under it.

P. 28, l. 310, Hymen.]—She addresses the Torch. The shadowy Marriage-God "Hymen" was a torch and a cry as much as anything more personal. As a torch he is the sign both of marriage and of death, of sunrise and of the consuming fire. The full Moon was specially connected with marriage ceremonies.

P. 30, l. 356, Loxias.]—The name of Apollo as an Oracular God.

Pp. 30–34, ll. 360–460, Cassandra's visions.—The allusions are to the various sufferings of Odysseus, as narrated in the *Odyssey*, and to the tragedies of the house of Atreus, as told for instance in Aeschylus' *Oresteia*. Agamemnon together with Cassandra, and in part because he brought Cassandra, was murdered—felled with an axe—on his return home by his wife Clytaemnestra and her lover Aegisthus. Their bodies were cast into a pit among the rocks. In vengeance for this, Orestes, Agamemnon's son, committed "mother-murder," and in consequence was driven by the Erinyes (Furies) of his mother into madness and exile.

P. 30, l. 370, This their king so wise.]—Agamemnon made the war for the sake of his brother Menelaus, and slew his daughter, Iphigenia, as a sacrifice at Aulis, to enable the ships to sail for Troy.

P. 31, ll. 394, 398, Hector and Paris.]—The point about Hector is clear, but as to Paris, the feeling that, after all, it was a glory that he and the half-divine Helen loved each other, is scarcely to be found anywhere else in Greek literature. (Cf., however, Isocrates' "Praise of Helen.") Paris and Helen were never idealised like Launcelot and Guinevere, or Tristram and Iseult.

P. 32, l. 423, A wise queen.]—Penelope, the faithful wife of Odysseus.

P. 33, l. 425, O Heralds, yea, Voices of Death.]— There is a play on the word for "heralds" in the Greek here, which I have evaded by a paraphrase. (Κήρ-υκες as though from Κήρ the death-spirit, "the one thing abhorred of all mortal men.")

P. 33, l. 430, That in this place she dies.]—The death of Hecuba is connected with a certain heap of stones on the shore of the Hellespont, called *Kunos-sêma*, or "Dog's Tomb." According to one tradition (Eur. *Hec.* 1259 ff.) she threw herself off the ship into the sea; according to another she was stoned by the Greeks for her curses upon the fleet; but in both she is changed after death into a sort of Hell-hound. M. Victor Bérard suggests that the dog first comes into the story owing to the accidental resemblance of the (hypothetical) Semitic word *S'qoulah*, "Stone" or "Stoning," and the Greek *Skulax*, dog. The Homeric Scylla (*Skulla*) was also both a Stone and a Dog (*Phèniciens et Odyssèe*, i. 213). Of course in the present passage there is no direct reference to these wild sailor-stories.

P. 34, l. 456, The wind comes quick.]—*i.e.* The storm of the Prologue. Three Powers: the three Erinyes.

P. 36, l. 511 ff., Chorus.]—The Wooden 'Horse is always difficult to understand, and seems to have an obscuring effect on the language of poets who treat of it. I cannot help suspecting that the story arises from a real historical incident misunderstood. Troy, we are told, was still holding out after ten years and could not be taken, until at last by the divine suggestions of Athena, a certain Epeios devised a "Wooden Horse."

What was the "device"? According to the *Odyssey* and most Greek poets, it was a gigantic wooden figure of a horse. A party of heroes, led by Odysseus, got inside it and waited. The Greeks made a show of giving up the siege and sailed away, but only as far as Tenedos. The Trojans came out and found the horse, and after wondering greatly what it was meant for and what to do with it, made a breach in their walls and dragged it into the Citadel as a thank-offering to Pallas. In the night the Greeks returned; the heroes in the horse came out and opened the gates, and Troy was captured.

It seems possible that the "device" really was the

building of a wooden siege-tower, as high as the walls, with a projecting and revolving neck. Such engines were (1) capable of being used at the time in Asia, as a rare and extraordinary device, because they exist on early Assyrian monuments; (2) certain to be misunderstood in Greek legendary tradition, because they were not used in Greek warfare till many centuries later. (First, perhaps, at the sieges of Perinthus and Byzantium by Philip of Macedon, 340 B.C.)

It is noteworthy that in the great picture by Polygnôtus in the Leschê at Delphi "above the wall of Troy appears the head alone of the Wooden Horse" (*Paus.* x. 26). Aeschylus also (*Ag.* 816) has some obscure phrases pointing in the same direction: " A horse's brood, a shield-bearing people, launched with a leap about the Pleiads' setting, sprang clear above the wall," &c. Euripides here treats the horse metaphorically as a sort of war-horse trampling Troy.

P. 37, l. 536, Her that spareth not, Heaven's yokeless rider.]—Athena like a northern Valkyrie, as often in the *Iliad*. If one tries to imagine what Athena, the War-Goddess worshipped by the Athenian mob, was like—what a mixture of bad national passions, of superstition and statecraft, of slip-shod unimaginative idealisation—one may partly understand why Euripides made her so evil. Allegorists and high-minded philosophers might make Athena entirely noble by concentrating their minds on the beautiful elements in the tradition, and forgetting or explaining away all that was savage; he was determined to pin her down to the worsts facts recorded of her, and let people worship such a being if they liked!

P. 38, l. 554, To Artemis.]—Maidens at the shrine of Artemis are a fixed datum in the tradition. (Cf. *Hec.* 935 ff.)

P. 39 ff., l. 576 ff., Andromache and Hecuba.]—

This very beautiful scene is perhaps marred to most modern readers by an element which is merely a part of the convention of ancient mourning. Each of the mourners cries: "There is no affliction like mine!" and then proceeds to argue, as it were, against the other's counter claim. One can only say that it was, after all, what they expected of each other; and I believe the same convention exists in most places where keening or wailing is an actual practice.

P. 41, l. 604, Even as the sound of a song.]—I have filled in some words which seem to be missing in the Greek here.

Pp. 41-50, Andromache.]—This character is wonderfully studied. She seems to me to be a woman who has not yet shown much character or perhaps had very intense experience, but is only waiting for sufficiently great trials to become a heroine and a saint. There is still a marked element of conventionality in her description of her life with Hector; but one feels, as she speaks, that she is already past it. Her character is built up of "Sophrosyne," of self-restraint and the love of goodness—qualities which often seem second-rate or even tiresome until they have a sufficiently great field in which to act. Very characteristic is her resolution to make the best, and not the worst, of her life in Pyrrhus' house, with all its horror of suffering and apparent degradation. So is the self-conquest by which she deliberately refrains from cursing her child's murderers, for the sake of the last poor remnant of good she can still do to him, in getting him buried. The nobility of such a character depends largely, of course, on the intensity of the feelings conquered.

It is worth noting, in this connection, that Euripides is contradicting a wide-spread tradition (Robert, *Bild und Lied*, pp. 63 ff.). Andromache, in the pictures of the Sack of Troy, is represented with a great pestle or some such instrument fighting with the Soldiers to rescue Astyanax ('Ανδρο-μάχη = " Man-fighting ").

Observe, too, what a climax of drama is reached by means of the very fact that Andromache, to the utmost of her power, tries to do nothing "dramatic," but only what will be best. Her character in Euripides' play, *Andromache*, is, on the whole, similar to this, but less developed.

P. 51, l. 799 ff., In Salamis, filled with the foaming, &c.]—A striking instance of the artistic value of the Greek chorus in relieving an intolerable strain. The relief provided is something much higher than what we ordinarily call "relief"; it is a stream of pure poetry and music in key with the sadness of the surrounding scene, yet, in a way happy just because it is beautiful. (Cf. note on *Hippolytus*, l. 732.)

The argument of the rather difficult lyric is: "This is not the first time Troy has been taken. Long ago Heracles made war against the old king Laomedon, because he had not given him the immortal steeds that he promised. And Telamon joined him; Telamon who might have been happy in his island of Salamis, among the bees and the pleasant waters, looking over the strait to the olive-laden hills of Athens, the beloved City! And they took ship and slew Laomedon. Yea, twice Zeus has destroyed Ilion!

(Second part.) Is it all in vain that our Trojan princes have been loved by the Gods? Ganymêdês pours the nectar of Zeus in his banquets, his face never troubled, though his motherhood is burned with fire! And, to say nothing of Zeus, how can the Goddess of Morning rise and shine upon us uncaring? She loved Tithônus, son of Laomedon, and bore him

up from us in a chariot to be her husband in the skies.
But all that once made them love us is gone!"

P. 52, 1. 833, Pools of thy bathing.]—It is probable that Ganymêdês was himself originally a pool
or a spring on Ida, now a pourer of nectar in heaven.

Pp. 54–63, Menelaus and Helen.]—The meeting
of Menelaus and Helen after the taking of Troy was
naturally one of the great moments in the heroic
legend. The versions, roughly speaking, divide themselves into two. In one (*Little Iliad*, Ar. *Lysistr*. 155,
Eur. *Andromache* 628) Menelaus is about to kill her,
but as she bares her bosom to the sword, the sword
falls from his hand. In the other (Stesichorus, *Sack
of Ilion* (?) Menelaus or some one else takes her to
the ships to be stoned, and the men cannot stone her.
As Quintus of Smyrna says, "They looked on her as
they would on a God!"

Both versions have affected Euripides here. And
his Helen has just the magic of the Helen of legend.
That touch of the supernatural which belongs of right
to the Child of Heaven—a mystery, a gentleness, a
strange absence of fear or wrath—is felt through all
her words. One forgets to think of her guilt or
innocence; she is too wonderful a being to judge
too precious to destroy. This supernatural element,
being the thing which, if true, separates Helen from
other women, and in a way redeems her, is for that
reason exactly what Hecuba denies. The contro-
versy has a certain eternal quality about it: the
hypothesis of heavenly enchantment and the hypothesis
of mere bad behaviour, neither of them entirely con-
vincing! But the very curses of those that hate her
make a kind of superhuman atmosphere about Helen
in this play; she fills the background like a great
well-spring of pain.

This Menelaus, however, is rather different from

the traditional Menelaus. Besides being the husband of Helen, he is the typical Conqueror, for whose sake the Greeks fought and to whom the central prize of the war belongs. And we take him at the height of his triumph, the very moment for which he made the war! Hence the peculiar bitterness with which he is treated, his conquest turning to ashes in his mouth, and his love a confused turmoil of hunger and hatred, contemptible and yet terrible.

The exit of the scene would leave a modern audience quite in doubt as to what happened, unless the action were much clearer than the words. But all Athenians knew from the *Odyssey* that the pair were swiftly reconciled, and lived happily together as King and Queen of Sparta.

P. 54, l. 884, Thou deep base of the world.]—These lines, as a piece of religious speculation, were very famous in antiquity. And dramatically they are most important. All through the play Hecuba is a woman of remarkable intellectual power and of fearless thought. She does not definitely deny the existence of the Olympian gods, like some characters in Euripides, but she treats them as beings that have betrayed her, and whose name she scarcely deigns to speak. It is the very godlessness of Hecuba's fortitude that makes it so terrible and, properly regarded, so noble. (Cf. p. 35 "Why call on things so weak?" and p. 74 "They know, they know . . .") Such Gods were as a matter of fact the moral inferiors of good men, and Euripides will never blind his eyes to their inferiority. And as soon as people see that their god is bad, they tend to cease believing in his existence at all. (Hecuba's answer to Helen is not inconsistent with this, it is only less characteristic.)

Behind this Olympian system, however, there is a possibility of some real Providence or impersonal

Governance of the world, to which here, for a moment, Hecuba makes a passionate approach. If there is *any* explanation, *any* justice, even in the form of mere punishment of the wicked, she will be content and give worship! But it seems that there is not. Then at last there remains—what most but not all modern freethinkers would probably have begun to doubt at the very beginning—the world of the departed, the spirits of the dead, who are true, and in their dim way love her still (p. 71 "Thy father far away shall comfort thee," and the last scene of the play).

This last religion, faint and shattered by doubt as it is, represents a return to the most primitive "Pelasgian" beliefs, a worship of the Dead which existed long before the Olympian system, and has long outlived it.

P. 57, l. 922, The fire-brand's image.]—Hecuba, just before Paris' birth, dreamed that she gave birth to a fire-brand. The prophets therefore advised that the babe should be killed; but Priam disobeyed them.

P. 57, l. 924, Three Crowns of Life.]—On the Judgment of Paris see Miss Harrison, *Prolegomena*, pp. 292 ff. Late writers degrade the story into a beauty contest between three thoroughly personal goddesses— and a contest complicated by bribery. But originally the Judgment is rather a Choice between three possible lives, like the Choice of Heracles between Work and Idleness. The elements of the choice vary in different versions: but in general Hera is royalty; Athena is prowess in war or personal merit; Aphrodite, of course, is love. And the goddesses are not really to be distinguished from the gifts they bring. They are what they give, and nothing more. Cf. the wonderful lyric *Androm.* 274 ff., where they come to "a young man walking to and fro alone, in an empty hut in the firelight."

There is an extraordinary effect in Helen herself *being* one of the Crowns of Life—a fair equivalent for the throne of the world.

P. 57, l. 940 ff., Alexander . . . Paris.]—Two plays on words in the Greek.

P. 58, l. 956, The old Gate-Warden.]—He and the Watchers are, of course, safely dead. But on the general lines of the tradition it may well be that Helen is speaking the truth. She loved both Menelaus and Paris; and, according to some versions, hated Dêïphobus, the Trojan prince who seized her after Paris' death. There is a reference to Dêïphobus in the MSS. of the play here, but I follow Wilamowitz in thinking it spurious.

Pp. 63 ff., Chorus.]—On the Trojan Zeus see above, on p. 11. Mount Ida caught the rays of the rising sun in some special manner and distributed them to the rest of the world; and in this gleam of heavenly fire the God had his dwelling, which is now the brighter for the flames of his City going up like incense!

Nothing definite is known of the Golden Images and the Moon-Feasts.

P. 64, l. 1088, Towers of the Giants.]—The prehistoric castles of Tiryns and Mycênae.

P. 65, l. 1111, May Helen be there.]—(Cf. above.) Pitanê was one of the five divisions of Sparta. Athena had a " Bronzen House " on the acropolis of Sparta. Simoïs, of course, the river of Troy.

P. 71, l. 1232, I make thee whole.]—Here as elsewhere Hecuba fluctuates between fidelity to the oldest and most instinctive religion, and a rejection of all Gods.

P. 72, l. 1240, Lo, I have seen the open hand of God.]—The text is, perhaps, imperfect here; but Professor Wilamowitz agrees with me that Hecuba has seen something like a vision. The meaning of this speech is of the utmost importance. It expresses the inmost theme of the whole play, a search for an answer to the injustice of suffering in the very splendour and beauty of suffering. Of course it must be suffering of a particular kind, or, what comes to the same thing, suffering borne in a particular way; but in that case the answer seems to me to hold. One does not really think the world evil because there are martyrs or heroes in it. For them the elements of beauty which exist in any great trial of the spirit become so great as to overpower the evil that created them—to turn it from shame and misery into tragedy. Of course to most sufferers, to children and animals and weak people, or those without inspiration, the doctrine brings no help. It is a thing invented by a poet for himself.

P. 75, l. 1288, Thou of the Ages.]—The Phrygian All-Father, identified with Zeus, son of Kronos. (Cf. on p. 11.)

P. 76, l. 1304, Now hast thou found thy prayer.]— The Gods have deserted her, but she has still the dead. (Cf. above, on p. 71.)

P. 79, l. 1332, Forth to the dark Greek ships.]— Curiously like another magnificent ending of a great poem, that of the *Chanson de Roland*, where Charlemagne is called forth on a fresh quest:

"Deus," dist li Reis, "si penuse est ma vie!"
Pluret des oilz, sa barbe blanche tiret. . . .

EURIPIDES

THE MEDEA

TRANSLATED INTO ENGLISH RHYMING VERSE

WITH EXPLANATORY NOTES BY

GILBERT MURRAY

O.M., D.C.L.

FORMERLY REGIUS PROFESSOR OF GREEK IN THE
UNIVERSITY OF OXFORD

LONDON
GEORGE ALLEN & UNWIN LTD
MUSEUM STREET

INTRODUCTION

THE *Medea*, in spite of its background of wonder and enchantment, is not a romantic play but a tragedy of character and situation. It deals, so to speak, not with the romance itself, but with the end of the romance, a thing which is so terribly often the reverse of romantic. For all but the very highest of romances are apt to have just one flaw somewhere, and in the story of Jason and Medea the flaw was of a fatal kind.

The wildness and beauty of the Argo legend run through all Greek literature, from the mass of Corinthian lays older than our present Iliad, which later writers vaguely associate with the name of Eumêlus, to the Fourth Pythian Ode of Pindar and the beautiful Argonautica of Apollonius Rhodius. Our poet knows the wildness and the beauty; but it is not these qualities that he specially seeks. He takes them almost for granted, and pierces through them to the sheer tragedy that lies below.

Jason, son of Aeson, King of Iôlcos, in Thessaly, began his life in exile. His uncle Pelias had seized his father's kingdom, and Jason was borne away to the mountains by night and given, wrapped in a purple robe, to Chiron, the Centaur. When he reached manhood he came down to Iôlcos to demand, as Pindar tells us, his ancestral honour, and stood in the market-place, a world-famous figure, onesandalled, with his pard-skin, his two spears and his long hair, gentle and wild and fearless, as the Wise Beast had reared him. Pelias, cowed but loath to yield, promised to give up the kingdom if Jason would make his way to the unknown land of Colchis and perform a double quest. First, if I read Pindar aright, he must fetch back the soul of his kinsman Phrixus, who had died there far from home; and, secondly, find the fleece of the Golden Ram which Phrixus had sacrificed. Jason undertook the quest: gathered the most daring heroes from all parts of Hellas; built the first ship, Argo, and set to sea. After all manner of desperate adventures he reached the land of Aiêtês, king of the Colchians, and there hope failed him. By policy, by tact, by sheer courage he did all that man could do. But Aiêtês was both hostile and treacherous. The Argonauts were surrounded, and their destruction seemed only a question of days when, suddenly, unasked, and by the mercy of Heaven, Aiêtês' daughter, Mêdêa, an enchantress as well as a princess, fell in love with Jason. She helped him through all his trials; slew for him her own sleepless serpent, who guarded the fleece; deceived her father, and secured both the fleece and the soul of Phrixus. At the last moment it appeared that her brother, Absyrtus, was about to lay an ambush for Jason. She invited Absyrtus to her room, stabbed him dead, and fled with Jason over the seas. She had given up all, and expected in return a perfect love.

And what of Jason? He could not possibly avoid taking Medea with him. He probably rather loved her. She formed at the least a brilliant addition to the glory of his enterprise. Not many heroes could produce a barbarian princess ready to leave all and follow them in blind trust. For of course, as every one knew without the telling in fifth-century Athens, no legal marriage was possible between a Greek and a barbarian from Colchis.

All through the voyage home, a world-wide baffled voyage by the Ister and the Eridanus and the African Syrtes, Medea was still in her element, and proved a constant help and counsellor to the Argonauts. When they reached Jason's home, where Pelias was still king, things began to be different. An ordered and law-abiding Greek state was scarcely the place for the untamed Colchian. We only know the catastrophe. She saw with smothered rage how Pelias hated Jason and was bent on keeping the kingdom from him, and she determined to do her lover another act of splendid service. Making the most of her fame as an enchantress, she persuaded Pelias that he could, by a certain process, regain his youth. He eagerly caught at the hope. His daughters tried the process upon him, and Pelias died in agony. Surely Jason would be grateful now!

The real result was what it was sure to be in a civilised country. Medea and her lover had to fly for their lives, and Jason was debarred for ever from succeeding to the throne of Iôlcos. Probably there was another result also in Jason's mind: the conclusion that at all costs he must somehow separate himself from this wild beast of a woman who was ruining his life. He directed their flight to Corinth, governed at the time by a ruler of some sort, whether " tyrant " or king, who was growing old and had an only daughter. Creon would naturally want a son-in-law to support and succeed him. And where in all Greece could he find one stronger or more famous than the chief of the Argonauts? If only Medea were not there! No doubt Jason owed her a great debt for her various services. Still, after all, he was not married to her. And a man must not be weak in such matters as these. Jason accepted the princess's hand, and when Medea became violent, found it difficult to be really angry with Creon for instantly condemning her to exile. At this point the tragedy begins.

The *Medea* is one of the earliest of Euripides' works now preserved to us. And those of us who have in our time glowed at all with the religion of realism will probably feel in it many of the qualities of youth. Not, of course, the more normal, sensuous, romantic youth, the youth of *Romeo and Juliet*; but another kind—crude, austere, passionate—the youth of the poet who is also a sceptic and a devotee of truth, who so hates the conventionally and falsely beautiful that he is apt to be unduly ascetic towards beauty itself. When a writer really deficient in poetry walks in this path, the result is purely disagreeable. It produces its best results when the writer, like Euripides or Tolstoy, is so possessed by an inward flame of poetry that it breaks out at the great moments and consumes the cramping theory that would hold it in. One can feel in the *Medea* that the natural and inevitable romance of the story is kept rigidly down. One word about Medea's ancient serpent, two or three references to the Clashing Rocks, one startling flash of light upon the real love of Jason's life, love for the ship Argo, these are almost all the concessions made to us by the merciless delineator of disaster into whose hands we are fallen. Jason is a middle-aged man, with much glory, indeed, and some illusions; but a man entirely set upon building up a great career, to whom love and all its works, though at times he has found them convenient, are for the most part only irrational and disturbing elements in a world which he can otherwise mould to his will. And yet, most cruel touch of all, one feels this man to be the real Jason. It is not that he has fallen from his heroic past. It is that he was really like this always. And so with Medea. It is not only that her beauty has begun to fade; not only that she is set in surroundings which vaguely belittle and weaken her, making her no more a bountiful princess, but only an ambiguous and much criticised foreigner. Her very devotion of love for Jason, now turned to hatred, shows itself to have been always of that somewhat rank and ugly sort to which such a change is natural.

For concentrated dramatic quality and sheer intensity of passion few plays ever written can vie with the *Medea*. Yet it obtained only a third prize at its first production; and, in spite of its immense fame, there are not many scholars who would put it among their favourite tragedies. The comparative failure of the first production was perhaps due chiefly to the extreme originality of the play. The Athenians in 432 B.C. had not yet learnt to understand or tolerate such work as this, though it is likely enough that they fortified their unfavourable opinion by the sort of criticisms which we still find attributed to Aristotle and Dicæarchus.

At the present time it is certainly not the newness of the subject: I do not think it is Aegeus, nor yet the dragon chariot, much less Medea's involuntary burst of tears in the second scene with Jason, that really produces the feeling of dissatisfaction with which many people must rise from this great play. It is rather the general scheme on which the drama is built. It is a scheme which occurs again and again in Euripides, a study of oppression and revenge. Such a subject in the hands of a more ordinary writer would probably take the form of a triumph of oppressed virtue. But Euripides gives us nothing so sympathetic, nothing so cheap and unreal. If oppression usually made people virtuous, the problems of the world would be very different from what they are. Euripides seems at times to hate the revenge of the oppressed almost as much as the original cruelty of the oppressor; or, to put the same fact in a different light, he seems deliberately to dwell upon the twofold evil of cruelty, that it not only causes pain to the victim, but actually by means of the pain makes him a worse man, so that when his turn of triumph comes, it is no longer a triumph of justice or a thing to make men rejoice. This is a grim lesson; taught often enough by history, though seldom by the fables of the poets.

Seventeen years later than the *Medea* Euripides expressed this sentiment in a more positive way in the *Trojan Women*, where a depth of wrong borne without revenge becomes, or seems for the moment to become, a thing beautiful and glorious. But more plays are constructed like the *Medea*. The *Hecuba* begins with a noble and injured Queen, and ends

with her hideous vengeance on her enemy and his
innocent sons.   In the *Orestes* all our hearts go out to
the suffering and deserted prince, till we find at last
that we have committed ourselves to the blood-thirst
of a madman.   In the *Electra*, the workers of the
vengeance themselves repent.

The dramatic effect of this kind of tragedy is
curious.   No one can call it undramatic or tame.
Yet it is painfully unsatisfying.   At the close of the
Medea I actually find myself longing for a *deus ex
machinâ*, for some being like Artemis in the *Hippolytus*
or the good Dioscuri of the *Electra*, to speak a word
of explanation or forgiveness, or at least leave some
sound of music in our ears to drown that dreadful and
insistent clamour of hate.   The truth is that in this
play Medea herself is the *dea ex machinâ*.   The woman
whom Jason and Creon intended simply to crush has
been transformed by her injuries from an individual
human being into a sort of living Curse.   She is
inspired with superhuman force.   Her wrongs and
her hate fill all the sky.   And the judgment pronounced on Jason comes not from any disinterested
or peace-making God, but from his own victim
transfigured into a devil.

From any such judgment there is an instant appeal
to sane human sympathy.   Jason has suffered more
than enough.   But that also is the way of the world.
And the last word upon these tragic things is most
often something not to be expressed by the sentences
of even the wisest articulate judge, but only by the
unspoken *lacrimæ rerum.*

CHARACTERS OF THE PLAY

MEDEA, *daughter of Aiêtês, King of Colchis.*
JASON, *chief of the Argonauts; nephew of Pelias, King of Iôlcos in Thessaly.*
CREON, *ruler of Corinth.*
AEGEUS, *King of Athens.*
NURSE *of Medea.*
TWO CHILDREN *of Jason and Medea.*
ATTENDANT *on the children.*
A MESSENGER.

CHORUS of Corinthian Women, with their LEADER.
Soldiers and Attendants.

The scene is laid in Corinth. The play was first acted when Pythodôrus was Archon, Olympiad 87, year 1 (431 B.C.). Euphorion was first, Sophocles second, Euripides third, with Medea, Philoctêtes, Dictys, and the Harvesters, a Satyr-play.

MEDEA

The Scene represents the front of MEDEA'S *House in Corinth. A road to the right leads towards the royal castle, one on the left to the harbour. The* NURSE *is discovered alone.*

NURSE.

Would God no Argo e'er had winged the seas
To Colchis through the blue Symplêgades:
No shaft of riven pine in Pêlion's glen
Shaped that first oar-blade in the hands of men
Valiant, who won, to save King Pelias' vow,
The fleece All-golden! Never then, I trow,
Mine own princess, her spirit wounded sore
With love of Jason, to the encastled shore
Had sailed of old Iôlcos: never wrought
The daughters of King Pelias, knowing not,
To spill their father's life: nor fled in fear,
Hunted for that fierce sin, to Corinth here
With Jason and her babes. This folk at need
Stood friend to her, and she in word and deed
Served alway Jason. Surely this doth bind,
Through all ill days, the hurts of humankind,
When man and woman in one music move.
  But now, the world is angry, and true love

Sick as with poison.   Jason doth forsake
My mistress and his own two sons, to make
His couch in a king's chamber.   He must wed:
Wed with this Creon's child, who now is head
And chief of Corinth.   Wherefore sore betrayed
Medea calleth up the oath they made,
They two, and wakes the claspèd hands again,
The troth surpassing speech, and cries amain
On God in heaven to mark the end, and how
Jason hath paid his debt.

> All fasting now
And cold, her body yielded up to pain,
Her days a waste of weeping, she hath lain,
Since first she knew that he was false.   Her eyes
Are lifted not; and all her visage lies
In the dust.   If friends will speak, she hears no more
Than some dead rock or wave that beats the shore:
Only the white throat in a sudden shame
May writhe, and all alone she moans the name
Of father, and land, and home, forsook that day
For this man's sake, who casteth her away.
Not to be quite shut out from home . . . alas,
She knoweth now how rare a thing that was!
Methinks she hath a dread, not joy, to see
Her children near.   'Tis this that maketh me
Most tremble, lest she do I know not what.
Her heart is no light thing, and useth not
To brook much wrong.   I know that woman, aye,
And dread her!   Will she creep alone to die
Bleeding in that old room, where still is laid
Lord Jason's bed?   She hath for that a blade
Made keen.   Or slay the bridegroom and the king,
And win herself God knows what direr thing?

'Tis a fell spirit.   Few, I ween, shall stir
Her hate unscathed, or lightly humble her.
    Ha!   'Tis the children from their games again,
Rested and gay; and all their mother's pain
Forgotten!   Young lives ever turn from gloom!
        [*The* CHILDREN *and their* ATTENDANT *come in.*

ATTENDANT.

Thou ancient treasure of my lady's room,
What mak'st thou here before the gates alone,
And alway turning on thy lips some moan
Of old mischances?   Will our mistress be
Content, this long time to be left by thee?

NURSE.

Grey guard of Jason's children, a good thrall
Hath his own grief, if any hurt befall
His masters.   Aye,   it   holds   one's   heart!   . . .
    Meseems
I have strayed out so deep in evil dreams,
I longed to rest me here alone, and cry
Medea's wrongs to this still Earth and Sky.

ATTENDANT.

How?   Are the tears yet running in her eyes?

NURSE.

'Twere good to be like thee! . . . Her sorrow lies
Scarce wakened yet, not half its perils wrought.

ATTENDANT.

Mad spirit! . . . if a man may speak his thought
Of masters mad.—And nothing in her ears
Hath sounded yet of her last cause for tears!
   [*He moves towards the house, but the* NURSE
   checks him.

NURSE.

What cause, old man? . . . Nay, grudge me not one
   word.

ATTENDANT.

'Tis nothing.   Best forget what thou hast heard.

NURSE.

Nay, housemate, by thy beard!   Hold it not hid
From me. . . . I will keep silence if thou bid.

ATTENDANT.

I heard an old man talking, where he sate
At draughts in the sun, beside the fountain gate,
And never thought of me, there standing still
Beside him.   And he said, 'Twas Creon's will,
Being lord of all this land, that she be sent,
And with her her two sons, to banishment.
Maybe 'tis all false.   For myself, I know
No further, and I would it were not so.

NURSE.

Jason will never bear it—his own sons
Banished,—however hot his anger runs
Against their mother!

ATTENDANT.

Old love burneth low
When new love wakes, men say.   He is not now
Husband nor father here, nor any kin.

NURSE.

But this is ruin!   New waves breaking in
To wreck us, ere we are righted from the old!

ATTENDANT.

Well, hold thy peace.   Our mistress will be told
All in good time.   Speak thou no word hereof.

NURSE.

My babes!   What think ye of your father's love?
God curse him not, he is my master still:
But, oh, to them that loved him, 'tis an ill
Friend. . . .

ATTENDANT.

And what man on earth is different?   How?
Hast thou lived all these years, and learned but now
That every man more loveth his own head
Than other men's?   He dreameth of the bed
Of this new bride, and thinks not of his sons.

NURSE.

Go: run into the house, my little ones:
All will end happily! . . . Keep them apart:
Let not their mother meet them while her heart

Is darkened.   Yester night I saw a flame
Stand in her eyes, as though she hated them,
And would I know not what.   For sure her wrath
Will never turn nor slumber, till she hath . . .
Go: and if some must suffer, may it be
Not we who love her, but some enemy!

VOICE (*within*).
O shame and pain: O woe is me!
Would I could die in my misery!
[*The* CHILDREN *and the* ATTENDANT *go in.*

NURSE.
Ah, children, hark!   She moves again
Her frozen heart, her sleeping wrath.
In, quick!   And never cross her path,
Nor rouse that dark eye in its pain;

That fell sea-spirit, and the dire
Spring of a will untaught, unbowed.
Quick, now!—Methinks this weeping cloud
Hath in its heart some thunder-fire,

Slow gathering, that must flash ere long.
I know not how, for ill or well,
It turns, this uncontrollable
Tempestuous spirit, blind with wrong.

VOICE (*within*).
Have I not suffered?   Doth it call
No tears? . . . Ha, ye beside the wall
Unfathered children, God hate you
As I am hated, and him, too,
That gat you, and this house and all!

NURSE.

For pity! What have they to do,
  Babes, with their father's sin? Why call
  Thy curse on these? . . . Ah, children, all
These days my bosom bleeds for you.

Rude are the wills of princes: yea,
  Prevailing alway, seldom crossed,
  On fitful winds their moods are tossed:
'Tis best men tread the equal way.

Aye, not with glory but with peace
  May the long summers find me crowned:
  For gentleness—her very sound
Is magic, and her usages

All wholesome: but the fiercely great
  Hath little music on his road,
  And falleth, when the hand of God
Shall move, most deep and desolate.
[*During the last words the* LEADER *of the Chorus
  has entered. Other women follow her.*

LEADER.

I heard a voice and a moan,
  A voice of the eastern seas:
  Hath she found not yet her ease?
    Speak, O agèd one.
  For I stood afar at the gate,
    And there came from within a cry,

And wailing desolate.
Ah, no more joy have I,
For the griefs this house doth see,
And the love it hath wrought in me.

NURSE.

There is no house! 'Tis gone. The lord
Seeketh a prouder bed: and she
Wastes in her chamber, nor one word
Will hear of care or charity.

VOICE (*within*).

O Zeus, O Earth, O Light,
Will the fire not stab my brain?
What profiteth living? Oh,
Shall I not lift the slow
Yoke, and let Life go,
As a beast out in the night,
To lie, and be rid of pain.

CHORUS.

Some Women.

A.

"O Zeus, O Earth, O Light:"
The cry of a bride forlorn
Heard ye, and wailing born
Of lost delight?

B.

Why weariest thou this day,
    Wild heart, for the bed abhorrèd,
The cold bed in the clay?
Death cometh though no man pray,
    Ungarlanded, un-adorèd.
        Call him not thou.

C.

If another's arms be now
    Where thine have been,
    On his head be the sin:
Rend not thy brow!

D.

All that thou sufferest,
    God seeth: Oh, not so sore
Waste nor weep for the breast
    That was thine of yore.

VOICE (*within*).

Virgin of Righteousness,
Virgin of hallowed Troth,
Ye marked me when with an oath
I bound him; mark no less
That oath's end.   Give me to see
Him and his bride, who sought
My grief when I wronged her not,
Broken in misery,

And all her house. . . . O God,
My mother's home, and the dim
Shore that I left for him,
And the voice of my brother's blood. . . .

NURSE.

Oh, wild words! Did ye hear her cry
    To them that guard man's faith forsworn,
    Themis and Zeus? . . . This wrath new-born
Shall make mad workings ere it die.

CHORUS.
Other Women.

A.

Would she but come to seek
    Our faces, that love her well,
    And take to her heart the spell
Of words that speak?

B.

Alas for the heavy hate
    And anger that burneth ever!
Would it but now abate,
Ah God, I love her yet.
    And surely my love's endeavour
    Shall fail not here.

C.

Go: from that chamber drear
    Forth to the day
Lead her, and say, Oh, say
    That we love her dear.

D.

Go, lest her hand be hard
  On the innocent: Ah, let be!
For her grief moves hitherward,
  Like an angry sea.

Nurse.

That will I: though what words of mine
  Or love shall move her?   Let them lie
  With the old lost labours! . . . Yet her eye—
Know ye the eyes of the wild kine,

The lion flash that guards their brood?
  So looks she now if any thrall
  Speak comfort, or draw near at all
My mistress in her evil mood.

[*The* Nurse *goes into the house.*

Chorus.

A Woman.

Alas, the bold blithe bards of old
  That all for joy their music made,
For feasts and dancing manifold,
  That Life might listen and be glad.

But all the darkness and the wrong,
  Quick deaths and dim heart-aching things,
Would no man ease them with a song
  Or music of a thousand strings?

Then song had served us in our need.
What profit, o'er the banquet's swell
That lingering cry that none may heed?
The feast hath filled them: all is well!

Others.

I heard a song, but it comes no more,
        Where the tears ran over:
A keen cry but tired, tired:
A woman's cry for her heart's desired,
        For a traitor's kiss and a lost lover.
But a prayer, methinks, yet riseth sore
        To God, to Faith, God's ancient daughter—
The Faith that over sundering seas
Drew her to Hellas, and the breeze
Of midnight shivered, and the door
        Closed of the salt unsounded water.
[*During the last words* MEDEA *has come out from
        the house.*

MEDEA.

Women of Corinth, I am come to show
My face, lest ye despise me.   For I know
Some heads stand high and fail not, even at night
Alone—far less like this, in all men's sight:
And we, who study not our wayfarings
But feel and cry—Oh we are drifting things,
And evil!   For what truth is in men's eyes,
Which search no heart, but in a flash despise

A strange face, shuddering back from one that ne'er
Hath wronged them? . . . Sure, far-comers any-
    where,
I know, must bow them and be gentle. Nay,
A Greek himself men praise not, who alway
Should seek his own will recking not. . . . But I—
This thing undreamed of, sudden from on high,
Hath sapped my soul: I dazzle where I stand,
The cup of all life shattered in my hand,
Longing to die—O friends! He, even he,
Whom to know well was all the world to me,
The man I loved, hath proved most evil.—Oh,
Of all things upon earth that bleed and grow,
A herb most bruised is woman. We must pay
Our store of gold, hoarded for that one day,
To buy us some man's love; and lo, they bring
A master of our flesh! There comes the sting
Of the whole shame. And then the jeopardy,
For good or ill, what shall that master be;
Reject she cannot: and if he but stays
His suit, 'tis shame on all that woman's days.
So thrown amid new laws, new places, why,
'Tis magic she must have, or prophecy—
Home never taught her that—how best to guide
Toward peace this thing that sleepeth at her side.
And she who, labouring long, shall find some way
Whereby her lord may bear with her, nor fray
His yoke too fiercely, blessed is the breath
That woman draws! Else, let her pray for death.
Her lord, if he be wearied of the face
Withindoors, gets him forth, some merrier place
Will ease his heart: but she waits on, her whole
Vision enchainèd on a single soul.

And then, forsooth, 'tis they that face the call
Of war, while we sit sheltered, hid from all
Peril!—False mocking!   Sooner would I stand
Three times to face their battles, shield in hand,
Than bear one child.
              But peace!   There cannot be
Ever the same tale told of thee and me.
Thou hast this city, and thy father's home,
And joy of friends, and hope in days to come:
But I, being citiless, am cast aside
By him that wedded me, a savage bride
Won in far seas and left—no mother near,
No brother, not one kinsman anywhere
For harbour in this storm.   Therefore of thee
I ask one thing.   If chance yet ope to me
Some path, if even now my hand can win
Strength to requite this Jason for his sin,
Betray me not!   Oh, in all things but this,
I know how full of fears a woman is,
And faint at need, and shrinking from the light
Of battle: but once spoil her of her right
In man's love, and there moves, I warn thee well,
No bloodier spirit between heaven and hell.

LEADER.

I will betray thee not.   It is but just,
Thou smite him.—And that weeping in the dust
And stormy tears, how should I blame them? . . .
    Stay:
'Tis Creon, lord of Corinth, makes his way
Hither, and bears, methinks, some word of weight.

[Enter from the right CREON, *the King, with armed Attendants.*

CREON

Thou woman sullen-eyed and hot with hate
Against thy lord, Medea, I here command
That thou and thy two children from this land
Go forth to banishment.   Make no delay:
Seeing ourselves, the King, are come this day
To see our charge fulfilled; nor shall again
Look homeward ere we have led thy children twain
And thee beyond our realm's last boundary.

MEDEA

Lost! Lost!
Mine haters at the helm with sail flung free
Pursuing; and for us no beach nor shore
In the endless waters! . . . Yet, though stricken sore,
I still will ask thee, for what crime, what thing
Unlawful, wilt thou cast me out, O King?

CREON.

What crime?   I fear thee, woman—little need
To cloak my reasons—lest thou work some deed
Of darkness on my child.   And in that fear
Reasons enough have part.   Thou comest here
A wise-woman confessed, and full of lore
In unknown ways of evil. Thou art sore
In heart, being parted from thy lover's arms.
And more, thou hast made menace . . . so the
     alarms

But now have reached mine ear . . . on bride and
    groom,
And him who gave the bride, to work thy doom
Of vengeance.   Which, ere yet it be too late,
I sweep aside.   I choose to earn thine hate
Of set will now, not palter with the mood
Of mercy, and hereafter weep in blood.

MEDEA.

'Tis not the first nor second time, O King,
That fame hath hurt me, and come nigh to bring
My ruin. . . . How can any man, whose eyes
Are wholesome, seek to rear his children wise
Beyond men's wont?   Much helplessness in arts
Of common life, and in their townsmen's hearts
Envy deep-set . . . so much their learning brings!
Come unto fools with knowledge of new things,
They deem it vanity, not knowledge.   Aye,
And men that erst for wisdom were held high,
Feel thee a thorn to fret them, privily
Held higher than they.   So hath it been with me.
A wise-woman I am; and for that sin
To divers ill names men would pen me in;
A seed of strife; an eastern dreamer; one
Of brand not theirs; one hard to play upon . . .
Ah, I am not so wondrous wise!—And now,
To thee, I am terrible!   What fearest thou?
What dire deed?   Do I tread so proud a path—
Fear me not thou!—that I should brave the wrath
Of princes?   Thou: what hast thou ever done
To wrong me?   Granted thine own child to one
Whom thy soul chose.—Ah, *him* out of my heart
I hate; but thou, meseems, hast done thy part

Not ill.   And for thine houses' happiness
I hold no grudge.   Go: marry, and God bless
Your issues.   Only suffer me to rest
Somewhere within this land. Though sore oppressed,
I will be still, knowing mine own defeat.

CREON.

Thy words be gentle: but I fear me yet
Lest even now there creep some wickedness
Deep hid within thee.   And for that the less
I trust thee now than ere these words began.
A woman quick of wrath, aye, or a man,
Is easier watching than the cold and still.
    Up, straight, and find thy road! Mock not my will
With words. This doom is passed beyond recall;
Nor all thy crafts shall help thee, being withal
My manifest foe, to linger at my side.

MEDEA (*suddenly throwing herself down and
clinging to* CREON).
Oh, by thy knees!   By that new-wedded bride . . .

CREON.
'Tis waste of words.   Thou shalt not weaken me.

MEDEA.
Wilt hunt me?   Spurn me when I kneel to thee?

CREON.
'Tis mine own house that kneels to me, not thou.

MEDEA.

Home, my lost home, how I desire thee now!

CREON.

And I mine, and my child, beyond all things.

MEDEA.

O Loves of man, what curse is on your wings!

CREON.

Blessing or curse, 'tis as their chances flow.

MEDEA.

Remember, Zeus, the cause of all this woe!

CREON.

Oh, rid me of my pains! Up, get the · gone!

MEDEA.

What would I with thy pains? I have mine own.

CREON.

Up: or, 'fore God, my soldiers here shall fling . . .

MEDEA.

Not that! Not that! . . . I do but pray, O King . . .

CREON.

Thou wilt not? I must face the harsher task?

MEDEA.

I accept mine exile. 'Tis not that I ask.

CREON.

Why then so wild? Why clinging to mine hand?

MEDEA (*rising*).

For one day only leave me in thy land
At peace, to find some counsel, ere the strain
Of exile fall, some comfort for these twain,
Mine innocents; since others take no thought,
It seems, to save the babes that they begot.
　Ah! Thou wilt pity them! Thou also art
A father: thou hast somewhere still a heart
That feels. . . . I reck not of myself: 'tis they
That break me, fallen upon so dire a day.

CREON.

Mine is no tyrant's mood.　Aye, many a time
Ere this my tenderness hath marred the chime
Of wisest counsels.　And I know that now
I do mere folly.　But so be it!　Thou
Shalt have this grace . . . But this I warn thee clear,
If once the morrow's sunlight find thee here
Within my borders, thee or child of thine,
Thou diest! . . . Of this judgment not a line

Shall waver nor abate.   So linger on,
If thou needs must, till the next risen sun;
No further. . . . In one day there scarce can be
Those perils wrought whose dread yet haunteth me.

[*Exit* CREON *with his suite.*

CHORUS.

O woman, woman of sorrow,
   Where wilt thou turn and flee?
What town shall be thine to-morrow,
   What land of all lands that be,
What door of a strange man's home?
   Yea, God hath hunted thee,
Medea, forth to the foam
    Of a trackless sea.

MEDEA.

Defeat on every side; what else?—But Oh,
Not here the end is: think it not!   I know
For bride and groom one battle yet untried,
And goodly pains for him that gave the bride.
   Dost dream I would have grovelled to this man,
Save that I won mine end, and shaped my plan
For merry deeds?   My lips had never deigned
Speak word with him: my flesh been never stained
With touching. . . . Fool, Oh, triple fool! It lay
So plain for him to kill my whole essay
By exile swift: and, lo, he sets me free
This one long day: wherein mine haters three
Shall lie here dead, the father and the bride
And husband—mine, not hers!   Oh, I have tried

So many thoughts of murder to my turn,
I know not which best likes me. Shall I burn
Their house with fire? Or stealing past unseen
To Jason's bed—I have a blade made keen
For that—stab, breast to breast, that wedded pair?
Good, but for one thing. When I am taken there,
And killed, they will laugh loud who hate me. . . .
                                 Nay,
I love the old way best, the simple way
Of poison, where we too are strong as men.
Ah me!
And they being dead—what place shall hold me then?
What friend shall rise, with land inviolate
And trusty doors, to shelter from their hate
This flesh! . . . None anywhere! . . . A little
    more
I needs must wait: and, if there ope some door
Of refuge, some strong tower to shield me, good:
In craft and darkness I will hunt this blood.
Else, if mine hour be come and no hope nigh,
Then sword in hand, full-willed and sure to die,
I yet will live to slay them. I will wend
Man-like, their road of daring to the end.
  So help me She who of all Gods hath been
The best to me, of all my chosen queen
And helpmate, Hecatê, who dwells apart,
The flame of flame, in my fire's inmost heart:
For all their strength, they shall not stab my soul
And laugh thereafter! Dark and full of dole
Their bridal feast shall be, most dark the day
They joined their hands, and hunted me away.
  Awake thee now, Medea! Whatso plot
Thou hast, or cunning, strive and falter not.

On to the peril-point!　Now comes the strain
Of daring.　Shall they trample thee again?
How?　And with Hellas laughing o'er thy fall
While this chief's daughter weds, and weds withal
Jason? . . . A true king was thy father, yea,
And born of the ancient Sun! . . . Thou know'st
　　　the way;
And God hath made thee woman, things most vain
For help, but wondrous in the paths of pain.

　　　　　　　　　　　　[MEDEA *goes into the House.*

CHORUS.

Back streams the wave on the ever-running river:
　Life, life is changed and the laws of it o'ertrod.
Man shall be the slave, the affrighted, the low-liver!
　　　Man hath forgotten God.
And woman, yea, woman, shall be terrible in story:
　The tales too, meseemeth, shall be other than of
　　　yore.
For a fear there is that cometh out of Woman and a
　　　glory,
　And that hard hating voices shall encompass her no
　　　more!

The old bards shall cease, and their memory that
　　　lingers
　Of frail brides and faithless, shall be shrivelled as
　　　with fire.
For they loved us not, nor knew us: and our lips were
　　　dumb, our fingers
　　　Could wake not the secret of the lyre.

Else, else, O God the Singer, I had sung amid their
    rages
  A long tale of Man and his deeds for good and
    ill.
But the old World knoweth—'tis the speech of all
    his ages—
  Man's wrong and ours: he knoweth and is still.

Some Women.

Forth from thy father's home
  Thou camest, O heart of fire,
To the Dark Blue Rocks, to the clashing foam,
  To the seas of thy desire:

  Till the Dark Blue Bar was crossed;
    And, lo, by an alien river
  Standing, thy lover lost,
    Void-armed for ever,

  Forth yet again, O lowest
    Of landless women, a ranger
  Of desolate ways, thou goest,
    From the walls of the stranger.

Others.

And the great Oath waxeth weak;
  And Ruth, as a thing outstriven,
Is fled, fled, from the shores of the Greek,
  Away on the winds of heaven.

Dark is the house afar,
    Where an old king called thee daughter;
All that was once thy star
    In stormy water.

Dark: and, lo, in the nearer
    House that was sworn to love thee,
Another, queenlier, dearer,
    Is thronèd above thee.

Enter from the right JASON.

JASON.

Oft have I seen, in other days than these,
How a dark temper maketh maladies
No friend can heal. 'Twas easy to have kept
Both land and home. It needed but to accept
Unstrivingly the pleasure of our lords.
But thou, for mere delight in stormy words,
Wilt lose all! . . . Now thy speech provokes not me.
Rail on. Of all mankind let Jason be
Most evil; none shall check thee. But for these
Dark threats cast out against the majesties
Of Corinth, count as veriest gain thy path
Of exile. I myself, when princely wrath
Was hot against thee, strove with all good will
To appease the wrath, and wished to keep thee still
Beside me. But thy mouth would never stay
From vanity, blaspheming night and day
Our masters. Therefore thou shalt fly the land.
    Yet, even so, I will not hold my hand
From succouring mine own people. Here am I
To help thee, woman, pondering heedfully

Thy new state.　For I would not have thee flung
Provisionless away—aye, and the young
Children as well; nor lacking aught that will
Of mine can bring thee.　Many a lesser ill
Hangs on the heels of exile.　.　.　.　Aye, and though
Thou hate me, dream not that my heart can know
Or fashion aught of angry will to thee.

MEDEA.

Evil, most evil!　.　.　.　since thou grantest me
That comfort, the worst weapon left me now
To smite a coward.　.　.　.　Thou comest to me, thou,
Mine enemy!　(*Turning to the* CHORUS.)　Oh, say,
　　how call ye this,
To face, and smile, the comrade whom his kiss
Betrayed?　Scorn?　Insult?　Courage?　None of
　　these:
'Tis but of all man's inward sicknesses
The vilest, that he knoweth not of shame
Nor pity!　Yet I praise him that he came .　.　.
To me it shall bring comfort, once to clear
My heart on thee, and thou shalt wince to hear.
　I will begin with that, 'twixt me and thee,
That first befell.　I saved thee.　I saved thee—
Let thine own Greeks be witness, every one
That sailed on Argo—saved thee, sent alone
To yoke with yokes the bulls of fiery breath,
And sow that Acre of the Lords of Death;
And mine own ancient Serpent, who did keep
The Golden Fleece, the eyes that knew not sleep,
And shining coils, him also did I smite
Dead for thy sake, and lifted up the light

That bade thee live.   Myself, uncounsellèd,
Stole forth from father and from home, and fled
Where dark Iôlcos under Pelion lies,
With thee—Oh, single-hearted more than wise!
I murdered Pelias, yea, in agony,
By his own daughters' hands, for sake of thee;
I swept their house like War.—And hast thou then
Accepted all—O evil yet again!—
And cast me off and taken thee for bride
Another?   And with children at thy side!
One could forgive a childless man.   But no:
I have borne thee children . . .
                                        Is sworn faith so low
And weak a thing?   I understand it not.
Are the old gods dead?   Are the old laws forgot,
And new laws made?   Since not my passioning,
But thine own heart, doth cry thee for a thing
Forsworn.

    [*She catches sight of her own hand which she
    has thrown out to denounce him.*

        Poor, poor right hand of mine, whom he
Did cling to, and these knees, so cravingly,
We are unclean, thou and I; we have caught the stain
Of bad men's flesh . . . and dreamed our dreams in
    vain.
    Thou comest to befriend me?   Give me, then,
Thy counsel.   'Tis not that I dream again
For good from thee: but, questioned, thou wilt show
The viler.   Say: now whither shall I go?
Back to my father?   Him I did betray,
And all his land, when we two fled away.
To those poor Peliad maids?   For them 'twere good
To take me in, who spilled their father's blood. . . .

Aye, so my whole life stands! There were at home
Who loved me well: to them I am become
A curse. And the first friends who sheltered me,
Whom most I should have spared, to pleasure thee
I have turned to foes. Oh, therefore hast thou laid
My crown upon me, blest of many a maid
In Hellas, now I have won what all did crave,
Thee, the world-wondered lover and the brave;
Who this day looks and sees me banished, thrown
Away with these two babes all, all, alone . . .
Oh, merry mocking when the lamps are red:
" Where go the bridegroom's babes to beg their bread
In exile, and the woman who gave all
To save him? "
    O great God, shall gold withal
Bear thy clear mark, to sift the base and fine,
And o'er man's living visage runs no sign
To show the lie within, ere all too late?

LEADER.

Dire and beyond all healing is the hate
When hearts that loved are turned to enmity.

JASON.

In speech at least, meseemeth, I must be
Not evil; but, as some old pilot goes
Furled to his sail's last edge, when danger blows
Too fiery, run before the wind and swell,
Woman, of thy loud storms.—And thus I tell
My tale. Since thou wilt build so wondrous high
Thy deeds of service in my jeopardy,

To all my crew and quest I know but one
Saviour, of Gods or mortals one alone,
The Cyprian.   Oh thou hast both brain and wit,
Yet underneath . . . nay, all the tale of it
Were graceless telling; how sheer love, a fire
Of poison-shafts, compelled thee with desire
To save me.   But enough.   I will not score
That count too close.   'Twas good help: and there-
    for
I give thee thanks, howe'er the help was wrought.
Howbeit, in my deliverance, thou hast got
Far more than given.   A good Greek land hath
    been
Thy lasting home, not barbary.   Thou hast seen
Our ordered life, and justice, and the long
Still grasp of law not changing with the strong
Man's pleasure.   Then, all Hellas far and near
Hath learned thy wisdom, and in every ear
Thy fame is.   Had thy days run by unseen
On that last edge of the world, where then had been
The story of great Medea?   Thou and I . . .
What worth to us were treasures heapèd high
In rich kings' rooms; what worth a voice of gold
More sweet than ever rang from Orpheus old,
Unless our deeds have glory?
                   Speak I so,
Touching the Quest I wrought, thyself did throw
The challenge down.   Next for thy cavilling
Of wrath at mine alliance with a king,
Here thou shalt see I both was wise, and free
From touch of passion, and a friend to thee
Most potent, and my children . . . Nay, be still!
   When first I stood in Corinth, clogged with ill

From many a desperate mischance, what bliss
Could I that day have dreamed of, like to this,
To wed with a king's daughter, I exiled
And beggared?   Not—what makes thy passion
    wild—
From loathing of thy bed; not over-fraught
With love for this new bride; not that I sought
To upbuild mine house with offspring: 'tis enough,
What thou hast borne: I make no word thereof:
But, first and greatest, that we all might dwell
In a fair house and want not, knowing well
That poor men have no friends, but far and near
Shunning and silence.   Next, I sought to rear
Our sons in nurture worthy of my race,
And, raising brethren to them, in one place
Join both my houses, and be all from now
Prince-like and happy.   What more need hast
    thou
Of children?   And for me, it serves my star
To link in strength the children that now are
With those that shall be.

                        Have I counselled ill?
Not thine own self would say it, couldst thou still
One hour thy jealous flesh.—'Tis ever so!
Who looks for more in women?   When the flow
Of love runs plain, why, all the world is fair:
But, once there fall some ill chance anywhere
To baulk that thirst, down in swift hate are trod
Men's dearest aims and noblest.   Would to God
We mortals by some other seed could raise
Our fruits, and no blind women block our ways!
Then had there been no curse to wreck man-
    kind.

LEADER.

Lord Jason, very subtly hast thou twined
Thy speech: but yet, though all athwart thy will
I speak, this is not well thou dost, but ill,
Betraying her who loved thee and was true.

MEDEA.

Surely I have my thoughts, and not a few
Have held me strange.   To me it seemeth, when
A crafty tongue is given to evil men
'Tis like to wreck, not help them.   Their own brain
Tempts them with lies to dare and dare again,
Till . . . no man hath enough of subtlety.
As thou—be not so seeming-fair to me
Nor deft of speech.   One word will make thee fall.
Wert thou not false, 'twas thine to tell me all,
And charge me help thy marriage path, as I
Did love thee; not befool me with a lie.

JASON.

An easy task had that been!   Aye, and thou
A loving aid, who canst not, even now,
Still that loud heart that surges like the tide!

MEDEA.

That moved thee not.   Thine old barbarian bride,
The queen out of the east who loved thee sore,
She grew grey-haired, she served thy pride no more.

Jason.

Now understand for once! The girl to me
Is nothing, in this web of sovranty
I hold. I do but seek to save, even yet,
Thee: and for brethren to our sons beget
Young kings, to prosper all our lives again.

Medea.

God shelter me from prosperous days of pain,
And wealth that maketh wounds about my heart.

Jason.

Wilt change that prayer, and choose a wiser part?
Pray not to hold true sense for pain, nor rate
Thyself unhappy, being too fortunate.

Medea.

Aye, mock me; thou hast where to lay thine head,
But I go naked to mine exile.

Jason.

                              Tread
Thine own path! Thou hast made it all to be.

Medea.

How? By seducing and forsaking thee?

JASON.

By those vile curses on the royal halls
Let loose. . . .

MEDEA.

On thy house also, as chance falls,
I am a living curse.

JASON.

Oh, peace! Enough
Of these vain wars: I will no more thereof.
If thou wilt take from all that I possess
Aid for these babes and thine own helplessness
Of exile, speak thy bidding. Here I stand
Full-willed to succour thee with stintless hand,
And send my signet to old friends that dwell
On foreign shores, who will entreat thee well.
Refuse, and thou shalt do a deed most vain.
But cast thy rage away, and thou shalt gain
Much, and lose little for thine anger's sake.

MEDEA.

I will not seek thy friends. I will not take
Thy givings. Give them not. Fruits of a stem
Unholy bring no blessing after them.

JASON.

Now God in heaven be witness, all my heart
Is willing, in all ways, to do its part

For thee and for thy babes.   But nothing good
Can please thee.   In sheer savageness of mood
Thou drivest from thee every friend.   Wherefore
I warrant thee, thy pains shall be the more.

[*He goes slowly away.*

MEDEA.

Go: thou art weary for the new delight
Thou wooest, so long tarrying out of sight
Of her sweet chamber.   Go, fulfil thy pride,
O bridegroom!   For it may be, such a bride
Shall wait thee,—yea, God heareth me in this—
As thine own heart shall sicken ere it kiss.

CHORUS.

Alas, the Love that falleth like a flood,
     Strong-winged and transitory:
Why praise ye him?   What beareth he of good
     To man, or glory?
Yet Love there is that moves in gentleness,
Heart-filling, sweetest of all powers that bless.
Loose not on me, O Holder of man's heart,
     Thy golden quiver,
Nor steep in poison of desire the dart
     That heals not ever.

The pent hate of the word that cavilleth,
     The strife that hath no fill,
Where once was fondness; and the mad heart's breath
     For strange love panting still:
O Cyprian, cast me not on these; but sift,
Keen-eyed, of love the good and evil gift.

Make Innocence my friend, God's fairest star,
    Yea, and abate not
The rare sweet beat of bosoms without war,
    That love, and hate not.

Others.

Home of my heart, land of my own,
    Cast me not, nay, for pity,
Out on my ways, helpless, alone,
Where the feet fail in the mire and stone,
    A woman without a city.
Ah, not that! Better the end:
    The green grave cover me rather,
If a break must come in the days I know,
And the skies be changed and the earth below;
For the weariest road that man may wend
    Is forth from the home of his father.

Lo, we have seen: 'tis not a song
    Sung, nor learned of another.
For whom hast thou in thy direst wrong
For comfort? Never a city strong
    To hide thee, never a brother.
Ah, but the man—cursèd be he,
    Cursèd beyond recover,
Who openeth, shattering, seal by seal,
A friend's clean heart, then turns his heel,
Deaf unto love: never in me
    Friend shall he know nor lover.
    [*While* MEDEA *is waiting downcast, seated upon*
    her door-step, there passes from the left a
    traveller with followers. As he catches sight
    of MEDEA *he stops.*

AEGEUS.

Have joy, Medea! 'Tis the homeliest
Word that old friends can greet with, and the best.

MEDEA (*looking up, surprised*).

Oh, joy on thee, too, Aegeus, gentle king
Of Athens!—But whence com'st thou journeying?

AEGEUS.

From Delphi now and the old encaverned stair. . . .

MEDEA.

Where Earth's heart speaks in song?   What mad'st
thou there?

AEGEUS.

Prayed heaven for children—the same search alway.

MEDEA.

Children?   Ah God!   Art childless to this day?

AEGEUS.

So God hath willed.   Childless and desolate.

MEDEA.

What word did Phœbus speak, to change thy fate?

AEGEUS.

Riddles, too hard for mortal man to read.

MEDEA.

Which I may hear?

AEGEUS.

Assuredly: they need

A rarer wit.

MEDEA.

How said he?

AEGEUS.

Not to spill

Life's wine, nor seek for more. . . .

MEDEA.

Until?

AEGEUS.

Until

I tread the hearth-stone of my sires of yore.

MEDEA.

And what should bring thee here, by Creon's shore?

AEGEUS.

One Pittheus know'st thou, high lord of Trozên?

MEDEA.

Aye, Pelops' son, a man most pure of sin.

AEGEUS.

Him I would ask, touching Apollo's will.

MEDEA.

Much use in God's ways hath he, and much skill.

AEGEUS.

And, long years back he was my battle-friend,
The truest e'er man had.

MEDEA.

                    Well, may God send
Good hap to thee, and grant all thy desire.

AEGEUS.

But thou . . . ?   Thy frame is wasted, and the fire
Dead in thine eyes.

MEDEA.

                    Aegeus, my husband is
The falsest man in the world.

AEGEUS.

                    What word is this?
Say clearly what thus makes thy visage dim?

MEDEA.

He is false to me, who never injured him.

AEGEUS.

What hath he done?   Show all, that I may see.

MEDEA.

Ta'en him a wife; a wife, set over me
To rule his house!

AEGEUS.

           He hath not dared to do,
Jason, a thing so shameful?

MEDEA.

             Aye, 'tis true:
And those he loved of yore have no place now.

AEGEUS.

Some passion sweepeth him?   Or is it thou
He turns from?

MEDEA.

           Passion, passion to betray
His dearest!

AEGEUS.

        Shame be his, so fallen away
From honour!

MEDEA.

Passion to be near a throne,
A king's heir!

AEGEUS.

How, who gives the bride?   Say on.

MEDEA.

Creon, who o'er all Corinth standeth chief.

AEGEUS.

Woman, thou hast indeed much cause for grief.

MEDEA.

'Tis ruin.—And they have cast me out as well.

AEGEUS.

Who?   'Tis a new wrong this, and terrible.

MEDEA.

Creon the king, from every land and shore. . . .

AEGEUS.

And Jason suffers him?   Oh, 'tis too sore!

MEDEA.

He loveth to bear bravely ills like these!
But, Aegeus, by thy beard, oh, by thy knees,
I pray thee, and I give me for thine own,
Thy suppliant, pity me! Oh, pity one
So miserable. Thou never wilt stand there
And see me cast out friendless to despair.
Give me a home in Athens . . . by the fire
Of thine own hearth! Oh, so may thy desire
Of children be fulfilled of God, and thou
Die happy! . . . Thou canst know not; even now
Thy prize is won! I, I will make of thee
A childless man no more. The seed shall be,
I swear it, sown. Such magic herbs I know.

AEGEUS.

Woman, indeed my heart goes forth to show
This help to thee, first for religion's sake,
Then for thy promised hope, to heal my ache
Of childlessness. 'Tis this hath made mine whole
Life as a shadow, and starved out my soul.
But thus it stands with me. Once make thy way
To Attic earth, I, as in law I may,
Will keep thee and befriend. But in this land,
Where Creon rules, I may not raise my hand
To shelter thee. Move of thine own essay
To seek my house, there thou shalt alway stay,
Inviolate, never to be seized again.
But come thyself from Corinth. I would fain
Even in foreign eyes be alway just.

MEDEA.

'Tis well.   Give me an oath wherein to trust
And all that man could ask thou hast granted me.

AEGEUS.

Dost trust me not?   Or what thing troubleth thee?

MEDEA.

I trust thee.   But so many, far and near,
Do hate me—all King Pelias' house, and here
Creon.   Once bound by oaths and sanctities
Thou canst not yield me up for such as these
To drag from Athens.   But a spoken word,
No more, to bind thee, which no God hath heard. . . .
The embassies, methinks, would come and go:
They all are friends to thee. . . . Ah me, I know
Thou wilt not list to me!   So weak am I,
And they full-filled with gold and majesty.

AEGEUS.

Methinks 'tis a far foresight, this thine oath.
Still, if thou so wilt have it, nothing loath
Am I to serve thee.   Mine own hand is so
The stronger, if I have this plea to show
Thy persecutors: and for thee withal
The bond more sure.—On what God shall I call?

141

MEDEA.

Swear by the Earth thou treadest, by the Sun,
Sire of my sires, and all the gods as one. . . .

AEGEUS.

To do what thing or not do?   Make all plain.

MEDEA.

Never thyself to cast me out again.
Nor let another, whatsoe'er his plea,
Take me, while thou yet livest and art free.

AEGEUS.

Never: so hear me, Earth, and the great star
Of daylight, and all other gods that are!

MEDEA.

'Tis well: and if thou falter from thy vow . . .?

AEGEUS.

God's judgment on the godless break my brow!

MEDEA.

Go!   Go thy ways rejoicing.—All is bright
And clear before me.   Go: and ere the night
Myself will follow, when the deed is done
I purpose, and the end I thirst for won.
            [AEGEUS *and his train depart.*

Chorus.

Farewell: and Maia's guiding Son
　　Back lead thee to thy hearth and fire,
　　Aegeus; and all the long desire
That wasteth thee, at last be won:
Our eyes have seen thee as thou art,
A gentle and a righteous heart.

Medea.

God, and God's Justice, and ye blinding Skies!
At last the victory dawneth!　Yea, mine eyes
See, and my foot is on the mountain's brow.
Mine enemies!　Mine enemies, oh, now
Atonement cometh!　Here at my worst hour
A friend is found, a very port of power
To save my shipwreck.　Here will I make fast
Mine anchor, and escape them at the last
In Athens' walled hill.—But ere the end
'Tis meet I show thee all my counsel, friend:
Take it, no tale to make men laugh withal!
　　Straightway to Jason I will send some thrall
To entreat him to my presence.　Comes he here,
Then with soft reasons will I feed his ear,
How his will now is my will, how all things
Are well, touching this marriage-bed of kings
For which I am betrayed—all wise and rare
And profitable!　Yet will I make one prayer,
That my two children be no more exiled
But stay. . . . Oh, not that I would leave a child

Here upon angry shores till those have laughed
Who hate me: 'tis that I will slay by craft
The king's daughter.   With gifts they shall be sent,
Gifts to the bride to spare their banishment,
Fine robings and a carcanet of gold.
Which raiment let her once but take, and fold
About her, a foul death that girl shall die
And all who touch her in her agony.
Such poison shall they drink, my robe and wreath!
   Howbeit, of that no more.   I gnash my teeth
Thinking on what a path my feet must tread
Thereafter.   I shall lay those children dead—
Mine, whom no hand shall steal from me away!
Then, leaving Jason childless, and the day
As night above him, I will go my road
To exile, flying, flying from the blood
Of these my best-beloved, and having wrought
All horror, so but one thing reach me not,
The laugh of them that hate us.
                        Let it come!
What profits life to me?   I have no home,
No country now, nor shield from any wrong.
That was my evil hour, when down the long
Halls of my father out I stole, my will
Chained by a Greek man's voice, who still, oh, still,
If God yet live, shall all requited be.
For never child of mine shall Jason see
Hereafter living, never child beget
From his new bride, who this day, desolate
Even as she made me desolate, shall die
Shrieking amid my poisons. . . . Names have I
Among your folk?   One light?   One weak of hand?
An eastern dreamer?—Nay, but with the brand

Of strange suns burnt, my hate, by God above,
A perilous thing, and passing sweet my love!
For these it is that make life glorious.

LEADER.

Since thou hast bared thy fell intent to us
I, loving thee, and helping in their need
Man's laws, adjure thee, dream not of this deed!

MEDEA.

There is no other way.—I pardon thee
Thy littleness, who art not wronged like me.

LEADER.

Thou canst not kill the fruit thy body bore!

MEDEA.

Yes: if the man I hate be pained the more.

LEADER.

And thou made miserable, most miserable?

MEDEA.

Oh, let it come!   All words of good or ill
Are wasted now.
        [*She claps her hands: the* NURSE *comes out from
            the house.*
                    Ho, woman; get thee gone
And lead lord Jason hither. . . . There is none

Like thee, to work me these high services.
But speak no word of what my purpose is,
As thou art faithful, thou, and bold to try
All succours, and a woman even as I !

[*The* NURSE *departs.*

CHORUS.

The sons of Erechtheus, the olden,
    Whom high gods planted of yore
In an old land of heaven upholden,
    A proud land untrodden of war:
They are hungered, and, lo, their desire
    With wisdom is fed as with meat:
In their skies is a shining of fire,
    A joy in the fall of their feet:
And thither, with manifold dowers,
    From the North, from the hills, from the morn,
The Muses did gather their powers,
    That a child of the Nine should be born;
And Harmony, sown as the flowers,
    Grew gold in the acres of corn.

And Cephîsus, the fair-flowing river—
    The Cyprian dipping her hand
Hath drawn of his dew, and the shiver
    Of her touch is as joy in the land.
For her breathing in fragrance is written,
    And in music her path as she goes,
And the cloud of her hair, it is litten
    With stars of the wind-woven rose.
So fareth she ever and ever,
    And forth of her bosom is blown,

As dews on the winds of the river,
  An hunger of passions unknown,
Strong Loves of all godlike endeavour,
  Whom Wisdom shall throne on her throne.

Some Women.

But Cephîsus the fair-flowing,
  Will he bear thee on his shore?
    Shall the land that succours all, succour thee,
  Who art foul among thy kind,
  With the tears of children blind?
Dost thou see the red gash growing,
      Thine own burden dost thou see?
        Every side, Every way,
      Lo, we kneel to thee and pray:
        By thy knees, by thy soul, O woman wild!
      One at least thou canst not slay,
          Not thy child!

Others.

Hast thou ice that thou shalt bind it
  To thy breast, and make thee dead
    To thy children, to thine own spirit's pain?
  When the hand knows what it dares,
  When thine eyes look into theirs,
Shalt thou keep by tears unblinded
      Thy dividing of the slain?
        These be deeds Not for thee:
      These be things that cannot be!
        Thy babes—though thine hardihood be fell,
      When they cling about thy knee,
          'Twill be well!

Enter JASON.

JASON.

I answer to thy call.   Though full of hate
Thou be, I yet will not so far abate
My kindness for thee, nor refuse mine ear.
Say in what new desire thou hast called me here.

MEDEA.

Jason, I pray thee, for my words but now
Spoken, forgive me.   My bad moods. . . . Oh, thou
At least wilt strive to bear with them!   There be
Many old deeds of love 'twixt me and thee.
Lo, I have reasoned with myself apart
And chidden: "Why must I be mad, O heart
Of mine: and raging against one whose word
Is wisdom: making me a thing abhorred
To them that rule the land, and to mine own
Husband, who doth but that which, being done,
Will help us all—to wed a queen, and get
Young kings for brethren to my sons?   And yet
I rage alone, and cannot quit my rage—
What aileth me?—when God sends harbourage
So simple?   Have I not my children?   Know
I not we are but exiles, and must go
Beggared and friendless else?"   Thought upon
      thought
So pressed me, till I knew myself full-fraught
With bitterness of heart and blinded eyes.
So now—I give thee thanks: and hold thee wise

To have caught this anchor for our aid.   The fool
Was I; who should have been thy friend, thy tool;
Gone wooing with thee, stood at thy bed-side
Serving, and welcomed duteously thy bride.
But, as we are, we are—I will not say
Mere evil—women!   Why must thou to-day
Turn strange, and make thee like some evil thing,
Childish, to meet my childish passioning?
See, I surrender: and confess that then
I had bad thoughts, but now have turned again
And found my wiser mind.   [*She claps her hands.*
                                Ho, children!   Run
Quickly!   Come hither, out into the sun,
        [*The* CHILDREN *come from the house, followed by
            their* ATTENDANT.
And greet your father.   Welcome him with us,
And throw quite, quite away, as mother does,
Your anger against one so dear.   Our peace
Is made, and all the old bad war shall cease
For ever.—Go, and take his hand. . . .
        [*As the* CHILDREN *go to* JASON, *she suddenly
            bursts into tears.   The* CHILDREN *quickly
            return to her: she recovers herself, smiling
            amid her tears.*
                                Ah me,
I am full of hidden horrors! . . . Shall it be
A long time more, my children, that ye live
To reach to me those dear, dear arms? . . . Forgive!
I am so ready with my tears to-day,
And full of dread. . . . I sought to smooth **away**
The long strife with your father, and, lo, now
I have all drowned with tears this little brow!
        [*She wipes the child's face.*

LEADER.

O'er mine eyes too there stealeth a pale tear:
Let the evil rest, O God, let it rest here!

JASON.

Woman, indeed I praise thee now, nor say
Ill of thine other hour. 'Tis nature's way,
A woman needs must stir herself to wrath,
When work of marriage by so strange a path
Crosseth her lord. But thou, thine heart doth
    wend
The happier road. Thou hast seen, ere quite the
    end,
What choice must needs be stronger: which to do
Shows a wise-minded woman. . . . And for you,
Children; your father never has forgot
Your needs. If God but help him, he hath wrought
A strong deliverance for your weakness. Yea,
I think you, with your brethren, yet one day
Shall be the mightiest voices in this land.
Do you grow tall and strong. Your father's hand
Guideth all else, and whatso power divine
Hath alway helped him. . . . Ah, may it be mine
To see you yet in manhood, stern of brow,
Strong-armed, set high o'er those that hate me. . . .
           How?
Woman, thy face is turned. Thy cheek is swept
With pallor of strange tears. Dost not accept
Gladly and of good will my benisons?

MEDEA.

'Tis nothing.   Thinking of these little ones. . . .

JASON.

Take heart, then.   I will guard them from all ill.

MEDEA.

I do take heart.   Thy word I never will
Mistrust.   Alas, a woman's bosom bears
But woman's courage, a thing born for tears.

JASON.

What ails thee?—All too sore thou weepest there.

MEDEA.

I was their mother!   When I heard thy prayer
Of long life for them, there swept over me
A horror, wondering how these things shall be.
    But for the matter of my need that thou
Should speak with me, part I have said, and now
Will finish.—Seeing it is the king's behest
To cast me out from Corinth . . . aye, and best,
Far best, for me—I know it—not to stay
Longer to trouble thee and those who sway
The realm, being held to all their house a foe. . . .
Behold, I spread my sails, and meekly go

To exile. But our children. . . . Could this land
Be still their home awhile: could thine own hand
But guide their boyhood. . . . Seek the king, and
    pray
His pity, that he bid thy children stay!

JASON.

He is hard to move. Yet surely 'twere well done.

MEDEA.

Bid her—for thy sake, for a daughter's boon. . . .

JASON.

Well thought! Her I can fashion to my mind.

MEDEA.

Surely. She is a woman like her kind. . . .
Yet I will aid thee in thy labour; I
Will send her gifts, the fairest gifts that lie
In the hands of men, things of the days of old,
Fine robings and a carcanet of gold,
By the boys' hands.—Go, quick, some handmaiden,
And fetch the raiment.
                        [*A handmaid goes into the house.*
                    Ah, her cup shall then
Be filled indeed! What more should woman crave,
Being wed with thee, the bravest of the brave,

And girt with raiment which of old the sire
Of all my house, the Sun, gave, steeped in fire,
To his own fiery race?
        [*The handmaid has returned bearing the Gifts.*
              Come, children, lift
With heed these caskets.   Bear them as your gift
To her, being bride and princess and of right
Blessed!—I think she will not hold them light.

JASON.

Fond woman, why wilt empty thus thine hand
Of treasure?   Doth King Creon's castle stand
In stint of raiment, or in stint of gold?
Keep these, and make no gift.   For if she hold
Jason of any worth at all, I swear
Chattels like these will not weigh more with her.

MEDEA.

Ah, chide me not!   'Tis written, gifts persuade
The gods in heaven; and gold is stronger made
Than words innumerable to bend men's ways.
Fortune is hers.   God maketh great her days:
Young and a crownèd queen!   And banishment
For those two babes. . . . I would not gold were
    spent,
But life's blood, ere that come.
                  My children, go
Forth into those rich halls, and, bowing low,
Beseech your father's bride, whom I obey,
Ye be not, of her mercy, cast away

Exiled: and give the caskets—above all
Mark this!—to none but her, to hold withal
And keep. . . . Go quick!   And let your mother
    know
Soon the good tidings that she longs for. . . . Go!
    [*She goes quickly into the house. * JASON *and the*
        CHILDREN *with their* ATTENDANT *depart.*

CHORUS.

Now I have no hope more of the children's living;
    No hope more.   They are gone forth unto death.
The bride, she taketh the poison of their giving:
    She taketh the bounden gold and openeth;
And the crown, the crown, she lifteth about her brow,
Where the light brown curls are clustering.   No
    hope now!

O sweet and cloudy gleam of the garments golden!
    The robe, it hath clasped her breast and the crown
    her head.
Then, then, she decketh the bride, as a bride of
    olden
    Story, that goeth pale to the kiss of the dead.
For the ring hath closed, and the portion of death
    is there;
And she flieth not, but perisheth unaware.

Some Women.

O bridegroom, bridegroom of the kiss so cold,
Art thou wed with princes, art thou girt with gold,

Who know'st not, suing
For thy child's undoing,
And, on her thou lovest, for a doom untold?
How art thou fallen from thy place of old!

Others.

O Mother, Mother, what hast thou to reap,
When the harvest cometh, between wake and sleep?
For a heart unslaken,
For a troth forsaken,
Lo, babes that call thee from a bloody deep:
And thy love returns not.   Get thee forth and weep!

[Enter the ATTENDANT *with the two* CHILDREN:
MEDEA *comes out from the house.*

ATTENDANT.

Mistress, these children from their banishment
Are spared.   The royal bride hath mildly bent
Her hand to accept thy gifts, and all is now
Peace for the children.—Ha, why standest thou
Confounded, when good fortune draweth near?

MEDEA.

Ah God!

ATTENDANT.

This chimes not with the news I bear.

MEDEA.

O God, have mercy!

ATTENDANT.

Is some word of wrath
Here hidden that I knew not of?   And hath
My hope to give thee joy so cheated me?

MEDEA.

Thou givest what thou givest: I blame not thee.

ATTENDANT.

Thy brows are all o'ercast: thine eyes are filled. . . .

MEDEA.

For bitter need, Old Man! The gods have willed,
And mine own evil mind, that this should come.

ATTENDANT.

Take heart! Thy sons one day will bring thee home.

MEDEA.

Home? . . . I have others to send home.   Woe's me!

ATTENDANT.

Be patient.   Many a mother before thee
Hath parted from her children.   We poor things
Of men must needs endure what fortune brings.

MEDEA.

I will endure.—Go thou within, and lay
All ready that my sons may need to-day.

[*The* ATTENDANT *goes into the house.*

O children, children mine: and you have found
A land and home, where, leaving me discrowned
And desolate, for ever you will stay,
Motherless children! And I go my way
To other lands, an exile, ere you bring
Your fruits home, ere I see you prospering
Or know your brides, or deck the bridal bed,
All flowers, and lift your torches overhead.
  Oh, cursèd be mine own hard heart! 'Twas all
In vain, then, that I reared you up, so tall
And fair; in vain I bore you, and was torn
With those long pitiless pains, when you were
    born.
Ah, wondrous hopes my poor heart had in you,
How you would tend me in mine age, and do
The shroud about me with your own dear hands,
When I lay cold, blessèd in all the lands
That knew us. And that gentle thought is dead!
You go, and I live on, to eat the bread
Of long years, to myself most full of pain.
And never your dear eyes, never again,
Shall see your mother, far away being thrown
To other shapes of life. . . . My babes, my own,
Why gaze ye so?—What is it that ye see?—
And laugh with that last laughter? . . . Woe is me,
What shall I do?
                    Women, my strength is gone,
Gone like a dream, since once I looked upon

157

Those shining faces. . . . I can do it not.
Good-bye to all the thoughts that burned so hot
Aforetime!   I will take and hide them far,
Far, from men's eyes.   Why should I seek a war
So blind: by these babes' wounds to sting again
Their father's heart, and win myself a pain
Twice deeper?   Never, never!   I forget
Henceforward all I laboured for.
                                        And yet,
What is it with me?   Would I be a thing
Mocked at, and leave mine enemies to sting
Unsmitten?   It must be.   O coward heart,
Ever to harbour such soft words!—Depart
Out of my sight, ye twain.   [*The* CHILDREN *go in.*
                                   And they whose eyes
Shall hold it sin to share my sacrifice,
On their heads be it!   My hand shall swerve not
    now.

    Ah, Ah, thou Wrath within me!   Do not thou,
Do not. . . . Down, down, thou tortured thing, and
    spare
My children!   They will dwell with us, aye, there
Far off, and give thee peace.
                              Too late, too late!
By all Hell's living agonies of hate,
They shall not take my little ones alive
To make their mock with!   Howsoe'er I strive
The thing is doomed; it shall not escape now
From being.   Aye, the crown is on the brow,
And the robe girt, and in the robe that high
Queen dying.
                I know all.   Yet . . . seeing that I

Must go so long a journey, and these twain
A longer yet and darker, I would fain
Speak with them, ere I go.

> *[A handmaid brings the* CHILDREN *out again.*

               Come, children; stand
A little from me.   There.   Reach out your hand,
Your right hand—so—to mother: and good-bye!

> *[She has kept them hitherto at arm's-length: but*
> *at the touch of their hands, her resolution*
> *breaks down, and she gathers them pas-*
> *sionately into her arms.*

Oh, darling hand!   Oh, darling mouth, and eye,
And royal mien, and bright brave faces clear,
May you be blessèd, but not here!   What here
Was yours, your father stole. . . . Ah God, the glow
Of cheek on cheek, the tender touch; and Oh,
Sweet scent of childhood. . . . Go! Go! . . . Am I
    blind? . . .
Mine eyes can see not, when I look to find
Their places.   I am broken by the wings
Of evil. . . . Yea, I know to what bad things
I go, but louder than all thought doth cry
Anger, which maketh man's worst misery.

> *[She follows the* CHILDREN *into the house.*

CHORUS.

> My thoughts have roamed a cloudy land,
> And heard a fierier music fall
> Than woman's heart should stir withal:
> And yet some Muse majestical,
> Unknown, hath hold of woman's hand,
> Seeking for Wisdom—not in all:

A feeble seed, a scattered band,
Thou yet shalt find in lonely places,
Not dead amongst us, nor our faces
Turned alway from the Muses' call.

And thus my thought would speak: that she
Who ne'er hath borne a child nor known   .
Is nearer to felicity:
Unlit she goeth and alone,
With little understanding what
A child's touch means of joy or woe,
And many toils she beareth not.

But they within whose garden fair
That gentle plant hath blown, they go
Deep-written all their days with care—
To rear the children, to make fast
Their hold, to win them wealth; and then
Much darkness, if the seed at last
Bear fruit in good or evil men!
And one thing at the end of all
Abideth, that which all men dread:
The wealth is won, the limbs are bred
To manhood, and the heart withal
Honest: and, lo, where Fortune smiled,
Some change, and what hath fallen?   Hark!
'Tis death slow winging to the dark,
And in his arms what was thy child.

What therefore doth it bring of gain
To man, whose cup stood full before,

That God should send this one thing more
Of hunger and of dread, a door
Set wide to every wind of pain?
[MEDEA *comes out alone from the house.*

MEDEA.

Friends, this long hour I wait on Fortune's eyes,
And strain my senses in a hot surmise
What passeth on that hill.—Ha! even now
There comes . . . 'tis one of Jason's men, I trow.
His wild-perturbèd breath doth warrant me
The tidings of some strange calamity.
[*Enter* MESSENGER.

MESSENGER.

O dire and ghastly deed! Get thee away,
Medea! Fly! Nor let behind thee stay
One chariot's wing, one keel that sweeps the seas. . . .

MEDEA.

And what hath chanced, to cause such flights as these?

MESSENGER.

The maiden princess lieth—and her sire,
The king—both murdered by thy poison-fire.

MEDEA.

Most happy tiding! Which thy name prefers
Henceforth among my friends and well-wishers.

MESSENGER.

What say'st thou? Woman, is thy mind within
Clear, and not raving? Thou art found in sin
Most bloody wrought against the king's high head,
And laughest at the tale, and hast no dread?

MEDEA.

I have words also that could answer well
Thy word. But take thine ease, good friend, and tell,
How died they? Hath it been a very foul
Death, prithee? That were comfort to my soul.

MESSENGER.

When thy two children, hand in hand entwined,
Came with their father, and passed on to find
The new-made bridal rooms, Oh, we were glad,
We thralls, who ever loved thee well, and had
Grief in thy grief. And straight there passed a word
From ear to ear, that thou and thy false lord
Had poured peace offering upon wrath foregone.
A right glad welcome gave we them, and one
Kissed the small hand, and one the shining hair:
Myself, for very joy, I followed where
The women's rooms are. There our mistress . . . she
Whom now we name so . . . thinking not to see
Thy little pair, with glad and eager brow
Sate waiting Jason. Then she saw, and slow
Shrouded her eyes, and backward turned again,
Sick that thy children should come near her. Then

Thy husband quick went forward, to entreat
The young maid's fitful wrath.   "Thou wilt not
    meet
Love's coming with unkindness?   Nay, refrain
Thy suddenness, and turn thy face again,
Holding as friends all that to me are dear,
Thine husband.   And accept these robes they bear
As gifts: and beg thy father to unmake
His doom of exile on them—for my sake."
When once she saw the raiment, she could still
Her joy no more, but gave him all his will.
And almost ere the father and the two
Children were gone from out the room, she drew
The flowerèd garments forth, and sate her down
To her arraying: bound the golden crown
Through her long curls, and in a mirror fair
Arranged their separate clusters, smiling there
At the dead self that faced her.   Then aside
She pushed her seat, and paced those chambers
    wide
Alone, her white foot poising delicately—
So passing joyful in those gifts was she!—
And many a time would pause, straight-limbed, and
    wheel.
Her head to watch the long fold to her heel
Sweeping.   And then came something strange.   Her
    cheek
Seemed pale, and back with crooked steps and
    weak
Groping of arms she walked, and scarcely found
Her old seat, that she fell not to the ground.
   Among the handmaids was a woman old
And grey, who deemed, I think, that Pan had hold

Upon her, or some spirit, and raised a keen
Awakening shout; till through her lips was seen
A white foam crawling, and her eyeballs back
Twisted, and all her face dead pale for lack
Of life: and while that old dame called, the cry
Turned strangely to its opposite, to die
Sobbing. Oh, swiftly then one woman flew
To seek her father's rooms, one for the new
Bridegroom, to tell the tale. And all the place
Was loud with hurrying feet.

                    So long a space
As a swift walker on a measured way
Would pace a furlong's course in, there she lay
Speechless, with veilèd lids. Then wide her eyes
She oped, and wildly, as she strove to rise,
Shrieked: for two diverse waves upon her rolled
Of stabbing death. The carcanet of gold
That gripped her brow was molten in a dire
And wondrous river of devouring fire.
And those fine robes, the gift thy children gave—
God's mercy!—everywhere did lap and lave
The delicate flesh; till up she sprang, and fled,
A fiery pillar, shaking locks and head
This way and that, seeking to cast the crown
Somewhere away. But like a thing nailed down
The burning gold held fast the anadem,
And through her locks, the more she scattered
    them,
Came fire the fiercer, till to earth she fell
A thing—save to her sire—scarce nameable,
And strove no more. That cheek of royal mien,
Where was it—or the place where eyes had
   been?

Only from crown and temples came faint blood
Shot through with fire.   The very flesh, it stood
Out from the bones, as from a wounded pine
The gum starts, where those gnawing poisons fine
Bit in the dark—a ghastly sight!   And touch
The dead we durst not.   We had seen too much.
  But that poor father, knowing not, had sped,
Swift to his daughter's room, and there the dead
Lay at his feet.   He knelt, and groaning low,
Folded her in his arms, and kissed her: " Oh,
Unhappy child, what thing unnatural hath
So hideously undone thee?   Or what wrath
Of gods, to make this old grey sepulchre
Childless of thee?   Would God but lay me there
To die with thee, my daughter! "   So he cried.
But after, when he stayed from tears, and tried
To uplift his old bent frame, lo, in the folds
Of those fine robes it held, as ivy holds
Strangling among young laurel boughs.   Oh, then
A ghastly struggle came!   Again, again,
Up on his knee he writhed; but that dead breast
Clung still to his: till, wild, like one possessed,
He dragged himself half free; and, lo, the live
Flesh parted; and he laid him down to strive
No more with death, but perish; for the deep
Had risen above his soul.   And there they sleep,
At last, the old proud father and the bride,
Even as his tears had craved it, side by side.
  For thee—Oh, no word more!   Thyself will know
How best to baffle vengeance. . . . Long ago
I looked upon man's days, and found a grey
Shadow.   And this thing more I surely say,

165

That those of all men who are counted wise,
Strong wits, devisers of great policies,
Do pay the bitterest toll.   Since life began,
Hath there in God's eye stood one happy man?
Fair days roll on, and bear more gifts or less
Of fortune, but to no man happiness.

[*Exit* MESSENGER.

CHORUS.

Some Women.

Wrath upon wrath, meseems, this day shall fall
From God on Jason!   He hath earned it all.

Other Women.

O miserable maiden, all my heart
Is torn for thee, so sudden to depart
From thy king's chambers and the light above
To darkness, all for sake of Jason's love!

MEDEA.

Women, my mind is clear.   I go to slay
My children with all speed, and then, away
From hence; not wait yet longer till they stand
Beneath another and an angrier hand
To die.   Yea, howsoe'er I shield them, die
They must.   And, seeing that they must, 'tis I
Shall slay them, I their mother, touched of none
Beside.   Oh, up, and get thine armour on,

My heart!   Why longer tarry we to win
Our crown of dire inevitable sin?
Take up thy sword, O poor right hand of mine,
Thy sword: then onward to the thin-drawn line
Where life turns agony.   Let there be naught
Of softness now: and keep thee from that thought,
"Born of thy flesh," "thine own belovèd."   Now,
For one brief day, forget thy children: thou
Shalt weep hereafter.   Though thou slay them, yet
Sweet were they. . . . I am sore unfortunate.

[She goes into the house.

CHORUS.

Some Women.

O Earth, our mother; and thou
　　All-seër, arrowy crown
Of Sunlight, manward now
　　Look down, Oh, look down!
Look upon one accurst,
　　Ere yet in blood she twine
　　Red hands—blood that is thine!
O Sun, save her first!
She is thy daughter still,
　　Of thine own golden line;
Save her!   Or shall man spill
　　The life divine?
Give peace, O Fire that diest not!   Send thy spell
　To stay her yet, to lift her afar, afar—
A torture-changèd spirit, a voice of Hell
　Wrought of old wrongs and war!

Others.
Alas for the mother's pain
    Wasted!   Alas the dear
Life that was born in vain!
    Woman, what mak'st thou here,
    Thou from beyond the Gate
        Where dim Symplêgades
        Clash in the dark blue seas,
    The shores where death doth wait?
    Why hast thou taken on thee,
        To make us desolate,
    This anger of misery
        And guilt of hate?
For fierce are the smitings back of blood once shed
    Where love hath been: God's wrath upon them
        that kill,
And an anguished earth, and the wonder of the dead
    Haunting as music still. . . .
                            [*A cry is heard within.*

A Woman.
Hark!   Did ye hear?   Heard ye the children's cry?

Another.
O miserable woman!   O abhorred!

A Child within.
What shall I do?   What is it?   Keep me fast
From mother!

The Other Child.
                I know nothing.   Brother!   Oh,
I think she means to kill us.

A Woman.

Let me go!
I will—Help! Help!—and save them at the
last.

A Child.

Yes, in God's name! Help quickly ere we die!

The Other Child.

She has almost caught me now. She has a sword.
[*Many of the Women are now beating at the
barred door to get in. Others are standing
apart.*

Women at the door.

Thou stone, thou thing of iron! Wilt verily
Spill with thine hand that life, the vintage stored
Of thine own agony?

The Other Women.

A Mother slew her babes in days of yore,
    One, only one, from dawn to eventide,
        Ino, god-maddened, whom the Queen of Heaven
        Set frenzied, flying to the dark: and she
        Cast her for sorrow to the wide salt sea,
    Forth from those rooms of murder unforgiven,
Wild-footed from a white crag of the shore,
    And clasping still her children twain, she died.

O Love of Woman, charged with sorrow sore,
    What hast thou wrought upon us? What beside
        Resteth to tremble for?
        [*Enter hurriedly* JASON *and Attendants.*

JASON.

Ye women by this doorway clustering
Speak, is the doer of the ghastly thing
Yet here, or fled?   What hopeth she of flight?
Shall the deep yawn to shield her?   Shall the height
Send wings, and hide her in the vaulted sky
To work red murder on her lords, and fly
Unrecompensed?   But let her go!   My care
Is but to save my children, not for her.
Let them she wronged requite her as they may.
I care not.   'Tis my sons I must some way
Save, ere the kinsmen of the dead can win
From them the payment of their mother's sin.

LEADER.

Unhappy man, indeed thou knowest not
What dark place thou art come to!   Else, God
     wot,
Jason, no word like these could fall from thee.

JASON.

What is it!—Ha!   The woman would kill me?

LEADER.

Thy sons are dead, slain by their mother's hand.

JASON.

How?   Not the children. . . . I scarce under-
     stand. . . .
O God, thou hast broken me!

LEADER.

Think of those twain
As things once fair, that ne'er shall bloom again.

JASON.

Where did she murder them?   In that old room?

LEADER.

Open, and thou shalt see thy children's doom.

JASON.

Ho, thralls!   Unloose me yonder bars!   Make more
Of speed!   Wrench out the jointing of the door.
And show my two-edged curse, the children dead,
The woman. . . . Oh, this sword upon her
        head. . . .
        [*While the Attendants are still battering at the
        door* MEDEA *appears on the roof, standing
        on a chariot of winged Dragons, in which are
        the children's bodies.*

MEDEA.

What make ye at my gates?   Why batter ye
With brazen bars, seeking the dead and me
Who slew them?   Peace! . . . And thou, if aught
        of mine
Thou needest, speak, though never touch of thine

171

Shall scathe me more.   Out of his firmament
My fathers' father, the high Sun, hath sent
This, that shall save me from mine enemies' rage.

JASON.

Thou living hate!   Thou wife in every age
Abhorrèd, blood-red mother, who didst kill
My sons, and make me as the dead: and still
Canst take the sunshine to thine eyes, and smell
The green earth, reeking from thy deed of hell;
I curse thee! Now, Oh, now mine eyes can see,
That then were blinded, when from savagery
Of eastern chambers, from a cruel land,
To Greece and home I gathered in mine hand
Thee, thou incarnate curse: one that betrayed
Her home, her father, her . . . Oh, God hath
     laid
Thy sins on me!—I knew, I knew, there lay
A brother murdered on thy hearth that day
When thy first footstep fell on Argo's hull. . . .
Argo, my own, my swift and beautiful!
     That was her first beginning.   Then a wife
I made her in my house.   She bore to life
Children: and now for love, for chambering
And men's arms, she hath murdered them!   A
     thing
Not one of all the maids of Greece, not one,
Had dreamed of; whom I spurned, and for mine
     own
Chose thee, a bride of hate to me and death,
Tigress, not woman, beast of wilder breath

Than Skylla shrieking o'er the Tuscan sea.
Enough!   No scorn of mine can reach to thee,
Such iron is o'er thine eyes.   Out from my road,
Thou crime-begetter, blind with children's blood!
And let me weep alone the bitter tide
That sweepeth Jason's days, no gentle bride
To speak with more, no child to look upon
Whom once I reared . . . all, all for ever gone!

MEDEA.

An easy answer had I to this swell
Of speech, but Zeus our father knoweth well,
All I for thee have wrought, and thou for me.
So let it rest.   This thing was not to be,
That thou shouldst live a merry life, my bed
Forgotten and my heart uncomforted,
Thou nor thy princess: nor the king that planned
Thy marriage drive Medea from his land,
And suffer not.   Call me what thing thou please,
Tigress or Skylla from the Tuscan seas:
My claws have gripped thine heart, and all things
    shine.

JASON.

Thou too hast grief.   Thy pain is fierce as mine.

MEDEA.

I love the pain, so thou shalt laugh no more.

JASON.

Oh, what a womb of sin my children bore!

MEDEA.

Sons, did ye perish for your father's shame?

JASON.

How?   It was not my hand that murdered them.

MEDEA.

'Twas thy false wooings, 'twas thy trampling pride.

JASON.

Thou hast said it!   For thy lust of love they died.

MEDEA.

And love to women a slight thing should be?

JASON.

To women pure!—All thy vile life to thee!

MEDEA.

Think of thy torment.   They are dead, they are dead!

JASON.

No: quick, great God; quick curses round thy head!

MEDEA.

The Gods know who began this work of woe.

JASON.

Thy heart and all its loathliness they know.

MEDEA.

Loathe on. . . . But, Oh, thy voice. It hurts me
sore.

JASON.

Aye, and thine me.   Wouldst hear me then no more?

MEDEA.

How?   Show me but the way.   'Tis this I crave.

JASON.

Give me the dead to weep, and make their grave.

MEDEA.

Never!   Myself will lay them in a still
Green sepulchre, where Hera by the Hill
Hath precinct holy, that no angry men
May break their graves and cast them forth again
To evil.   So I lay on all this shore
Of Corinth a high feast for evermore
And rite, to purge them yearly of the stain
Of this poor blood.   And I, to Pallas' plain
I go, to dwell beside Pandion's son,
Aegeus.—For thee, behold, death draweth on,
Evil and lonely, like thine heart: the hands
Of thine old Argo, rotting where she stands,

Shall smite thine head in twain, and bitter be
To the last end thy memories of me.
      [*She rises on the chariot and is slowly borne away.*

JASON.
May They that hear the weeping child
      Blast thee, and They that walk in blood!

MEDEA.
Thy broken vows, thy friends beguiled
      Have shut for thee the ears of God.

JASON.
Go, thou art wet with children's tears!

MEDEA.
Go thou, and lay thy bride to sleep.

JASON.
Childless, I go, to weep and weep.

MEDEA.
Not yet!   Age cometh and long years.

JASON.
My sons, mine own!
MEDEA.
                  Not thine, but mine . . .

JASON.
. . . Who slew them!

MEDEA.
                  Yes: to torture thee.

JASON.

Once let me kiss their lips, once twine
Mine arms, and touch. . . . Ah, woe is me!

MEDEA.

Wouldst love them and entreat?   But now
They were as nothing.

JASON.

At the last.
O God, to touch that tender brow!

MEDEA.

Thy words upon the wind are cast.

JASON.

Thou, Zeus, wilt hear me.   All is said
For naught. I am but spurned away
And trampled by this tigress, red
With children's blood.   Yet, come what may,
So far as thou hast granted, yea,
So far as yet my strength may stand,
I weep upon these dead, and say
Their last farewell, and raise my hand

To all the daemons of the air
In witness of these things; how she
Who slew them, will not suffer me
To gather up my babes, nor bear
To earth their bodies; whom, O stone
Of women, would I ne'er had known
Nor gotten, to be slain by thee!

[He casts himself upon the earth.

177

CHORUS.

Great treasure halls hath Zeus in heaven,
From whence to man strange dooms be given,
      Past hope or fear.
And the end men looked for cometh not,
And a path is there where no man thought:
      So hath it fallen here.

NOTES TO MEDEA

P. 3, l. 2, To Colchis through the blue Symplê-gades.]—The Symplêgades (" Clashing ") or Kuaneai (" Dark blue ") were two rocks in the sea which used to clash together and crush anything that was between them. They stood above the north end of the Bosphorus and formed the Gate (l. 1264, p. 70) to the Axeinos Pontos, or " Stranger-less Sea," where all Greeks were murdered. At the farthest eastern end of that sea was the land of Colchis.

P. 3, l. 3, Pêlion.]—The great mountain in Thessaly. Iôlcos, a little kingdom between Pêlion and the sea, ruled originally by Aeson, Jason's father, then by the usurping Pĕlias.

P. 3, l. 9, Daughters of Pĕlias.]—See Introduction, p. vii.

P. 4, l. 18, Wed.]—Medea was not legally married to Jason, and could not be, though in common parlance he is sometimes called her husband. Intermarriage between the subjects of two separate states was not possible in antiquity without a special treaty. And naturally there was no such treaty with Colchis.

This is, I think, the view of the play, and corresponds to the normal Athenian conceptions of society. In the original legend it is likely enough that Medea belongs to " matriarchal " times before the institution of marriage.

P. 4, l. 18, Head of Corinth.]—A peculiar word

(αἰσυμνᾶν) afterwards used to translate the Roman *dictator*. Creon is, however, apparently descended from the ancient king Sisyphus.

P. 4, l. 40, She hath a blade made keen, &c.]— These lines (40, 41) are repeated in a different context later on, p. 23, ll. 379, 380. The sword which to the Nurse suggested suicide was really meant for murder. There is a similar and equally dramatic repetition of the lines about the crown and wreath (786, 949, pp. 46, 54), and of those about the various characters popularly attributed to Medea (ll. 304, 808, pp. 18, 46).

P. 5, l. 48, ATTENDANT.]—Greek *Paidagôgos*, or "pedagogue"; a confidential servant who escorted the boys to and from school, and in similar ways looked after them. Notice the rather light and cynical character of this man, compared with the tenderness of the Nurse.

P. 5, l. 57, To this still earth and sky.]—Not a mere stage explanation. It was the ancient practice, if you had bad dreams or terrors of the night, to "show" them to the Sun in the morning, that he might clear them away.

P. 8, l. 111, Have I not suffered?]—Medea is apparently answering some would-be comforter. Cf. p. 4. ("If friends will speak," &c.)

P. 9, l. 131, CHORUS.]—As Dr. Verrall has remarked, the presence of the Chorus is in this play unusually awkward from the dramatic point of view. Medea's plot demands most absolute secrecy; and it is incredible that fifteen Corinthian women, simply because they were women, should allow a half-mad foreigner to murder several people, including their own Corinthian king and princess—who was a woman also — rather than reveal her plot. We must remember in palliation (1) that these women belong to the faction in Corinth which was friendly to Medea and hostile to Creon; (2) that the appeal to them as women had more force in antiquity than it would now, and the princess had really turned traitor to her sex. (See note on this subject at the end of the present writer's translation of the *Electra*.) (3) The non-interference of the Chorus seems monstrous: yet in ancient times, when law was weak and punishment was chiefly the concern of the injured persons, and of no one else, the reluctance of bystanders to interfere was much greater than it is now in an ordered society. Some oriental countries, and perhaps even California or Texas, could afford us some startling instances of impassiveness among bystanders.

P. 12, l. 167, Oh, wild words!]—The Nurse breaks in, hoping to drown her mistress's dangerous self-betrayal. Medea's murder of her brother (see Introduction, p. vi) was by ordinary standards her worst act, and seems not to have been known in Corinth. It forms the climax of Jason's denunciation, l. 1334, p. 74.

P. 13, l. 190, Alas, the bold blithe bards, &c.]— Who is the speaker? According to the MSS. the Nurse, and there is some difficulty in taking the lines from her. Yet (1) she has no reason to sing a song outside after saying that she is going in; and (2) it is quite necessary that she should take a little time indoors persuading Medea to come out. The words seems to suit the lips of an impersonal Chorus.

The general sense of the poem is interesting. It is

an apology for tragedy. It gives the tragic poet's conception of the place of his art in the service of humanity, as against the usual feeling of the public, whose serious work is devoted to something else, and who " go to a play to be amused."

P. 14, l. 214, Women of Corinth, I am come, &c.] —These opening lines are a well-known *crux interpretum.* It is interesting to note, (1) that the Roman poet Ennius (ca. 200 B.C.) who translated the *Medea,* did not understand them in the least; while, on the other hand, the earliest Greek commentators seem not to have noticed that there was any difficulty in them worth commenting upon. That implies that while the acting tradition was alive and unbroken, the lines were easily understood; but when once the tradition failed, the meaning was lost. (The first commentator who deals with the passage is Irenæus, a scholar of the Augustan time.)

P. 15, l. 231, A herb most bruised is woman.]— This fine statement of the wrongs of women in Athens doubtless contains a great deal of the poet's own mind; but from the dramatic point of view it is justified in several ways. (1) Medea is seeking for a common ground on which to appeal to the Corinthian women. (2) She herself is now in the position of all others in which a woman is most hardly treated as compared with a man. (3) Besides this, one can see that, being a person of great powers and vehement will, she feels keenly her lack of outlet. If she had men's work to do, she could be a hero: debarred from proper action (from τὸ πράσσειν, *Hip.* 1019) she is bound to make mischief. Cf. p. 24, ll. 408, 409. " Things most vain, &c."

There is a slight anachronism in applying the Attic system of dowries to primitive times. Medea's contemporaries either lived in a "matriarchal" system without any marriage, or else were bought by their husbands for so many cows.

P. 17, l. 271, CREON.]—Observe the somewhat archaic abruptness of this scene, a sign of the early date of the play.

P. 18, l. 295, Wise beyond men's wont.]—Medea was a "wise woman," which in her time meant much the same as a witch or enchantress. She did really know more than other women; but most of this extra knowledge consisted—or was supposed to consist—either in lore of poisons and charms, or in useless learning and speculation.

P. 18, l. 304, A seed of strife, an Eastern dreamer, &c.]—The meaning of these various "ill names" is not certain. Cf. l. 808, p. 46. Most scholars take θατέρου τρόπου (" of the other sort ") to mean " the opposite of a dreamer."

P. 20, ll. 333–4, What would I with thy pains?]— A conceit almost in the Elizabethan style, as if by taking "pains" away from Creon, she would have them herself.

P. 20, l. 335, Not that! Not that!]—Observe what a dislike Medea has of being touched: cf. l. 370 ("my flesh been never stained," &c.) and l. 496 ("poor, poor right hand of mine!"), pp. 22 and 28.

P. 22, l. 364, Defeat on every side.]—Observe (1) that in this speech Medea's vengeance is to take the form of a clear fight to the death against the three guilty persons. It is both courageous and, judged by the appropriate standard, just. (2) She wants to save her own life, not from cowardice, but simply to make her revenge more complete. To kill her enemies and escape is victory. To kill them and die with them is only a drawn battle. Other enemies will live and "laugh." (3) Already in this first soliloquy there is a suggestion of that strain of madness which becomes unmistakable later on in the play. ("Oh, I have tried so many thoughts of murder," &c., and especially the lashing of her own fury, "Awake thee now, Medea.")

P. 24, l. 405, Thief's daughter: lit. "a child of Sisyphus."]—Sisyphus, an ancient king of Corinth, was one of the well-known sinners punished in Tartarus. Medea's father, Aiêtês, was a brother of Circe, and born of the Sun.

P. 24, l. 409, Things most vain for help.]—See on ll. 230 ff.

P. 24, ll. 410-430, CHORUS.]—The song celebrates the coming triumph of Woman in her rebellion against Man; not by any means Woman as typifying the domestic virtues, but rather as the downtrodden, uncivilised, unreasoning, and fiercely emotional half of humanity. A woman who in defence of her honour and her rights will die sword in hand, slaying the man who wronged her, seems to the Chorus like a deliverer of the whole sex.

P. 24, l. 421, Old bards.]—Early literature in most countries contains a good deal of heavy satire on women: e.g. Hesiod's "Who trusts a woman trusts a thief;" or Phocylides' "Two days of a woman are very sweet: when you marry her and when you carry her to her grave."

It is curious how the four main Choruses of the *Medea* are divided each into two parts, distinct in subject and in metre.

P. 25, l. 439, Faith is no more sweet.]—Copied from a beautiful passage in Hesiod, *Works and Days*, 198 ff.: " There shall be no more sweetness found in the faithful man nor the righteous. . . . And at last up to Olympus from the wide-wayed earth, shrouding with white raiment their beautiful faces, go Ruth and Rebuking." (Aidos and Nemesis: *i.e.* the Ruth or Shame that you feel with reference to your own actions, and the Indignation or Disapproval that others feel.)

P. 27, ll. 478 ff., Bulls of fiery breath.]—Among the tasks set him by Aiêtês, Jason had to yoke two fire-breathing bulls, and plough with them a certain Field of Ares, sow the field with Dragon's teeth, and reap a harvest of earth-born or giant warriors which sprang from the seed. When all this was done, there remained the ancient serpent coiled round the tree where the Golden Fleece was hanging.

P. 29, l. 507, The first friends who sheltered me.]— *i.e.* the kindred of Pelias.

P. 29, l. 509, Blest of many a maid in Hellas.]— Jason was, of course, the great romantic hero of his time. Cf. his own words, l. 1340, p. 74.

Pp. 29 ff., ll. 523–575.—Jason's defence is made the weaker by his reluctance to be definitely insulting to Medea. He dares not say: " You think that, because you conceived a violent passion for me,—to which, I admit, I partly responded—I must live with you always; but the truth is, you are a savage with whom a civilised man cannot go on living." This point comes out unveiled in his later speech, l. 1329 ff., p. 74.

P. 30, ll. 536 ff., Our ordered life and justice.]—Jason has brought the benefits of civilisation to Medea! He is doubtless sincere, but the peculiar ironic cruelty of the plea is obvious.

P. 30, ll. 541 ff., The story of Great Medea, &c. . . . Unless our deeds have glory.]—This, I think, is absolutely sincere. To Jason ambition is everything. And, as Medea has largely shared his great deeds with him, he thinks that she cannot but feel the same. It seems to him contemptible that her mere craving for personal love should outweigh all the possible glories of life.

P. 31, l. 565, What more need hast thou of children?]—He only means, " of more children than you now have." But the words suggest to Medea a different meaning, and sow in her mind the first seed of the child-murder. See on the Aegeus scene below.

P. 34, l. 608, A living curse.]—Though she spoke no word, the existence of a being so deeply wronged would be a curse on her oppressors. So a murdered man's blood, or an involuntary cry of pain (Aesch. *Ag.* 237) on the part of an injured person is in itself fraught with a curse.

P. 35, ll. 627–641, CHORUS. Alas, the Love, &c.]—A highly characteristic Euripidean poem, keenly observant of fact, yet with a lyrical note penetrating all its realism. A love which really produces " good to man and glory," is treated in the next chorus, l. 844 ff., p. 49.

Pp. 37 ff., ll. 663–759, AEGEUS.]—This scene is generally considered to be a mere blot on the play, not, I think, justly. It is argued that the obvious purpose which the scene serves, the provision of an asylum for Medea, has no keen dramatic interest. The spectator would just as soon, or sooner, have her die. And, besides, her actual mode of escape is largely independent of Aegeus. Further, the arrival of Aegeus at this moment seems to be a mere coincidence (*Ar. Poetics*, 61 b, 23), and one cannot help suspecting that the Athenian poet was influenced by mere local interests in dragging in the Athenian king and the praises of Athens where they were not specially appropriate.

To these criticisms one may make some answer. (1) As to the coincidence, it is important to remember always that Greek tragedies are primarily historical plays, not works of fiction. They are based on definite *Logoi* or traditions (*Frogs*, l. 1052, p. 254) and therefore can, and should, represent accidental coincidences when it was a datum of the tradition that these coincidences actually happened. By Aristotle's time the practice had changed. The tragedies of his age were essentially fiction; and he tends to criticise the ancient tragedies by fictional standards.

Now it was certainly a datum in the Medea legend that she took refuge with Aegeus, King of Athens, and was afterwards an enemy to his son Theseus; but I think we may go further. This play pretty certainly has for its foundation the rites performed by the Corinthians at the Grave of the Children of Medea in the precinct of Hera Acraia near Corinth. See on l. 1379, p. 77. The legend in such cases is usually invented to explain the ritual; and I suspect that in the ritual, and, consequently, in the legend, there were two other data: first, a pursuit of Medea and her flight on a dragon-chariot, and, secondly, a meeting between Medea and Aegeus. (Both subjects are frequent on vase paintings, and may well be derived from historical pictures in some temple at Corinth.)

Thus, the meeting with Aegeus is probably not the free invention of Euripides, but one of the data supplied to him by his subject. But he has made it serve, as von Arnim was the first to perceive, a remarkable dramatic purpose. Aegeus was under a curse of childlessness, and his desolate condition suggests to Medea the ultimate form of her vengeance. She will make Jason childless. Cf. l. 670, " Children! Ah God, art childless? " (A childless king in antiquity was a miserable object: likely to be deposed and dishonoured, and to miss his due worship after death. See the fragments of Euripides' *Oineus*.)

There is also a further purpose in the scene, of a curious and characteristic kind. In several plays of Euripides, when a heroine hesitates on the verge of a crime, the thing that drives her over the brink is some sudden and violent lowering of her self-respect. Thus Phædra writes her false letter immediately after her public shame. Creûsa in the *Ion* turns murderous only after crying in the god's ears the story of her seduction. Medea, a princess and, as we have seen, a woman of rather proud chastity, feels, after the offer which she makes to Aegeus in this scene (l. 716 ff., p. 42), that she need shrink from nothing.

P. 38, l. 681, The hearth-stone of my sires of yore.] —This sounds as if it meant Aegeus' own house: in reality, by an oracular riddle, it meant the house of

Pittheus, by whose daughter, Aethra, Aegeus became the father of Theseus.

P. 43, l. 731, An oath wherein to trust.]—Observe that Medea is deceiving Aegeus. She intends to commit a murder before going to him, and therefore wishes to bind him down so firmly that, however much he wish to repudiate her, he shall be unable. Hence this insistence on the oath and the exact form of the oath. (At this time, apparently, she scarcely thinks of the children, only of her revenge.)

P. 46, l. 808, No eastern dreamer, &c.]—See on l. 304.

P. 47, l. 820, *The* NURSE *comes out.*]—There is no indication in the original to show who comes out. But it is certainly a woman; as certainly it is not one of the Chorus; and Medea's words suit the Nurse well. It is an almost devilish act to send the Nurse, who would have died rather than take such a message had she understood it.

P. 48, ll. 824–846, The sons of Erechtheus, &c.]— This poem is interesting as showing the ideal conception of Athens entertained by a fifth-century Athenian. One might compare with it Pericles' famous speech in Thucydides, ii, where the emphasis is laid on Athenian "plain living and high thinking" and the freedom of daily life. Or, again, the speeches of Aethra in Euripides' *Suppliant Women,* where more stress is laid on mercy and championship of the oppressed.

The allegory of " Harmony," as a sort of Korê, or Earth-maiden, planted by all the Muses in the soil of Attica, seems to be an invention of the poet. Not any given Art or Muse, but a spirit which unites and

harmonises all, is the special spirit of Athens. The
Attic connection with Erôs, on the other hand, is old
and traditional. But Euripides has transformed the
primitive nature-god into a mystic and passionate
longing for " all manner of high deed," a Love which,
different from that described in the preceding chorus,
really ennobles human life.

This first part of the Chorus is, of course, suggested
by Aegeus; the second is more closely connected
with the action of the play. " How can Medea dream
of asking that stainless land to shelter her crimes?
But the whole plan of her revenge is not only wicked
but impossible. She simply could not do such a thing,
if she tried."

Pp. 50 ff., l. 869, The second scene with Jason.]—
Dicæarchus, and perhaps his master Aristotle also,
seems to have complained of Medea's bursting into
tears in this scene, instead of acting her part con-
sistently—a very prejudiced criticism. What strikes
one about Medea's assumed rôle is that in it she
remains so like herself and so unlike another woman.
Had she really determined to yield to Jason, she
would have done so in just this way, keen-sighted
and yet passionate. One is reminded of the deceits of
half-insane persons, which are due not so much to conscious art as to the emergence of another side of the
personality.

P. 54, l. 949, Fine robings, &c.]—Repeated from
l. 786, p. 46, where it came full in the midst of
Medea's avowal of her murderous purpose. It
startles one here, almost as though she had spoken
out the word " murder " in some way which Jason
could not understand.

P. 56, l. 976, Chorus.]—The inaction of the
Chorus women during the last scene will not bear
thinking about, if we regard them as real human
beings, like, for instance, the Bacchæ and the Trojan
Women in the plays that bear their name. Still
there is not only beauty, but, I think, great dramatic
value in the conventional and almost mystical quality
of this Chorus, and also in the low and quiet tone of
that which follows, l. 1081 ff.

P. 59, ll. 1021 ff., Why does Medea kill her
children?]—She acts not for one clearly stated reason,
like a heroine in Sardou, but for many reasons, both
conscious and subconscious, as people do in real
life. Any analysis professing to be exact would
be misleading, but one may note some elements
in her feeling: (1) She had played dangerously long
with the notion of making Jason childless. (2) When
she repented of this (l. 1046, p. 60) the children
had already been made the unconscious murderers
of the princess. They were certain to be slain, perhaps with tortures, by the royal kindred. (3) Medea
might take them with her to Athens and trust to
the hope of Aegeus' being able and willing to protect
them. But it was a doubtful chance, and she would
certainly be in a position of weakness and inferiority
if she had the children to protect. (4) In the midst
of her passionate half-animal love for the children,
there was also an element of hatred, because they
were Jason's: cf. l. 112, p. 8. (5) She also seems
to feel, in a sort of wild-beast way, that by killing them
she makes them more her own: cf. l. 793, p. 46,
" Mine, whom no hand shall steal from me away; "
l. 1241, p. 68, " touched of none beside." (6) Euri-

pides had apparently observed how common it is, when a woman's mind is deranged by suffering, that her madness takes the form of child-murder. The terrible lines in which Medea speaks to the "Wrath" within her, as if it were a separate being (l. 1056, p. 60), seem to bear out this view.

P. 59, l. 1038, Other shapes of life.]—A mystical conception of death. Cf. *Ion*, 1067, where almost exactly the same phrase is used.

P. 61, l. 1078, I know to what bad deeds, &c.]— This expression of double consciousness was immensely famous in antiquity. It is quoted by Lucian, Plutarch, Clement, Galen, Synesius, Hierocles, Arrian, Simplicius, besides being imitated, *e.g.* by Ovid: " video meliora proboque, Deteriora sequor."

P. 63, l. 1123 ff., MESSENGER.]—A pendant to the Attendant's entrance above, l. 1002. The Attendant, bringing apparently good news, is received with a moan of despair, the Messenger of calamity with serene satisfaction. Cf. the Messenger who announces the death of Pentheus in the *Bacchæ*.

P. 65, l. 1162, Dead self.]—The reflection in the glass, often regarded as ominous or uncanny in some way.

P. 66, l. 1176, The cry turned strangely to its opposite.]—The notion was that an evil spirit could be scared away by loud cheerful shouts—*ololugæ*. But while this old woman is making an *ololugê*, she sees that the trouble is graver than she thought, and the cheerful cry turns into a wail.

P. 68, l. 1236, Women, my mind is clear.]— With the silence in which Medea passes over the success of her vengeance compare Theseus' words, *Hip.*,

l. 1260, "I laugh not, neither weep, at this fell doom."

P. 69, l. 1249, Thou shalt weep hereafter.]—Cf. *Othello*, v. ii., "Be thus when thou art dead, and I will kiss thee, And love thee after."

P. 69, ll. 1251 ff.—This curious prayer to the Sun to "save" Medea—both from the crime of killing her children and the misfortune of being caught by her enemies—is apparently meant to prepare us for the scene of the Dragon Chariot. Notice the emphasis laid on the divine origin of Medea's race and her transformation to "a voice of Hell."

P. 71, ll. 1278 ff., Death of the children.]—The door is evidently barred, since Jason has to use crow-bars to open it in l. 1317. Cf. the end of Maeterlinck's *Mort de Tintagiles*.

P. 71, l. 1281, A mother slew her babes in days of yore, &c.]—Ino, wife of Athamas, King of Thebes, nursed the infant Dionysus. For this Hera punished her with madness. She killed her two children, Learchus and Melicertes, and leaped into the sea. (There are various versions of the story.)—Observe the technique: just as the strain is becoming intolerable, we are turned away from tragedy to pure poetry. See on *Hip.* 731.

P. 74, l. 1320, This, that shall save me from mine enemies' rage.]—There is nothing in the words of the play to show what "this" is, but the Scholiast explains it as a chariot drawn by winged serpents, and the stage tradition seems to be clear on the subject. See note to the Aegeus scene (p. 88).

This first appearance of Medea "above, on the

tower " (Scholiast) seems to me highly effective. The result is to make Medea into something like a *dea ex machinâ*, who prophesies and pronounces judgment. See Introduction.

P. 76, l. 1370, They are dead, they are dead!]— This wrangle, though rather like some scenes in Norse sagas, is strangely discordant for a Greek play. It seems as if Euripides had deliberately departed from his usual soft and reflective style of ending in order to express the peculiar note of discord which is produced by the so-called " satisfaction " of revenge. Medea's curious cry: " Oh, thy voice! It hurts me sore! " shows that the effect is intentional.

P. 77, l. 1379, A still green sepulchre.]—There was a yearly festival in the precinct of Hera Acraia, near Corinth, celebrating the deaths of Medea's children. This festival, together with its ritual and " sacred legend," evidently forms the germ of the whole tragedy. Cf. the Trozenian rites over the tomb of Hippolytus, *Hip.* 1424 ff.

P. 77, l. 1386, The hands of thine old Argo.]— Jason, left friendless and avoided by his kind, went back to live with his old ship, now rotting on the shore. While he was sleeping under it, a beam of wood fell upon him and broke his head. It is a most grave mistake to treat the line as spurious.

THE

HIPPOLYTUS

OF

EURIPIDES

TRANSLATED INTO ENGLISH RHYMING VERSE
WITH EXPLANATORY NOTES BY

GILBERT MURRAY, LL.D., D.Litt.

REGIUS PROFESSOR OF GREEK IN THE UNIVERSITY OF OXFORD

LONDON : GEORGE ALLEN & UNWIN LTD.
RUSKIN HOUSE 40 MUSEUM STREET, W.C. 1

195

INTRODUCTION

In itself the *Hippolytus* needs little comment or explanation. It is a beautiful play. The harshest critics of Euripides admit its fine unity of construction, its sincere drawing of character, and its classic restraint. One might also remark on the singular skill with which the superhuman influences typified by Aphrodite and Artemis are wrought into the web of natural human action. But to the student of drama the play does present one curious problem, a problem of the relation of copies to originals, or later versions to earlier.

It has served as a model, with occasional close verbal borrowings, to two famous later tragedies, Seneca's *Phaedra* and Racine's *Phèdre*. Both plays have been greatly admired, and both show a determination to outbid their Greek original in dramatic effect. Seneca indeed may almost be said to treat it in the spirit of a modern commercial manager. " A fine plot," one can imagine him saying, " but for a modern audience it needs enlivening; it needs more invention, more incidents, stronger curtains." He sets to work to improve it.

First of all, obviously, the gods must go. A modern audience is not interested in gods. Then, Euripides has neglected the obvious *scène à faire*—Phaedra's declaration of love to Hippolytus. His hero and heroine never so much as speak to each other, and even the Nurse's proposals take place off the stage. Such propriety is surely excessive. The theatre demands a good strong Phaedra–Hippolytus scene, effectively prepared. Consequently Seneca gives us first a Nurse–Hippolytus dialogue in very general terms, the Nurse urging that young men should enjoy their youth, Hippolytus extolling chastity and the wild woods, and finally cursing all women. Phaedra, who has been eagerly

5

waiting, enters in time to hear these last words and, in her despair, faints. Hippolytus catches her as she is falling, and she wakes to find herself in his arms. Situation!

From this vantage point she proceeds to woo the embarrassed and unsuspecting young man; tells of her present unhappiness, and her intense unsatisfied love for Theseus —as he once was, " young, beautiful, virginal; like you! " Hippolytus at last understands, and in fury draws his sword upon her. " Yes," she cries: " that is how I wish to die, by your hand, in your arms. *Nunc me compotem voti facis*." Hippolytus flings the sword away in disgust and flies to his wild woods. The Nurse, returning, finds Phaedra dumb with despair, and sees that all is lost unless . . . " *Scelere velandum est scelus*. Accuse him before he can accuse us! —Ho! Help! Help! Hippolytus has tried to ravish the Queen, and threatened her with his sword." Attendants rush in. Curtain!

When, after the next chorus, Theseus returns—haggard and heroic from the realm of Hades—Phaedra repels him. She is unworthy to receive his embraces. She must die. " Why so? " She will not speak. " I must know," says Theseus: " if you are obstinate I will put your Nurse to the torture." Rather than permit that, Phaedra speaks, " I have been assaulted." " By whom? " " I will never say; but there is his sword." The sword is recognised. Hippolytus has fled. His guilt seems all too clear, and Theseus utters the fatal curse. In the next act, when the curse is duly fulfilled and Hippolytus slain (by a much magnified and improved sea-monster), Phaedra appears above the doorway with the sword in her hand, confesses all, and stabs herself. All first-rate theatrical stuff! Why could not Euripides have thought of it? Had he no sense of the theatre?

The curious thing is that, according to such evidence as

6

we have, not very abundant but fairly decisive, he did think of this sort of thing, tried it, and then deliberately threw it away. He saw on reflection that his drama would gain by greater restraint and simplicity. And no doubt it has gained in dignity, beauty, and depth of meaning, and perhaps even in dramatic effect.

Three or four ancient writers mention an earlier version of the Hippolytus which was considered " unseemly " or " unsuitable " by classical Greek taste. It was called " the Veil-face Hippolytus," presumably from some stronger development of the face-veiling incident at v. 947; the present play was "the Garland Hippolytus " evidently with reference to the " wreathèd garland " in v. 87. The ancient argument of our play, for instance, says: " This is the second, or, as it is called, the ' Garland' Hippolytus. That it is a later version is clear in the text; what was unseemly and open to reproach has been corrected." The earlier play has perished except for some twenty " fragments," that is, passages stated or credibly conjectured to be quotations from it. It contained apparently, among other incidents, the scene of Phaedra's declaration of love to Hippolytus, an attack by her on Theseus for his old infidelities, and a return of Theseus not merely from " abroad," but from Hades. Presumably Seneca took the earlier Hippolytus as his model, though we may be sure that no Greek tragedy of the fifth century B.C. could possibly have risen—or fallen, or contorted itself—into the ingenious extravagances of the silver-age Roman rhetorician.

Liveliness, epigram, variety, ingenuity, richness in incident, are all good qualities in literature, but they are dangerous in tragedy and fatal to the greatest tragedy. Who would wish the Book of Job to be cleverer, or the plot of *Paradise Lost* to be made more lively and exciting? The theme of the *Hippolytus*, as it stands, is simple and eternal. There

7

is such a Power as Cypris in the world; there is, much less conspicuous and violent but hardly less real, such a Power as Artemis. They do make human lives their playthings. That is what the *Hippolytus* makes us feel as we see the unconscious victims of these forces acting as they naturally would or must act.

Seneca was a consummate master of rhetoric in a period of bad taste. Racine was a great poet and dramatist in a famous period about which judgments differ. In *Phèdre* he followed Seneca's lead. He dropped the goddesses; he adopted the scene of Phaedra's declaration of love, the sword business, the infidelities of Theseus, the repentance and suicide. He further made the plot quite different and far more complex by inventing Aricie, a young princess beloved by Hippolytus, and thus adding motives of jealousy to Phaedra's other emotional complications, and, further, by developing the Hades story into a false report of Theseus' death. This report not only gives Phaedra an unexpected freedom, but also produces a political crisis with three rival claimants to the throne, Phaedra's son, Hippolytus himself, and Aricie, who belongs to an expelled branch of the royal family. The interwoven threads become irrelevant to the main theme and consequently a little tiresome. We have wandered far from the simple theme of the *Hippolytus*, the two eternal forces playing havoc with human life.

One cannot but notice also that, as with so many modern treatments of Greek stories, the cutting out of the supernatural element is incomplete and leaves behind it a sort of discord. While gods are at work behind the scenes, as in the *Hippolytus*, the Three Prayers and the mysterious Sea Bull are in their right atmosphere. When the gods are removed and our attention is concentrated on a masterly realistic picture of a somewhat morbid woman in love, we do not expect a sudden entrance of supernatural curses and

8

horned dragons. There is lovely verse in *Phèdre*; there
is subtle psychology; there is dramatic skill and power.
Yet, to me, in coming to *Phèdre* after the *Hippolytus* there
is a sense of irrecoverable loss, the loss of a quality of which
Racine himself was capable and which he perhaps attained
in *Athalie*.

Our evidence is not conclusive, but if we can trust it
Euripides did in the second *Hippolytus* a thing so rare as to
be almost unique in literature. The rule of the tradition
is that a later version regularly outbids or over-elaborates
the earlier. A simple example is given in one of Conington's
essays. Homer says he could not name all the Greeks
who went to Troy, not though he had ten tongues and
ten mouths (B 486). Vergil for a similar undertaking
thinks a hundred insufficient: *non mihi si linguae centum
sint, oraque centum, ferrea vox* (Georgics II. V. 43). While
certain later imitators are not content with a thousand.
That is the normal procedure. One may see it here in
Seneca and Racine, or again in Dryden's re-writing of
Shakespeare. It is an extraordinary instance of Greek
Sophrosynê in art that Euripides should actually have made
his second *Hippolytus* simpler and less sensational than his
first. One possible explanation suggests itself. The subject
of his play pretty certainly came to Euripides from a local
folk-tale attached to the sacred Tomb of Hippolytus in
Trozên, a story like that of Joseph and Potiphar's wife in
Genesis XXXIX, of Bellerophon and Anteia in the *Iliad*
(VI. 160), of Peleus and the wife of Acastus in Pindar
(Nem. IV. 57). It is a well-known type; one of those
traditional tales of "brides frail and faithless" which the
Chorus in the *Medea* promise to make an end of, as soon as
women come by their rights (*Med.* 421 ff.). These stories
are apt to have just the incidents which gave offence in the
first *Hippolytus*; the woman regularly makes overtures to

9

the man, is rejected by him, and then uses some garment or possession of his to back up her false accusation. It looks as if Euripides began by putting the Hippolytus story straight on to the stage, without any particular purging of its incidents. And the play somehow failed. Then he realized that what he wanted was a tragedy, and these tales in the first instance are not tragedies. They aim at entertainment, sometimes even at a snigger, rather than at tears or purgation of the soul. Hence the need of a second treatment of the subject, rejecting all that was small or mean, and concentrating on that which is great, simple, and of permanent human significance.

CHARACTERS OF THE PLAY

THE GODDESS APHRODITÊ.

THE GODDESS ARTEMIS.

THÊSEUS, *King of Athens and Trozên.*

PHAEDRA, *daughter of Minos, King of Crete, wife to Theseus.*

HIPPOLYTUS, *bastard son of Theseus and the Amazon Hippolytê.*

THE NURSE OF PHAEDRA.

AN OLD HUNTSMAN.

A HENCHMAN OF HIPPOLYTUS.

A CHORUS OF HUNTSMEN.

A CHORUS OF TROZENIAN WOMEN, WITH THEIR LEADER.

ATTENDANTS ON THE THREE ROYAL PERSONS.

"The scene is laid in Trozên. The play was first acted when Epameinon was Archon, Olympiad 87, year 4 (429 B.C.). Euripides was first, Iophon second, Ion third."

11

The scene represents the front of the royal castle of Trozên, the chief door being in the centre, facing the audience. Two statues are visible, that of ARTEMIS *on the right, that of* APHRODITE *or* CYPRIS *on the left. The goddess* APHRODITE *is discovered alone.*

.APHRODITE

Great among men, and not unnamed am I,
The Cyprian, in God's inmost halls on high.
And wheresoe'er from Pontus to the far
Red West men dwell, and see the glad day-star,
And worship Me, the pious heart I bless.
And wreck that life that lives in stubborness.
For that there is, even in a great God's mind,
That hungereth for the praise of human kind.
  So runs my word; and soon the very deed
Shall follow. For this Prince of Theseus' seed,
Hippolytus, child of that dead Amazon,
And reared by saintly Pittheus in his own
Strait ways, hath dared, alone of all Trozên,
To hold me least of spirits and most mean,
And spurns my spell and seeks no woman's kiss.
But great Apollo's sister, Artemis,
He holds of all most high, gives love and praise,
And through the wild dark woods for ever strays,
He and the Maid together, with swift hounds
To slay all angry beasts from out these bounds,
To more than mortal friendship consecrate!
  I grudge it not. No grudge know I, nor hate;
Yet, seeing he hath offended, I this day
Shall smite Hippolytus. Long since my way

13

Was opened, nor needs now much labour more.
For once from Pittheus' castle to the shore
Of Athens came Hippolytus over-seas
Seeking the vision of the Mysteries.
And Phaedra there, his father's Queen high-born,
Saw him, and, as she saw, her heart was torn
With great love, by the working of my will.
And for his sake, long since, on Pallas' hill,
Deep in the rock, that Love no more might roam,
She built a shrine, and named it *Love-at-home:*
And the rock held it, but its face alway
Seeks Trozên o'er the seas.   Then came the day
When Theseus, for the blood of kinsmen shed,
Spake doom of exile on himself, and fled,
Phaedra beside him, even to this Trozên.
And here that grievous and amazèd Queen,
Wounded and wondering, with ne'er a word,
Wastes slowly; and her secret none hath heard
Nor dreamed.
         But never thus this love shall end!
To Theseus' ear some whisper will I send,
And all be bare!   And that proud Prince, my foe,
His sire shall slay with curses.   Even so
Endeth that gift that great Poseidon made
To Theseus, the three Prayers not vainly prayed.
    And she, not in dishonour, yet shall die.
I would not rate this woman's pain so high
As not to pay mine haters in full fee
That vengeance that shall make all well with me.

But soft, here comes he, striding from the chase,
Our Prince Hippolytus!—I will go my ways.—
And hunters at his heels: and a loud throng
Glorying Artemis with praise and song!

14

Little he knows that Hell's gates opened are,
And this his last look on the great Day-star!
[APHRODITE *withdraws, unseen by* HIPPOLYTUS *and a band
of huntsmen, who enter from the left, singing. They pass
the Statue of* APHRODITE *without notice.*

HIPPOLYTUS

Follow, O follow me,
    Singing on your ways
Her in whose hand are we,
Her whose own flock we be,
The Zeus-Child, the Heavenly;
    To Artemis be praise!

HUNTSMEN

Hail to thee, Maiden blest,
Proudest and holiest:
God's Daughter, great in bliss,
Leto-born, Artemis!
Hail to thee, Maiden, far
Fairest of all that are,
    Yea, and most high thine home,
Child of the Father's hall;
Hear, O most virginal,
Hear, O most fair of all,
    In high God's golden dome.

[*The huntsmen have gathered about the altar of* ARTEMIS.
HIPPOLYTUS *now advances from them, and approaches the
Statue with a wreath in his hand.*

HIPPOLYTUS

To thee this wreathèd garland, from a green
And virgin meadow bear I, O my Queen,

15

Where never shepherd leads his grazing ewes
Nor scythe has touched.   Only the river dews
Gleam, and the spring bee sings, and in the glade
Hath Solitude her mystic garden made.
   No evil hand may cull it: only he
Whose heart hath known the heart of Purity,
Unlearned of man, and true whate'er befall.
Take therefore from pure hands this coronal,
O mistress loved, thy golden hair to twine.
For, sole of living men, this grace is mine,
To dwell with thee, and speak, and hear replies
Of voice divine, though none may see thine eyes.
   Oh, keep me to the end in this same road!
[*An* OLD HUNTSMAN, *who has stood apart from the rest,
here comes up to* HIPPOLYTUS.

HUNTSMAN
My Prince—for 'Master' name I none but God—
Gave I good counsel, wouldst thou welcome it?

HIPPOLYTUS
Right gladly, friend; else were I poor of wit.

HUNTSMAN
Knowest thou one law, that through the world has won.

HIPPOLYTUS
What wouldst thou?   And how runs thy law?   Say on.

HUNTSMAN
It hates that Pride that speaks not all men fair!

HIPPOLYTUS
And rightly.   Pride breeds hatred everywhere.

16

HUNTSMAN

And good words love, and grace in all men's sight?

HIPPOLYTUS

Aye, and much gain withal, for trouble slight.

HUNTSMAN

How deem'st thou of the Gods?   Are they the same?

HIPPOLYTUS

Surely: we are but fashioned on their frame.

HUNTSMAN

Why then wilt thou be proud, and worship not . . .

HIPPOLYTUS

Whom? If the name be speakable, speak out!

HUNTSMAN

She stands here at thy gate: the Cyprian Queen!

HIPPOLYTUS

I greet her from afar: my life is clean.

HUNTSMAN

Clean?   Nay, proud, proud; a mark for all to scan.

HIPPOLYTUS

Each mind hath its own bent, for God or man.

HUNTSMAN

God grant thee happiness . . . and wiser thought!

17

HIPPOLYTUS

These Spirits that reign in darkness like me not.

HUNTSMAN

What the Gods ask, O Son, that man must pay!

HIPPOLYTUS (*turning from him to the others*)
On, huntsmen, to the Castle! Make your way
Straight to the feast room; 'tis a welcome thing
After the chase, a board of banqueting.
And see the steeds be groomed, and in array
The chariot dight. I drive them forth to-day.
[*He pauses, and makes a slight gesture of reverence to the
Statue on the left. Then to the* OLD HUNTSMAN.
That for thy Cyprian, friend, and nought beside!
[HIPPOLYTUS *follows the huntsmen, who stream off by the
central door into the Castle. The* OLD HUNTSMAN
remains.

HUNTSMAN (*approaching the Statue and kneeling*)
O Cyprian—for a young man in his pride
I will not follow!—here before thee, meek,
In that one language that a slave may speak,
I pray thee; Oh, if some wild heart in froth
Of youth surges against thee, be not wroth
For ever! Nay, be far and hear not then:
Gods should be gentler and more wise than men!
[*He rises and follows the others into the Castle.*

*The Orchestra is empty for a moment, then there enter from
right and left several Trozenian women, young and old.
Their number eventually amounts to fifteen.*

18

Chorus

There riseth a rock-born river,
   Of Ocean's tribe, men say;
The crags of it gleam and quiver,
   And pitchers dip in the spray:
A woman was there with raiment white
To bathe and spread in the warm · sunlight,
   And she told a tale to me there by the river,
    The tale of the Queen and her evil day:

How, ailing beyond allayment,
   Within she hath bowed her head,
And with shadow of silken raiment
   The bright brown hair bespread.
For three long days she hath lain forlorn,
Her lips untainted of flesh or corn,
   For that secret sorrow beyond allayment
    That steers to the far sad shore of the dead.

Some Women

Is this some Spirit, O child of man?
Doth Hecat hold thee perchance, or Pan?
Doth She of the Mountains work her ban,
   Or the dread Corybantes bind thee?

Others

Nay, is it sin that upon thee lies,
Sin of forgotten sacrifice,
In thine own Dictynna's sea-wild eyes?
   Who in Limna here can find thee;
For the Deep's dry floor is her easy way,
And she moves in the salt wet whirl of the spray.

19

Other Women

Or doth the Lord of Erechtheus' race,
Thy Theseus, watch for a fairer face,
For secret arms in a silent place,
    Far from thy love or chiding?

Others

Or hath there landed, amid the loud
Hum of Piraeus' sailor-crowd,
Some Cretan venturer, weary-browed,
    Who bears to the Queen some tiding;
Some far home-grief, that hath bowed her low,
And chained her soul to a bed of woe?

An Older Woman

Nay—know ye not?—this burden hath alway lain
On the devious being of woman; yea, burdens twain,
The burden of Wild Will and the burden of Pain.
Through my heart once that wind of terror sped;
    But I, in fear confessèd,
Cried from the dark to Her in heavenly bliss,
The Helper of Pain, the Bow-Maid Artemis:
Whose feet I praise for ever, where they tread
    Far off among the blessèd!

THE LEADER

But see, the Queen's grey nurse at the door,
Sad-eyed and sterner, methinks, than of yore,
    With the Queen. Doth she lead her hither,
To the wind and sun?—Ah, fain would I know
What strange betiding hath blanched that brow,
    And made that young life wither.

20

[*The* NURSE *comes out from the central door, followed by*
PHAEDRA, *who is supported by two handmaids. They
make ready a couch for* PHAEDRA *to lie upon.*

NURSE

O sick and sore are the days of men!
What wouldst thou? What shall I change again?
Here is the Sun for thee; here is the sky;
Here they weary pillows windswept lie,
      By the castle door.
But the cloud of thy brow is dark, I ween;
And soon thou wilt back to thy bower within:
So swift to change is the path of thy feet,
And near things hateful, and far things sweet;
      So was it before!

Oh, pain were better than tending pain!
For that were single, and this is twain,
With grief of heart and labour of limb.
Yet all man's life is but ailing and dim,
      And rest upon earth comes never.
But if any far-off state there be,
Dearer than life to mortality;
The hand of the Dark hath hold thereof,
And mist is under and mist above.
And so we are sick for life, and cling
On earth to this nameless and shining thing.
For other life is a fountain sealed,
And the deeps below us are unrevealed,
      And we drift on legends for ever!

[PHAEDRA *during this has been laid on her couch; she speaks
to the handmaids.*

21

PHAEDRA

Yes; lift me: not my head so low.
There, hold my arms.—Fair arms they seem!—
My poor limbs scarce obey me now!
Take off that hood that weighs my brow,
And let my long hair stream.

NURSE

Nay, toss not, Child, so feveredly.
The sickness best will win relief
By quiet rest and constancy.
All men have grief.

PHAEDRA (*not noticing her*)

Oh for a deep and dewy spring,
With runlets cold to draw and drink!
And a great meadow blossoming,
Long-grassed, and poplars in a ring,
To rest me by the brink!

NURSE

Nay, Child! Shall strangers hear this tone
So wild, and thoughts so fever-flown?

PHAEDRA

Oh, take me to the Mountain! Oh,
Past the great pines and through the wood,
Up where the lean hounds softly go,
A-whine for wild things' blood,
And madly flies the dappled roe.
O God, to shout and speed them there,
An arrow by my chestnut hair
Drawn tight, and one keen glimmering spear—
Ah! if I could!

22

NURSE

What wouldst thou with them—fancies all!—
Thy hunting and thy fountain brink?
What wouldst thou? By the city wall
Canst hear our own brook plash and fall
    Downhill, if thou wouldst drink.

PHAEDRA

O Mistress of the Sea-lorn Mere
    Where horse-hoofs beat the sand and sing,
O Artemis that I were there
To tame Enetian steeds and steer
    Swift chariots in the ring!

NURSE

Nay, mountainward but now thy hands
    Yearned out, with craving for the chase;
And now toward the unseaswept sands
    Thou roamest, where the coursers pace!
O wild young steed, what prophet knows
The power that holds thy curb, and throws
    Thy swift heart from its race?

[*At these words* PHAEDRA *gradually recovers herself and
pays attention.*

PHAEDRA

What have I said? Woe's me! And where
    Gone straying from my wholesome mind?
Hath some god caught me in his snare?
    —Nurse, veil my head again, and blind
Mine eyes.—There is a tear behind
    That lash.—Oh I am sick with shame!

23

Aye, but it hath a sting,
To come to reason; yet the name
Of madness is an awful thing.—
Could I but die in one swift flame
Unthinking, unknowing!

NURSE

I veil thy face, Child.—Would that so
Mine own were veiled for evermore,
So sore I love thee! . . . Though the lore
Of long life mocks me, and I know
How love should be a lightsome thing
Not rooted in the deep o' the heart;
With gentle ties, to twine apart
If need so call, or closer cling.—
Why do I love thee so? O fool,
O fool, the heart that bleeds for twain,
And builds, men tell us, walls of pain,
To walk by love's unswerving rule,
The same for ever, stern and true!
For 'Thorough' is no word of peace:
'Tis 'Naught-too-much' makes trouble cease,
And many a wise man bows thereto.
[*The* LEADER OF THE CHORUS *here approaches the* NURSE.

LEADER

Nurse of our Queen, thou watcher old and true,
We see her great affliction, but no clue
Have we to learn the sickness. Wouldst thou tell
The name and sort thereof, 'twould like us well.

NURSE

Small leechcraft have I, and she tells no man.

24

LEADER

Thou know'st no cause? Nor when the unrest began?

NURSE

It all comes to the same. She will not speak.

LEADER (*turning and looking at* PHAEDRA)

How she is changed and wasted! And how weak!

NURSE

'Tis the third day she hath fasted utterly.

LEADER

What, is she mad? Or doth she seek to die?

NURSE

I know not. But to death it sure must lead.

LEADER

'Tis strange. And doth her husband take no heed?

NURSE

She hides her wound, and vows that all is well.

LEADER

Can he not look into her face and tell?

NURSE

Theseus has been abroad these many days.

LEADER

Canst thou not force her then? Or think of ways
To trap the secret of the sick heart's pain?

25

NURSE

Have I not tried all ways, and all in vain?
Yet will I cease not now, and thou shalt tell
If in her grief I serve my mistress well!
[*She goes across to where* PHAEDRA *lies; and presently, while
speaking, kneels by her.*
Dear daughter mine, all that before was said
Let both of us forget; and thou instead
Be kindlier, and unlock that prisoned brow.
And I, who followed then the wrong road, now
Will leave it and be wiser. If thou fear
Some secret sickness, there be women here
To give thee comfort.   [PHAEDRA *shakes her head.*
                              No; not secret? Then
Is it a sickness meet for aid of men?
Speak, that a leech may tend thee.
                                   Silent still!
Nay, Child, what profits silence? If 'tis ill
This that I counsel, make me see the wrong:
If well, then yield to me.
                         Nay, Child, I long
For one kind word, one look!
              [PHAEDRA *lies motionless. The* NURSE *rises.*
                         Oh, woe is me!
Women, we labour here all fruitlessly,
All as far off as ever from her heart.
She is still the same, all silent and apart,
Not hearing me.   [*Turning to* PHAEDRA *again*
                    Nay, hear thou shalt, and be,
If so thou will, more wild than the wild sea;
But know, thou art thy little ones' betrayer!
If thou die now, shall child of thine be heir
To Theseus' castle? Nay, not thine, I ween,
But hers! That barbèd Amazonian Queen

26

218

Hath left a child to bend thy children low,
A bastard royal-hearted—sayst not so?—
Hippolytus . . .

PHAEDRA

Ah!
[She starts up, sitting, and throws the veil off.

NURSE
That stings thee?

PHAEDRA

Nurse, most sore
Thou hast hurt me!   In God's name, speak that name no
more.

NURSE
Thou seest?   Thy mind is clear; but with thy mind
Thou wilt not save thy children, nor be kind
To thine own life.

PHAEDRA

My children?   Nay, most dear
I love them.—Far, far other grief is here.

NURSE (*after a pause, wondering*)
Thy hand is clean, O Child, from stain of blood?

PHAEDRA

My hand is clean; but is my heart, O God?

NURSE
Some enemy's spell hath made thy spirit dim?

PHAEDRA

He hates me not that slays me, nor I him.

27

NURSE

Theseus, the King, hath wronged thee in man's wise?

PHAEDRA

Ah, could but I stand guiltless in his eyes!

NURSE

O speak! What is this death-fraught mystery?

PHAEDRA

Nay, leave me to my wrong. I wrong not thee.

NURSE (*suddenly throwing herself in supplication at*
PHAEDRA's feet)

Not wrong me, whom thou wouldst all desolate leave!

PHAEDRA (*rising and trying to move away*)

What wouldst thou? Force me? Clinging to my sleeve?

NURSE

Yea, to thy knees; and weep; and let not go!

PHAEDRA

Woe to thee, Woman, if thou learn it, woe!

NURSE

I know no bitterer woe than losing thee.

PHAEDRA

I am lost! Yet the deed shall honour me.

NURSE

Why hide what honours thee? 'Tis all I claim!

28

PHAEDRA

Why, so I build up honour out of shame!

NURSE

Then speak, and higher still thy fame shall stand.

PHAEDRA

Go, in God's name!—Nay, leave me; loose my hand!

NURSE

Never, until thou grant me what I pray.

PHAEDRA (*yielding, after a pause*)

So be it.   I dare not tear that hand away.

NURSE (*rising and releasing* PHAEDRA)

Tell all thou wilt, Daughter   I speak no more.

PHAEDRA (*after a long pause*)

Mother, poor Mother, that didst love so sore!

NURSE

What mean'st thou, Child?   The Wild Bull of the Tide?

PHAEDRA

And thou, sad sister, Dionysus' bride!

NURSE

Child! wouldst thou shame the house where thou wast born?

PHAEDRA

And I the third, sinking most all-forlorn!

29

NURSE (*to herself*).
I am all lost and feared. What will she say?

PHAEDRA
From there my grief comes, not from yesterday.

NURSE
I come no nearer to thy parable.

PHAEDRA
Oh, would that thou couldst tell what I must tell!

NURSE
I am no seer in things I wot not of.

PHAEDRA (*again hesitating*)
What is it that they mean, who say men . . . love?

NURSE
A thing most sweet, my Child, yet dolorous.

PHAEDRA
Only the half, belike, hath fallen on us!

NURSE (*starting*)
On thee? Love?—Oh, what sayst thou? What man's
son?

PHAEDRA
What man's? There was a Queen, an Amazon . . .

NURSE
Hippolytus, sayst thou?

30

PHAEDRA (*again wrapping her face in the veil*)
                    Nay, 'twas thou, not I!

[PHAEDRA *sinks back on the couch and covers her face again.
The* NURSE *starts violently from her and walks up and
down.*

NURSE

O God! what wilt thou say, Child? Wouldst thou try
To kill me?—Oh, 'tis more than I can bear;
Women, I will no more of it, this glare
Of hated day, this shining of the sky.
I will fling down my body, and let it lie
Till life be gone!
                    Women, God rest with you,
My works are over! For the pure and true
Are forced to evil, against their own heart's vow,
And love it!

[*She suddenly sees the Statue of* CYPRIS, *and stands with her
eyes riveted upon it.*

                    Ah, Cyprian! No god art thou,
But more than god, and greater, that hath thrust
Me and my queen and all our house to dust!

[*She throws herself on the ground close to the statue.*

CHORUS

Some Women

O Women, have ye heard? Nay, dare ye hear
The desolate cry of the young Queen's misery?

A Woman

My Queen, I love thee dear,
    Yet liefer were I dead than framed like thee.

31

Others

Woe, woe to me for this thy bitter bane,
Surely the food man feeds upon is pain!

Others

How wilt thou bear thee through this livelong day,
    Lost, and thine evil naked to the light?
Strange things are close upon us—who shall say
    How strange?—save one thing that is plain to sight,
The stroke of the Cyprian and the fall thereof
On thee, thou child of the Isle of fearful Love!
[PHAEDRA *during this has risen from the couch and comes
    forward collectedly. As she speaks the* NURSE *gradually
    rouses herself and listens more calmly.*

PHAEDRA

O Women, dwellers in this portal-seat
Of Pelops' land, gazing towards my Crete,
How oft, in other days than these, have I
Through night's long hours thought of man's misery,
And how this life is wrecked! And, to mine eyes,
Not in man's knowledge, not in wisdom, lies
The lack that makes for sorrow. Nay, we scan
And know the right—for wit hath many a man—
But will not to the last end strive and serve.
For some grow too soon weary, and some swerve
To other paths, setting before the Right
The diverse far-off image of Delight;
And many are delights beneath the sun!
Long hours of converse; and to sit alone
Musing—a deadly happiness!—and Shame:
Though two things there be hidden in one name,
And Shame can be slow poison if it will!
    This is the truth I saw then, and see still;

32

224

Nor is there any magic that can stain
That white truth for me, or make me blind again.
Come, I will show thee how my spirit hath moved.
When the first stab came, and I knew I loved,
I cast about how best to face mine ill.
And the first thought that came, was to be still
And hide the sickness.—For no trust there is
In man's tongue, that so well admonishes
And counsels and betrays, and waxes fat
With griefs of its own gathering!—After that
I would my madness bravely bear, and try
To conquer by mine own heart's purity.

   My third mind, when these two availed me naught
To quell love, was to die—
[*Motion of protest among the Women.*

                         the best, best, thought
Of all—gainsay me not!—for such as me.
I would not hide my praise for none to see;
Why should I have my shame before men's eyes
Kept living?   And I knew, in deadly wise,
Shame was the deed and shame the suffering;
And I a woman, too, to face the thing,
Despised of all!
                Oh, utterly accurst
Be she of women, whoso dared the first
To cast her honour out to a strange man!
'Twas in some great house, surely, that began
This plague upon us; then the baser kind,
When the good led towards evil, followed blind
And joyous!   Cursed be they whose lips are clean
And wise and seemly, but their hearts within
Rank with bad daring!   How can they, O Thou
That walkest on the waves, great Cyprian, how

33

Smile in their husband's faces, and not fall,
Not cower before the Darkness that knows all,
Aye, dread the dead still chambers, lest one day
The stones find voice, and all be finished!
                                              Nay,
Friends, 'tis for this I die; lest I stand there
Having shamed my husband and the babes I bare.
In ancient Athens they shall some day dwell,
My babes, free men, free-spoken, honourable,
And when one asks their mother, proud of me!
For, oh, it cows a man, though bold he be,
To know a mother's or a father's sin.
   'Tis written, one way is there, one, to win
This life's race, could man keep it from his birth,
A true clean spirit. And through all this earth
To every false man, that hour comes apace
When Time holds up a mirror to his face,
And girl-like, marvelling, there he stares to see
How foul his heart! Be it not so with me!

LEADER OF CHORUS

Ah God, how sweet is virtue, and how wise,
And honour its due meed in all men's eyes!

NURSE (*who has now risen and recovered herself*)

Mistress, a sharp swift terror struck me low
A moment since, hearing of this thy woe.
But now—I was a coward! And men say
Our second thoughts are wiser every way.
   This is no monstrous thing; no grief too dire
To meet with quiet thinking. In her ire
A perilous goddess hath swept down on thee.
Thou lovest. Is that so strange? Many there be

34

Beside thee! . . . And because thou lovest, wilt fall
And die! And must all lovers die, then? All
That are or shall be? A blithe law for them!
Nay, when in might she swoops, no strength can stem
Cypris; and if man yields him, she is sweet;
But is he proud and stubborn? From his feet
She lifts him, and—how think you?—flings to scorn!

   She ranges with the stars of eve and morn,
She wanders in the heaving of the sea,
And all life lives from her.—Aye, this is she
That sows Love's seed and brings Love's fruit to birth;
And great Love's brethren are all we on earth!

   Nay, they who con grey books of ancient days
Or dwell among the Muses, tell—and praise—
How Zeus himself once yearned for Semelê;
How maiden Eôs in her radiancy
Swept Kephalos to heaven away, away,
For sore love's sake. And there they dwell, men say,
And fear not, fret not; for a thing too stern,
Meeting, hath crushed them!

               And must thou, then, turn
And struggle? Sprang there from thy father's blood
Thy little soul all lonely? Or the god
That rules thee, is he other than our gods?

   Nay, yield thee to men's ways, and kiss their rods!
How many, deem'st thou, of men good and wise,
Know their own home's blot, and avert their eyes?
How many fathers, when a son has strayed
And toiled beneath the Cyprian, bring him aid,
Not chiding? And man's wisdom e'er hath been
To keep what is not good to see, unseen!

   A straight and perfect life is not for man;
Nay, in a shut house, let him, if he can,

35

'Mid sheltered rooms, make all lines true. But here,
Out in the wide sea fallen, and full of fear,
Hopest thou so easily to swim to land?
   Canst thou but set thine ill days on one hand
And more good days on the other, verily,
O child of woman, life is well with thee!
[*She pauses, and then draws nearer to* PHAEDRA.
Nay, dear my daughter, cease thine evil mind,
Cease thy fierce pride! For pride it is, and blind,
To seek to outpass gods!—Love on and dare:
A god hath willed it! But since pain is there,
Make the pain sleep! Songs are there to bring calm,
And magic words. And I shall find the balm,
Be sure, to heal thee. Else in sore dismay
Were men, could not we women find our way!

LEADER OF THE CHORUS

Help is there, Queen, in all this woman says,
To ease thy suffering. But 'tis thee I praise;
Albeit that praise is harder to thine ear
Than all her chiding was, and bitterer!

PHAEDRA

Oh, this it is hath flung to dogs and birds
Men's lives and homes and cities—fair false words!
Oh, why speak things to please our ears? We crave
Not that. 'Tis honour, honour, we must save;

NURSE

Why prate so proud? 'Tis no words, brave nor base,
Thou cravest; 'tis a man's arms!
[PHAEDRA *moves indignantly.*

                             Up and face

The truth of what thou art, and name it straight!
Were not thy life thrown open here for Fate
To beat on; hadst thou been a woman pure
Or wise or strong; never had I for lure
Of joy nor heartache led thee on to this!
But when a whole life one great battle is,
To win or lose—no man can blame me then.

PHAEDRA

Shame on thee! Lock those lips, and ne'er again
Let word nor thought so foul have harbour there!

NURSE

Foul, if thou wilt: but better than the fair
For thee and me. And better, too, the deed
Behind them, if it save thee in thy need,
Than that word Honour thou wilt die to win!

PHAEDRA

Nay, in God's name,—such wisdom and such sin
Are all about thy lips!—urge me no more.
For all the soul within me is wrought o'er
By Love; and if thou speak and speak, I may
Be spent, and drift where now I shrink away.

NURSE

Well, if thou wilt!—'Twere best never to err,
But, having erred, to take a counsellor
Is second.—Mark me now. I have within
Love-philtres, to make peace where storm hath been,
That, with no shame, no scathe of mind, shall save
Thy life from anguish; wilt but thou be brave!
[*To herself reflecting.*

37

Ah, but from him, the well-beloved, some sign
We need, or word, or raiment's hem, to twine
Amid the charm, and one spell knit from twain.

PHAEDRA

Is it a potion or a salve? Be plain.

NURSE

Who knows? Seek to be helped, Child, not to know.

PHAEDRA

Why art thou ever subtle? I dread thee, so

NURSE

Thou wouldst dread everything!—What dost thou dread?

PHAEDRA

Lest to his ear some word be whisperèd

NURSE

Let be, Child! I will make all well with thee!
—Only do thou, O Cyprian of the Sea,
Be with me! And mine own heart, come what may,
Shall know what ear to seek, what word to say!
[*The* NURSE *having spoken these last words in prayer apart
to the Statue of* CYPRIS *turns back and goes into the house.*
PHAEDRA *sits pensive again on her couch till towards the
end of the following Song, when she rises and bends close
to the door.*

CHORUS

Erôs, Erôs, who blindest, tear by tear,
    Men's eyes with hunger; thou swift Foe, that
        pliest
Deep in our hearts joy like an edgèd spear;

38

Come not to me with Evil haunting near,
Wrath on the wind, nor jarring of the clear
    Wing's music as thou fliest!
There is no shaft that burneth, not in fire,
Not in wild stars, far off and flinging fear,
As in thine hands the shaft of All Desire,
        Erôs, Child of the Highest!

In vain, in vain, by old Alpheüs' shore
    The blood of many bulls doth stain the river,
And all Greece bows on Phœbus' Pythian floor;
Yet bring we to the Master of Man no store
The Keybearer, who standeth at the door
        Close-barred, where hideth ever
The heart of the shrine.   Yea, though he sack man's
            life
    Like a sacked city, and moveth evermore
Girt with calamity and strange ways of strife,
        Him have we worshipped never!

There roamed a Steed in Oechalia's wild,
    A Maid without yoke, without Master,
And Love she knew not, that far King's child:
But he came, he came, with a song in the night,
With fire, with blood; and she strove in flight,
A Torrent Spirit, a Maenad white,
        Faster and vainly faster,
Sealed unto Heracles by the Cyprian's Might.
    Alas, thou Bride of Disaster!

O Mouth of Dirce, O god-built wall,
    That Dirce's wells run under,
Ye know the Cyprian's fleet footfall!

39

Ye saw the heaven's around her flare,
When she lulled to her sleep that Mother fair
Of Twy-born Bacchus, and decked her there
The Bride of the bladed Thunder.
For her breath is on all that hath life, and she floats in
the air,
Bee-like, death-like, a wonder.

[*During the last lines* PHAEDRA *has approached the door
and is listening*

PHAEDRA

Silence, ye Women! Something is amiss.

LEADER

How? In the house?—Phaedra, what fear is this?

PHAEDRA

Let me but listen! There are voices. Hark!

LEADER

I hold my peace: yet is thy presage dark.

PHAEDRA

Oh, misery!
O God, that such a thing should fall on me!

LEADER

What sound, what word,
O Woman, Friend, makes that sharp terror start
Out at thy lips? What ominous cry half-heard
Hath leapt upon thine heart?

PHAEDRA

I am undone!—Bend to the door and hark,
Hark what a tone sounds there, and sinks away!

40

LEADER

Thou art beside the bars. 'Tis thine to mark
  The castle's floating message. Say, Oh, say
    What thing hath come to thee?

PHAEDRA (*calmly*)

  Why, what thing should it be?
The son of that proud Amazon speaks again
In bitter wrath: speaks to my handmaiden!

LEADER

I hear a noise of voices, nothing clear.
  For thee the din hath words, as through barred locks
    Floating, at thy heart it knocks.

PHAEDRA

"Pander of Sin" it says.—Now canst thou hear?—
And there: "Betrayer of a master's bed."

LEADER

  Ah me, betrayed! Betrayed!
Sweet Princess, thou art ill bested,
Thy secret brought to light, and ruin near,
    By her thou heldest dear,
By her that should have loved thee and obeyed!

PHAEDRA

Aye, I am slain. She thought to help my fall
With love instead of honour, and wrecked all.

LEADER

  Where wilt thou turn thee, where?
And what help seek, O wounded to despair?

41

PHAEDRA

I know not, save one thing, to die right soon.
For such as me God keeps no other boon.

[*The door in the centre bursts open, and* HIPPOLYTUS *comes
    forth, closely followed by the* NURSE   PHAEDRA *cowers
    aside.*

HIPPOLYTUS

O Mother Earth, O Sun that makest clean,
What poison have I heard, what speechless sin!

NURSE

Hush, O my Prince, lest others mark, and guess . . !

HIPPOLYTUS

I have heard horrors!   Shall I hold my peace?

NURSE

Yea, by this fair right arm, Son, by thy pledge   . .

HIPPOLYTUS

Down with that hand!   Touch not my garment's edge!

NURSE

Oh, by thy knees, be silent or I die!

HIPPOLYTUS

Why, when thy speech was all so guiltless?   Why?

NURSE

It is not meet, fair Son, for every ear!

HIPPOLYTUS

Good words can bravely forth, and have no fear.

42

NURSE

Thine oath, thine oath! I took thine oath before!

HIPPOLYTUS

'Twas but my tongue, 'twas not my soul that swore.

NURSE

O Son, what wilt thou? Wilt thou slay thy kin?

HIPPOLYTUS

I own no kindred with the spawn of sin!
[*He flings her from him.*

NURSE

Nay, spare me! Man was born to err; oh, spare!

HIPPOLYTUS

O God, why hast Thou made this gleaming snare,
Woman, to dog us on the happy earth?
Was it Thy will to make Man, why his birth
Through Love and Woman?   Could we not have rolled
Our store of prayer and offering, royal gold,
Silver and weight of bronze before Thy feet,
And bought of God new child-souls, as were meet
For each man's sacrifice, and dwelt in homes
Free, where nor Love nor Woman goes and comes?
　　How, is that daughter not a bane confessed,
Whom her own sire sends forth—(He knows her best!)—
And, will some man but take her, pays a dower!
And he, poor fool, takes home the poison-flower;
Laughs to hang jewels on the deadly thing
He joys in; labours for her robe-wearing,
Till wealth and peace are dead. He smarts the less
In whose high seat is set a Nothingness,

43

A woman naught availing. Worst of all
The wise deep-thoughted! Never in my hall
May she sit throned who thinks and waits and sighs!
For Cypris breeds most evil in the wise,
And least in her whose heart has naught within;
For puny wit can work but puny sin.

Why do we let their handmaids pass the gate?
Wild beasts were best, voiceless and fanged, to wait
About their rooms, that they might speak with none,
Nor ever hear one answering human tone!
But now dark women in still chambers lay
Plans that creep out into the light of day
On handmaids' lips—   [*Turning to the* NURSE
                    As thine accursèd head
Braved the high honour of my Father's bed,
And came to traffic. . . . Our white torrent's spray
Shall drench mine ears to wash those words away!
And couldst thou dream that *I* . . .? I feel impure
Still at the very hearing! Know for sure,
Woman, naught but mine honour saves ye both.
Hadst thou not trapped me with that guileful oath,
No power had held me secret till the King
Knew all! But now, while he is journeying,
I too will go my ways and make no sound.
And when he comes again, I shall be found
Beside him, silent, watching with what grace
Thou and thy mistress greet him face to face!
Then shall I have the taste of it, and know
What woman's guile is.—Woe upon you, woe!
How can I too much hate you, while the ill
Ye work upon the world grows deadlier still?
Too much? Make woman pure, and wild Love tame,
Or let me cry for ever on their shame!

44

[He goes off in fury to the left. PHAEDRA *still cowering in her place begins to sob.*

PHAEDRA

Sad, sad and evil-starred
  Is Woman's state.
What shelter now is left or guard?
What spell to loose the iron knot of fate?
  And this thing, O my God,
O thou sweet Sunlight, is but my desert!
I cannot fly before the avenging rod
  Falls, cannot hide my hurt.
What help, O ye who love me, can come near,
  What god or man appear,
To aid a thing so evil and so lost?
Lost, for this anguish presses, soon or late,
To that swift river that no life hath crossed.
No woman ever lived so desolate!

LEADER OF THE CHORUS

Ah me, the time for deeds is gone; the boast
Proved vain that spake thine handmaid; and all lost!
[At these words PHAEDRA *suddenly remembers the* NURSE, *who is cowering silently where* HIPPOLYTUS *had thrown her from him. She turns upon her.*

PHAEDRA

O wicked, wicked, wicked! Murderess heart
To them that loved thee! Hast thou played thy part?
Am I enough trod down?

     May Zeus, my sire,
Blast and uproot thee! Stab thee dead with fire!
Said I not—Knew I not thine heart?—to name
To no one soul this that is now my shame?

45

And thou couldst not be silent! So no more
I die in honour. But enough; a store
Of new words must be spoke and new things thought.
This man's whole being to one blade is wrought
Of rage against me. Even now he speeds
To abase me to the King with thy misdeeds;
Tell Pittheus; fill the land with talk of sin!
    Cursèd be thou, and whoso else leaps in
To bring bad aid to friends that want it not.
[*The* NURSE *has raised herself, and faces* PHAEDRA, *downcast but calm*

NURSE

Mistress, thou blamest me; and all thy lot
So bitter sore is, and the sting so wild,
I bear with all. Yet, if I would, my Child,
I have mine answer, couldst thou hearken aught
    I nursed thee, and I love thee; and I sought
Only some balm to heal thy deep despair,
And found—not what I sought for. Else I were
Wise, and thy friend, and good, had all sped right.
So fares it with us all in the world's sight.

PHAEDRA

First stab me to the heart, then humour me
With words! 'Tis fair; 'tis all as it should be!

NURSE

We talk too long, Child. I did ill; but, oh,
There is a way to save thee, even so!

PHAEDRA

A way? No more ways! One way hast thou trod
Already, foul and false and loathed of god!

46

Begone out of my sight; and ponder how
Thine own life stands! I need no helpers now.
[*She turns from the* NURSE *who creeps abashed away into
the Castle.*
Only do ye, high Daughters of Trozên,
Let all ye hear be as it had not been;
Know naught, and speak of naught! 'Tis my last prayer.

LEADER

By God's pure daughter, Artemis, I swear,
No word will I of these thy griefs reveal!

PHAEDRA

'Tis well. But now, yea, even while I reel
And falter, one poor hope, as hope now is,
I clutch at in this coil of miseries;
To save some honour for my children's sake;
Yea, for myself some fragment, though things break
In ruin around me. Nay, I will not shame
The old proud Cretan castle whence I came,
I will not cower before King Theseus' eyes,
Abased, for want of one life's sacrifice!

LEADER

What wilt thou? Some dire deed beyond recall?

PHAEDRA (*musing*)

Die; but how die?
LEADER
Let not such wild words fall!

PHAEDRA (*turning upon her*)

Give thou not such light counsel! Let me be
To sate the Cyprian that is murdering me!

47

To-day shall be her day; and, all strife past,
Her bitter Love shall quell me at the last.
    Yet, dying, shall I die another's bane!
He shall not stand so proud where I have lain
Bent in the dust!   Oh, he shall stoop to share
The life I live in, and learn mercy there!
[*She goes off wildly into the Castle.*

CHORUS

Could I take me to some cavern for mine hiding,
    In the hill-tops where the Sun scarce hath trod;
Or a cloud make the home of mine abiding,
    As a bird among the bird-droves of God!
        Could I wing me to my rest amid the roar
        Of the deep Adriatic on the shore,
Where the waters of Eridanus are clear,
    And Phaëthon's sad sisters by his grave
Weep into the river, and each tear
    Gleams, a drop of amber, in the wave.

To the strand of the Daughters of the Sunset,
    The Apple-tree, the singing and the gold;
Where the mariner must stay him from his onset,
    And the red wave is tranquil as of old;
        Yea, beyond that Pillar of the End
        That Atlas guardeth, would I wend;
Where a voice of living waters never ceaseth
    In God's quiet garden by the sea,
And Earth, the ancient life-giver, increaseth
    Joy among the meadows, like a tree.

———————

O shallop of Crete, whose milk-white wing
Through the swell and the storm-beating,

48

Bore us thy Prince's daughter,
Was it well she came from a joyous home
To a far King's bridal across the foam?
What joy hath her bridal brought her?
Sure some spell upon either hand
Flew with thee from the Cretan strand,
Seeking Athena's tower divine;
And there, where Munychus fronts the brine,
Crept by the shore-flung cables' line,
The curse from the Cretan water!

And, for that dark spell that about her clings,
Sick desires of forbidden things
The soul of her rend and sever;
The bitter tide of calamity
Hath risen above her lips; and she,
Where bends she her last endeavour?
She will hie her alone to her bridal room,
And a rope swing slow in the rafters' gloom;
And a fair white neck shall creep to the noose,
A-shudder with dread, yet firm to choose
The one strait way for fame, and lose
The Love and the pain for ever.

[*The Voice of the* NURSE *is heard from within, crying, at first
inarticulately, then clearly.*

VOICE

Help ho! The Queen! Help, whoso hearkeneth!
Help! Theseus' spouse caught in a noose of death!

A WOMAN

God, is it so soon finished? That bright head
Swinging beneath the rafters! Phaedra dead!

49

VOICE

O haste! This knot about her throat is made
So fast! Will no one bring me a swift blade?

A WOMAN

Say, friends, what think ye? Should we haste within,
And from her own hand's knotting loose the Queen?

ANOTHER

Nay, are there not men there? 'Tis an ill road
In life, to finger at another's load.

VOICE

Let it lie straight! Alas! the cold white thing
That guards his empty castle for the King!

A WOMAN

Ah! 'Let it lie straight!' Heard ye what she said?
No need for helpers now; the Queen is dead!
[*The Women intent upon the voices from the Castle, have
not noticed the approach of* THESEUS. *He enters from the
left; his dress and the garland on his head show that he has
returned from some oracle or special abode of a God. He
stands for a moment perplexed.*

THESEUS

Ho, Women, and what means this loud acclaim
Within the house? The vassals' outcry came
To smite mine ears far off. It were more meet
To fling out wide the Castle gates, and greet
With joy a herald from God's Presence!
[*The confusion and horror of the Women's faces gradually
affects him. A dirge-cry comes from the Castle*

50

How?
Not Pittheus?   Hath Time struck that hoary brow?
Old is he, old, I know.   But sore it were.
Returning thus, to find his empty chair!
[*The Women hesitate; then the Leader comes forward.*

LEADER

O Theseus, not on any old man's head
This stroke falls   Young and tender is the dead.

THESEUS

Ye Gods!   One of my children torn from me?

LEADER

Thy motherless children live, most grievously.

THESEUS

How sayst thou?   What?   My wife? . . .

Say how she died.

LEADER

In a high death-knot that her own hands tied.

THESEUS

A fit of the old cold anguish—Tell me all—
That held her?   Or did some fresh thing befall?

LEADER

We know no more.   But now arrived we be,
Theseus, to mourn for thy calamity.
[THESEUS *stays for a moment silent, and puts his hand to his
    brow.   He notices the wreath.*

I   51

THESEUS

What? And all garlanded I come to her
With flowers, most evil-starred God's-messenger!
    Ho, varlets, loose the portal bars; undo
The bolts; and let me see the bitter view
Of her whose death hath brought me to mine own.
[*The great central door of the Castle is thrown open wide and
the body of* PHAEDRA *is seen lying on a bier, surrounded
by a group of Handmaids, wailing.*

THE HANDMAIDS

Ah me, what thou hast suffered and hast done:
    A deed to wrap this roof in flame!
Why was thine hand so strong, thine heart so bold?
Wherefore, O dead in anger, dead in shame,
The long, long wrestling ere thy breath was cold?
            O ill-starred Wife,
What brought this blackness over all thy life?
[*A throng of Men and Women has gradually collected.*

THESEUS

            Ah me, this is the last
—Hear, O my countrymen!—and bitterest
Of Theseus' labours! Fortune all unblest,
How hath thine heavy heel across me passed!
Is it the stain of sins done long ago,
            Some fell God still remembereth,
That must so dim and fret my life with death?
I cannot win to shore; and the waves flow
Above mine eyes, to be surmounted not.
            Ah wife, sweet wife, what name
            Can fit thine heavy lot?
Gone like a wild bird, like a blowing flame,
In one swift gust, where all things are forgot!

52

Alas! this misery!
Sure 'tis some stroke of God's great anger rolled
        From age to age on me,
For some dire sin wrought by dim kings of old.

LEADER

Sire, this great grief hath come to many an one,
A true wife lost.   Thou art not all alone

THESEUS

Deep, deep beneath the Earth
        Dark may my dwelling be,
And Night my heart's one comrade, in the dearth,
O Love, of thy most sweet society.
This is my death, O Phaedra, more than thine.
[*He turns suddenly on the Attendants.*
Speak who speak can?   What was it?   What malign
Swift stroke, O heart discounselled, leapt on thee?
[*He bends over* PHAEDRA; *then as no one speaks, looks
    fiercely up.*
What, will ye speak?   Or are they dumb as death,
This herd of thralls my high house harboureth?
[*There is no answer.   He bends again over* PHAEDRA.
Ah me, why shouldst thou die?
A wide and royal grief I here behold,
Not to be borne in peace, not to be told.
        As a lost man am I.
My children motherless and my house undone,
        Since thou art vanished quite,
Purest of hearts that e'er the wandering Sun
Touched, or the star-eyed splendour of the Night.
[*He throws himself beside the body.*

53

Chorus

Unahppy one, O most unhappy one;
  With what strange evil is this Castle vexed!
Mine eyes are molten with the tears that run
  For thee and thine; but what thing follows next?
    I tremble when I think thereon!

[*They have noticed that there is a tablet with writing fastened
to the dead woman's wrist.* THESEUS *also sees it.*

THESEUS

Ha, what is this that hangs from her dear hand?
A tablet! It would make me understand
Some dying wish, some charge about her bed
And children. 'Twas the last prayer, ere her head
Was bowed for ever   [*Taking the tablet.*
      Fear not, my lost bride,
No woman born shall lie at Theseus' side,
Nor rule in Theseus' house!
            A seal! Ah, see
How her gold signet here looks up at me,
Trustfully. Let me tear this thread away,
And read what tale the tablet seeks to say
[*He proceeds to undo and read the tablet   The Chorus
breaks into horrified groups*

Some Women

Woe, woe! God brings to birth
A new grief here, close on the other's tread!
    My life hath lost its worth.
May all go now with what is finishèd!
The castle of my King is overthrown,
A house no more, a house vanished and gone!

54

OTHER WOMEN

O God, if it may be in any way,
Let not this house be wrecked! Help us who pray!
I know not what is here: some unseen thing
That shows the Bird of Evil on the wing.

[THESEUS *has read the tablet and breaks out in uncontrollable
emotion*

THESEUS

Oh, horror piled on horror!—Here is writ . . .
Nay, who could bear it, who could speak of it?

LEADER

What, O my King? If I may hear it, speak!

THESEUS

Doth not the tablet cry aloud, yea, shriek,
Things not to be forgotten?—Oh, to fly
And hide mine head! No more a man am I.
Ah, God, what ghastly music echoes here!

LEADER

How wild thy voice! Some terrible thing is near.

THESEUS

No; my lips' gates will hold it back no more;
        This deadly word,
That struggles on the brink and will not o'er,
        Yet will not stay unheard.
[*He raises his hand, to make proclamation to all present.*
        Ho, hearken all this land!
[*The people gather expectantly about him.*
Hippolytus by violence hath laid hand
On this my wife, forgetting God's great eye.
[*Murmurs of amazement and horror;* THESEUS, *apparently
calm, raises both arms to heaven.*

55

Therefore, O Thou my Father, hear my cry,
Poseidon! Thou didst grant me for mine own
Three prayers; for one of these, slay now my son,
Hippolytus; let him not outlive this day,
If true thy promise was! Lo, thus I pray.

LEADER

Oh, call that wild prayer back! O King, take heed!
I know that thou wilt live to rue this deed.

THESEUS

It may not be.—And more, I cast him out
From all my realms. He shall be held about
By two great dooms. Or by Poseidon's breath
He shall fall swiftly to the house of Death;
Or wandering, outcast, o'er strange land and sea,
Shall live and drain the cup of misery.

LEADER

Ah, see! here comes he at the point of need.
Shake off that evil mood, O King: have heed
For all thine house and folk.—Great Theseus, hear!
[THESEUS *stands silent in fierce gloom.* HIPPOLYTUS *comes
in from the right.*

HIPPOLYTUS

Father, I heard thy cry, and sped in fear
To help thee.—But I see not yet the cause
That racked thee so.—Say, Father, what it was.
[*The murmurs in the crowd the silent gloom of his Father,
and the horror of the Chorus-women gradually work on*
HIPPOLYTUS *and bewilder him. He catches sight of
the bier.*

56

Ah, what is that! Nay, Father, not the Queen
Dead! (*Murmurs in the crowd.*)
     'Tis most strange. 'Tis passing strange, I ween.
'Twas here I left her. Scarce an hour hath run
Since here she stood and looked on this same sun.
What is it with her? Wherefore did she die?
[THESEUS *remains silent. The murmurs increase.*
Father, to thee I speak. Oh, tell me, why,
Why art thou silent? What doth silence know
Of skill to stem the bitter flood of woe?
And human hearts in sorrow crave the more
For knowledge, though the knowledge grieve them sore.
It is not love, to veil thy sorrows in
From one most near to thee, and more than kin.

       THESEUS (*to himself*)
Fond race of men, so striving and so blind,
Ten thousand arts and wisdoms can ye find,
Desiring all and all imagining:
But ne'er have reached nor understood one thing,
To make a true heart there where no heart is!

       HIPPOLYTUS
That were indeed beyond man's mysteries,
To make a false heart true against his will.
But why this subtle talk? It likes me ill,
Father; thy speech runs wild beneath this blow.

       THESEUS (*as before*)
O would that God had given us here below
Some test of love, some sifting of the soul,
To tell the false and true! Or through the whole
Of men two voices ran, one true and right,
The other as chance willed it; that we might

57

Convict the liar by the true man's tone,
And not live duped forever, every one!

HIPPOLYTUS (*misunderstanding him; then guessing at
                    something of the truth*)
What?   Hath some friend proved false?

                                              Or in thine ear
Whispered some slander?   Stand I tainted here,
Though utterly innocent?   [*Murmurs from the crowd.*
                          Yea, dazed am I;
'Tis thy words daze me, falling all awry,
Away from reason, by fell fancies vexed!

THESEUS
O heart of man, what height wilt venture next?
What end comes to thy daring and thy crime?
For if with each man's life 'twill higher climb,
And every age break out in blood and lies
Beyond its fathers, must not God devise
Some new world far from ours, to hold therein
Such brood of all unfaithfulness and sin?

   Look, all, upon this man, my son, his life
Sprung forth from mine!   He hath defiled my wife;
And standeth here convicted by the dead,
A most black villain!
[HIPPOLYTUS *falls back with a cry and covers his face with
    his robe.*

                          Nay, hide not thine head!
Pollution, is it?   Thee it will not stain
Look up, and face thy Father's eyes again!
   Thou friend of Gods, of all mankind elect;
Thou the pure heart, by thoughts of ill unflecked!
I care not for thy boasts.   I am not mad,
To deem that Gods love best the base and bad.

58

Now is thy day! Now vaunt thee; thou so pure,
No flesh of life may pass thy lips! Now lure
Fools after thee; call Orpheus King and Lord;
Make ecstasies and wonders! Thumb thine hoard
Of ancient scrolls and ghostly mysteries—
Now thou art caught and known!

                    Shun men like these,
I charge ye all! With solemn words they chase
Their prey, and in their hearts plot foul disgrace.
  My wife is dead.—'Ha, so that saves thee now?'
That is what grips thee worst, thou caitiff, thou!
What oaths, what subtle words, shall stronger be
Than this dead hand, to clear the guilt from thee?
 'She hated thee,' thou sayest; 'the bastard born
Is ever sore and bitter as a thorn
To the true brood.'—A sorry bargainer
In the ills and goods of life thou makest her,
If all her best-beloved she cast away
To wreak blind hate on thee!—What, wilt thou say,
'Through every woman's nature one blind strand
Of passion winds, that men scarce understand?'—
Are we so different? Know I not the fire
And perilous flood of a young man's desire,
Desperate as any woman, and as blind,
When Cypris stings? Save that the man behind
Has all men's strength to aid him. Nay, 'twas thou...
 But what avail to wrangle with thee now,
When the dead speaks for all to understand,
A perfect witness!

                Hie thee from this land
To exile with all speed. Come never more
To god-built Athens, not to the utmost shore
Of any realm where Theseus' arm is strong!
What? Shall I bow my head beneath this wrong,

1*   59

And cower to thee? Not Isthmian Sinis so
Will bear men witness that I laid him low,
Nor Skiron's rocks, that share the salt sea's prey,
Grant that my hand hath weight vile things to slay!

LEADER

Alas! whom shall I call of mortal men
Happy? The highest are cast down again

HIPPOLYTUS

Father, the hot strained fury of thy heart
Is terrible. Yet, albeit so swift thou art
Of speech, if all this matter were laid bare,
Speech were not then so swift; nay, nor so fair. . . .
[*Murmurs again in the crowd.*
I have no skill before a crowd to tell
My thoughts. 'Twere best with few, that know me well.—
Nay, that is natural; tongues that sound but rude
In wise men's ears, speak to the multitude
With music.
       None the less, since there is come
This stroke upon me, I must not be dumb,
But speak perforce. . . . And there will I begin
Where thou beganst, as though to strip my sin
Naked, and I not speak a word!
          Dost see
This sunlight and this earth? I swear to thee
There dwelleth not in these one man—deny
What lists thee!—cleaner of this crime than I.

Two things I have learned to know; God's worship first,
Next to win friends about me, few, that thirst
To hold them clean of all unrighteousness;
For whom 'twere shame to proffer sin, nor less

60

With tolerance base to smooth the sinner's way.
How could I dupe the men whom day by day
I live with? They have proved me to the end,
Near and far off the same, who call me friend.
And most in that one thing, where now thy mesh
Would grip me, stainless quite! No woman's flesh
Hath e'er this body touched. Of all such deed
Naught wot I, save what things a man may read
In pictures or hear spoke; nor am I fain,
Being virgin-souled, to read or hear again,

So be it! My strict life has no worth for thee,
But show at least what hath corrupted me.
Was that poor flesh so passing fair, beyond
All women's loveliness?

                            Was I some fond
False plotter, that I schemed to win through her
Thy castle's heirdom? Fond indeed I were!
Nay, a stark madman! 'But a crown,' thou sayst,
'Usurped, is sweet.' Nay, rather most unblest
To all wise-hearted; sweet to fools and them
Whose eyes are blinded by the diadem.
In contests of all valour fain would I
Lead Hellas; but in rank and majesty
Not lead, but be at ease, with good men near
To love me, free to work and not to fear.
That brings more joy than any crown or throne.

[*He sees from the demeanour of* THESEUS *and of the crowd
   that his words are not winning them, but rather making
   them bitterer than before. It comes to his lips to speak the
   whole truth.*

I have said my say; save one thing . . . one alone.
   O had I here some witness in my need,
As I was witness! Could she hear me plead,

61

Face me and face the sunlight; well I know,
Our deeds would search us out for thee, and show
Who lies!

           But now, I .swear—so hear me both,
The Earth beneath and Zeus who Guards the Oath—
I never touched this woman that was thine!
No words could win me to it, nor incline
My heart to dream it. May God strike me down,
Nameless and fameless, without home or town,
An outcast and a wanderer of the world;
May my dead bones rest never, but be hurled
From sea to land, from land to angry sea,
If evil is my heart and false to thee!
[*He waits a moment; but sees that his Father is unmoved.*
  The truth again comes to his lips.
If 'twas some fear that made her cast away
Her life . . . I know not. More I must not say.
Right hath she done when in her was no right;
And Right I follow to mine own despite!

LEADER

It is enough! God's name is witness large,
And thy great oath, to assoil thee of this charge

THESEUS

Is not the man a juggler and a mage,
Cool wits and one right oath—what more?—to assuage
Sin and the wrath of injured fatherhood!

HIPPOLYTUS

Am I so cool? Nay, Father, 'tis thy mood
That makes me marvel! By my faith, wert thou
The son, and I the sire; and deemed I now

62

In very truth thou hadst my wife assailed,
I had not exiled thee, nor stood and railed,
But lifted once mine arm, and struck thee dead!

THESEUS

Thou gentle judge! Thou shalt not so be sped
To simple death, nor by thine own decree.
Swift death is bliss to men in misery.
Far off, friendless forever, thou shalt drain
Amid strange cities the last dregs of pain!

HIPPOLYTUS

Wilt verily cast me now beyond thy pale,
Not wait for Time, the lifter of the veil?

THESEUS

Aye, if I could, past Pontus, and the red
Atlantic marge! So do I hate thine head.

HIPPOLYTUS

Wilt weigh nor oath nor faith nor prophet's word
To prove me? Drive me from thy sight unheard?

THESEUS

This tablet here, that needs no prophet's lot
To speak from, tells me all. I ponder not
Thy fowls that fly above us! Let them fly.

HIPPOLYTUS

O ye great Gods, wherefore unlock not I
My lips, ere yet ye have slain me utterly,
Ye whom I love most? No. It may not be!
The one heart that I need I ne'er should gain
To trust me. I should break mine oath in vain.

63

THESEUS

Death! but he chokes me with his saintly tone!—
Up, get thee from this land! Begone! Begone!

HIPPOLYTUS

Where shall I turn me? Think. To what friend's door
Betake me, banished on a charge so sore?

THESEUS

Whoso delights to welcome to his hall
Vile ravishers . . . to guard his hearth withal!

HIPPOLYTUS

Thou seekst my heart, my tears? Aye, let it be
Thus! I am vile to all men, and to thee!

THESEUS

There was a time for tears and thought; the time
Ere thou didst up and gird thee to thy crime.

HIPPOLYTUS

Ye stones, will ye not speak? Ye castle walls!
Bear witness if I be so vile, so false!

THESEUS

Aye, fly to voiceless witnesses! Yet here
A dumb deed speaks against thee, and speaks clear!

HIPPOLYTUS

Alas!
Would I could stand and watch this thing, and see
My face, and weep for very pity of me!

64

THESEUS

Full of thyself, as ever! Not a thought
For them that gave thee birth; nay, they are naught!

HIPPOLYTUS

O my wronged Mother! O my birth of shame!
May none I love e'er bear a bastard's name!

THESEUS (*in a sudden blaze of rage*)

Up, thralls, and drag him from my presence! What?
'Tis but a foreign felon! Heard ye not?
[*The thralls still hesitate in spite of his fury.*

HIPPOLYTUS

They touch me at their peril! Thine own hand
Lift, if thou canst, to drive me from the land.

THESEUS

That will I straight, unless my will be done!
[HIPPOLYTUS *comes close to him and kneels.*
Nay! Not for thee my pity! Get thee gone!
[HIPPOLYTUS *rises, makes a sign of submission, and slowly
    moves away.* THESEUS *as soon as he sees him going turns
    rapidly and enters the Castle. The door is closed again.*
    HIPPOLYTUS *has stopped for a moment before the Statue
    of* ARTEMIS, *and, as* THESEUS *departs, breaks out in prayer.*

HIPPOLYTUS

So; it is done! O dark and miserable!
I see it all, but see not how to tell
The tale.—O thou belovèd, Leto's Maid,
Chase-comrade, fellow-rester in the glade,

65

Lo, I am driven with a caitiff's brand
Forth from great Athens! Fare ye well, O land
And city of old Erechtheus! Thou, Trozên,
What riches of glad youth mine eyes have seen
In thy broad plain! Farewell! This is the end;
The last word, the last look!
                              Come, every friend
And fellow of my youth that still may stay,
Give me god-speed and cheer me on my way.
Ne'er shall ye see a man more pure of spot
Than me, though mine own Father loves me not!

[HIPPOLYTUS *goes away to the right followed by many Hunts-*
men and other young men. The rest of the crowd has
by this time dispersed except the Women of the Chorus
and some Men of the Chorus of Huntsmen.

CHORUS
Men

Surely the thought of the Gods hath balm in it alway, to
    win me
    Far from my griefs; and a thought, deep in the dark
      of my mind,
Clings to a great Understanding. Yet all the spirit
    within me
    Faints, when I watch men's deeds matched with the
      guerdon they find.
        For Good comes in Evil's traces,
        And the Evil the Good replaces;
        And Life, 'mid the changing faces,
        Wandereth weak and blind.

Women

What wilt thou grant me, O God? Lo, this is the prayer
    of my travail—

66

Some well-being; and chance not very bitter thereby;
A Spirit uncrippled by pain; and a mind not deep to unravel
Truth unseen, nor yet dark with the brand of a lie.
With a veering mood to borrow
Its light from every morrow,
Fair friends and no deep sorrow,
Well could man live and die!

Men

Yet my spirit is no more clean,
And the weft of my hope is torn,
For the deed of wrong that mine eyes have seen,
The lie and the rage and the scorn;
A Star among men, yea, a Star
That in Hellas was bright,
By a Father's wrath driven far
To the wilds and the night.
Oh, alas for the sands of the shore!
Alas for the brakes of the hill,
Where the wolves shall fear thee no more,
And thy cry to Dictynna is still!

Women

No more in the yoke of thy car
Shall the colts of Enetia fleet;
Nor Limma's echoes quiver afar
To the clatter of galloping feet.
The sleepless music of old,
That leaped in the lyre,
Ceaseth now, and is cold,
In the halls of thy sire.
The bowers are discrowned and unladen
Where Artemis lay on the lea;
And the love-dream of many a maiden
Lost, in the losing of thee.

67

A Maiden

And I, even I,
  For thy fall, O Friend,
  Amid tears and tears,
  Endure to the end
  Of the empty years,
Of a life run dry.
  In vain didst thou bear him,
    Thou Mother forlorn!
  Ye Gods that did snare him,
  Lo, I cast in your faces
    My hate and my scorn!
  Ye love-linkèd Graces,
    (Alas for the day!)
  Was he naught, then, to you,
  That ye cast him away,
    The stainless and true,
From the old happy places?

Look yonder! Surely from the Prince 'tis one
That cometh, full of haste and woe-begone.
[A HENCHMAN *enters in haste.*

HENCHMAN

Ye women, whither shall I go to seek
King Theseus? Is he in this dwelling? Speak!

LEADER

Lo, where he cometh through the Castle gate!
[THESEUS *comes out from the Castle.*

68

HENCHMAN

O King, I bear thee tidings of dire weight
To thee, aye, and to every man, I ween,
From Athens to the marches of Trozên.

THESEUS

What? Some new stroke hath touched, unknown to me,
The sister cities of my sovranty?

HENCHMAN

Hippolytus is . . . Nay, not dead; but stark
Outstretched, a hairsbreadth this side of the dark.

THESEUS (*as though unmoved*)

How slain? Was there some other man, whose wife
He had like mine defiled, that sought his life?

HENCHMAN

His own wild team destroyed him, and the dire
Curse of thy lips.
                    The boon of thy great Sire
Is granted thee, O King, and thy son slain.

THESEUS

Ye Gods! And thou, Poseidon! Not in vain
I called thee Father; thou hast heard my prayer!
  How did he die? Speak on. How closed the snare
Of Heaven to slay the shamer of my blood?

HENCHMAN

'Twas by the bank of beating sea we stood,
We thralls and decked the steeds, and combed each mane;
Weeping; for word had come that ne'er again

69

The foot of our Hippolytus should roam
This land, but waste in exile by thy doom.
　So stood we till he came, and in his tone
No music now save sorrow's, like our own,
And in his train a concourse without end
Of many a chase-fellow and many a friend.
At last he brushed his sobs away, and spake:
'Why this fond loitering? I would not break
My Father's law.—Ho, there! My coursers four
And chariot, quick! This land is mine no more.'
　Thereat, be sure, each man of us made speed.
Swifter than speech we brought them up, each steed
Well dight and shining, at our Prince's side.
He grasped the reins upon the rail: one stride
And there he stood, a perfect charioteer,
Each foot in its own station set. Then clear
His voice rose, and his arms to heaven were spread:
'O Zeus, if I be false, strike thou me dead!
But, dead or living, let my Father see
One day, how falsely he hath hated me!'
　Even as he spake, he lifted up the goad
And smote; and the steeds sprang. And down the road
We henchmen followed, hard beside the rein,
Each hand, to speed him, toward the Argive plain
And Epidaurus.
　　　　　　So we made our way
Up toward the desert region, where the bay
Curls to a promontory near the verge
Of our Trozên, facing the southward surge
Of Saron's gulf. Just there an angry sound,
Slow-swelling, like God's thunder underground,
Broke on us, and we trembled. And the steeds
Pricked their ears skyward, and threw back their heads.

And wonder came on all men, and affright,
Whence rose that awful voice.   And swift our sight
Turned seaward, down the salt and roaring sand.
  And there, above the horizon, seemed to stand
A wave unearthly, crested in the sky;
Till Skiron's Cape first vanished from mine eye,
Then sank the Isthmus hidden, then the rock
Of Epidaurus.   Then it broke, one shock
And roar of gasping sea and spray flung far,
And shoreward swept, where stood the Prince's car.
  Three lines of wave together raced, and, full
In the white crest of them, a wild Sea-Bull
Flung to the shore, a fell and marvellous Thing.
The whole land held his voice, and answering
Roared in each echo.   And all we, gazing there,
Gazed seeing not; 'twas more than eyes could bear,
  Then straight upon the team wild terror fell.
Howbeit, the Prince, cool-eyed and knowing well
Each changing mood a horse has, gripped the reins
Hard in both hands; then as an oarsman strains
Up from his bench, so strained he on the thong,
Back in the chariot swinging.   But the young
Wild steeds bit hard the curb, and fled afar;
Nor rein nor guiding hand nor morticed car
Stayed them at all.   For when he veered them round,
And aimed their flying feet to grassy ground,
In front uprose that Thing, and turned again
The four great coursers, terror-mad.   But when
Their blind rage drove them toward the rocky places,
Silent, and ever nearer to the traces,
It followed, rockward, till one wheel-edge grazed.
  The chariot tript and flew, and all was mazed
In turmoil.   Up went wheel-box with a din,
Where the rock jagged, and nave and axle-pin.

71

And there—the long reins round him—there was he
Dragging, entangled irretrievably.
A dear head battering at the chariot side,
Sharp rocks, and ripped flesh, and a voice that cried:
'Stay, stay, O ye who fattened at my stalls,
Dash me not into nothing!—O thou false
Curse of my Father!—Help! Help, whoso can,
An innocent, innocent and stainless man!'
   Many there were that laboured then, I wot,
To bear him succour, but could reach him not,
Till—who knows how?—at last the tangled rein
Unclasped him, and he fell, some little vein
Of life still pulsing in him.
                        All beside,
The steeds, the hornèd Horror of the Tide,
Had vanished—who knows where?—in that wild land
   O King, I am a bondsman of thine hand;
Yet love nor fear nor duty me shall win
To say thine innocent son hath died in sin.
All women born may hang themselves, for me,
And swing their dying words from every tree
On Ida! For I know that he was true!

LEADER

O God, so cometh new disaster, new
Despair! And no escape from what must be!

THESEUS

Hate of the man thus stricken lifted me
At first to joy at hearing of thy tale;
But now, some shame before the Gods, some pale
Pity for mine own blood, hath o'er me come.
I laugh not, neither weep, at this fell doom.

72

HENCHMAN

How then? Behoves it bear him here, or how
Best do thy pleasure?—Speak, Lord.   Yet if thou
Wilt mark at all my word, thou wilt not be
Fierce-hearted to thy child in misery.

THESEUS

Aye, bring him hither. Let me see the face
Of him who durst deny my deep disgrace
And his own sin; yea, speak with him, and prove
His clear guilt by God's judgments from above.
[*The* HENCHMAN *departs to fetch* HIPPOLYTUS; THESEUS
sits waiting in stern gloom while the CHORUS *sing. At
the close of their song a Divine Figure is seen approaching
on a cloud in the air and the voice of* ARTEMIS *speaks.*

CHORUS

Thou comest to bend the pride
        Of the hearts of God and man,
Cypris; and by thy side,
        In earth-encircling span,
        He of the changing plumes,
        The Wing that the world illumes,
As over the leagues of land flies he,
Over the salt and sounding sea.

For mad is the heart of Love,
        And gold the gleam of his wing;
And all to the spell thereof
        Bend, when he makes his spring;
All life that is wild and young
        In mountain and wave and stream,
All that of earth is sprung,
        Or breathes in the red sunbeam;

73

Yea, and Mankind. O'er all a royal throne,
Cyprian, Cyprian, is thine alone!

A VOICE FROM THE CLOUD

O thou that rulest in Aegeus' Hall,
I charge thee, hearken!
                            Yea, it is I,
Artemis, Virgin of God most High.
Thou bitter King, art thou glad withal
        For thy murdered son?
For thine ear bent low to a lying Queen,
For thine heart so swift amid things unseen?
Lo, all may see what end thou hast won!
Go, sink thine head in the waste abyss;
Or aloft to another world than this,
        Birdwise with wings,
        Fly far to thine hiding,
Far over this blood that clots and clings;
For in righteous men and in holy things
        No rest is thine nor abiding!

[*The cloud has become stationary in the air.*

Hear, Theseus, all the story of thy grief!
Verily, I bring but anguish, not relief;
Yet, 'twas for this I came, to show how high
And clean was thy son's heart, that he may die
Honoured of men; aye, and to tell no less
The frenzy, or in some sort the nobleness,
Of thy dead wife. One Spirit there is, whom we
That know the joy of white virginity,
Most hate in heaven. She sent her fire to run
In Phaedra's veins, so that she loved thy son.
Yet strove she long with love, and in the stress
Fell not, till by her Nurse's craftiness

74

Betrayed, who stole, with oaths of secrecy,
To entreat thy son. And he, most righteously,
Nor did her will, nor, when thy railing scorn
Beat on him, broke the oath that he had sworn,
For God's sake. And thy Phaedra, panic-eyed,
Wrote a false writ, and slew thy son, and died,
Lying; but thou wast nimble to believe!
[THESEUS, *at first bewildered then dumbfounded now*
    utters a deep groan.
It stings thee, Theseus?—Nay, hear on, and grieve
Yet sorer. Wottest thou three prayers were thine
Of sure fulfilment, from thy Sire divine?
Hast thou no foes about thee, then, that one—
Thou vile King!—must be turned against thy son?
The deed was thine. Thy Sea-born Sire but heard
The call of prayer, and bowed him to his word.
But thou in his eyes and in mine art found
Evil, who wouldst not think, nor probe, nor sound
The deeps of prophet's lore, nor day by day
Leave Time to search; but, swifter than man may,
Let loose the curse to slay thine innocent son!

THESEUS
O Goddess, let me die!

ARTEMIS
            Nay; thou hast done
A heavy wrong; yet even beyond this ill
Abides for thee forgiveness. 'Twas the will
Of Cypris that these evil things should be,
Sating her wrath. And this immutably
Hath Zeus ordained in heaven: no God may thwart
A God's fixed will; we grieve but stand apart,

75

Else, but for fear of the Great Father's blame,
Never had I to such extreme of shame
Bowed me, be sure, as here to stand and see
Slain him I loved best of mortality!

  Thy fault, O King, its ignorance sunders wide
From very wickedness; and she who died
By death the more disarmed thee, making dumb
The voice of question. And the storm has come
Most bitterly of all on thee! Yet I
Have mine own sorrow, too. When good men die,
There is no joy in heaven, albeit our ire.
On child and house of the evil falls like fire.

[*A throng is seen approaching;* HIPPOLYTUS *enters supported by his attendants.*

CHORUS

  Lo, it is he! The bright young head
      Yet upright there!
Ah, the torn flesh and the blood-stained hair;
      Alas for the kindred's trouble!
It falls as fire from a God's hand sped,
      Two deaths, and mourning double.

HIPPOLYTUS

  Ah, pain, pain, pain!
O unrighteous curse! O unrighteous sire!
No hope.—My head is stabbed with fire,
And a leaping spasm about my brain.
  Stay, let me rest. I can no more.
O fell, fell steeds that my own hand fed,
Have ye maimed me and slain, that loved me of yore?
—Soft there, ye thralls! No trembling hands
As ye lift me, now!—Who is that that stands

At the right?—Now firm, and with measured tread,
Lift one accursèd and stricken sore
      By a father's sinning.

Thou, Zeus, dost see me?   Yea, it is I;
The proud and pure, the server of God,
The white and shining in sanctity!
To a visible death, to an open sod,
      I walk my ways;
And all the labour of saintly days
      Lost, lost, without meaning!

            Ah God, it crawls
               This agony, over me!
            Let be, ye thralls!
               Come, Death, and cover me;
            Come, O thou Healer blest!

            But a little more,
               And my soul is clear,
            And the anguish o'er!
               Oh, a spear, a spear!
            To rend my soul to its rest!

Oh, strange, false Curse!   Was there some blood-stained
         head,
Some father of my line, unpunishèd,
      Whose guilt lived in his kin,
And passed, and slept, till after this long day
It lights. . . . Oh, why on me?   Me, far away
      And innocent of sin?

77

O words that cannot save!
When will this breathing end in that last deep
Pain that is painlessness?   'Tis sleep I crave.
When wilt thou bring me sleep,
Thou dark and midnight magic of the grave!

ARTEMIS

Sore-stricken man, bethink thee in this stress,
Thou dost but die for thine own nobleness.

HIPPOLYTUS

Ah!
O breath of heavenly fragrance!   Though my pain
Burns, I can feel thee and find rest again.
The Goddess Artemis is with me here.

ARTEMIS

With thee and loving thee, poor sufferer!

HIPPOLYTUS

Dost see me, Mistress, nearing my last sleep?

ARTEMIS

Aye, and would weep for thee, if Gods could weep.

HIPPOLYTUS

Who now shall hunt with thee or hold thy quiver?

ARTEMIS

He dies; but my love cleaves to him for ever

HIPPOLYTUS

Who guide thy chariot, keep thy shrine-flowers fresh?

78

ARTEMIS

The accursèd Cyprian caught him in her mesh!

HIPPOLYTUS

The Cyprian? Now I see it!—Aye, 'twas she.

ARTEMIS

She missed her worship, loathed thy chastity!

HIPPOLYTUS

Three lives by her one hand! 'Tis all clear now.

ARTEMIS

Yea, three; thy father and his Queen and thou.

HIPPOLYTUS

My father; yea, he too is pitiable!

ARTEMIS

A plotting Goddess tripped him, and he fell.

HIPPOLYTUS

Father, where art thou? . . Oh, thou sufferest sore!

THESEUS

Even unto death, child. There is joy no more.

HIPPOLYTUS

I pity thee in this coil; aye, more than me.

THESEUS

Would I could lie there dead instead of thee!

79

HIPPOLYTUS

Oh, bitter bounty of Poseidon's love!

THESEUS

Would God my lips had never breathed thereof!

HIPPOLYTUS (*gently*)

Nay, thine own rage had slain me then, some wise!

THESEUS

A lying spirit had made blind mine eyes!

HIPPOLYTUS

Ah me!
Would that a mortal's curse could reach to God!

ARTEMIS

Let be! For not, though deep beneath the sod
Thou liest, not unrequited nor unsung
Shall this fell stroke, from Cypris' rancour sprung,
Quell thee, mine own, the saintly and the true!
   My hand shall win its vengeance, through and through
Piercing with flawless shaft what heart soe'er
Of all men living is most dear to Her.
Yea, and to thee, for this sore travail's sake,
Honours most high in Trozên will I make;
For yokeless maids before their bridal night
Shall shear for thee their tresses; and a rite
Of honouring tears be thine in ceaseless store;
And virgins' thoughts in music evermore
Turn toward thee, and praise thee in the Song
Of Phaedra's far-famed love and thy great wrong.

80

O seed of ancient Aegeus, bend thee now
And clasp thy son. Aye, hold and fear not thou!
Not knowingly hast thou slain him; and man's way,
When Gods send error, needs must fall astray.
   And thou, Hippolytus, shrink not from the King,
Thy father. Thou wast born to bear this thing.
   Farewell! I may not watch man's fleeting breath,
Nor stain mine eyes with the effluence of death.
And sure that Terror now is very near.
[*The cloud slowly rises and floats away.*

HIPPOLYTUS

Farewell, farewell, most Blessèd! Lift thee clear
Of soiling men! Thou wilt not grieve in heaven
For my long love! . . . Father, thou art forgiven.
It was Her will. I am not wroth with thee. . . .
I have obeyed Her all my days!   . .
                              Ah me,
The dark is drawing down upon mine eyes;
It hath me! . . . Father! . . . Hold me! Help me rise!

THESEUS (*supporting him in his arms*)
Ah, woe! How dost thou torture me, my son!

HIPPOLYTUS
I see the Great Gates opening. I am gone.

THESEUS
Gone? And my hand red-reeking from this thing!

HIPPOLYTUS
Nay, nay; thou art assoiled of manslaying.

81

THESEUS

Thou leav'st me clear of murder?   Sayst thou so?

HIPPOLYTUS

Yea, by the Virgin of the Stainless Bow!

THESEUS

Dear Son!   Ah, now I see thy nobleness!

HIPPOLYTUS

Pray that a true-born child may fill my place.

THESEUS

Ah me, thy righteous and godfearing heart!

HIPPOLYTUS

Farewell;
A long farewell, dear Father, ere we part!
[THESEUS *bends down and embraces him passionately.*

THESEUS

Not yet!—O hope and bear while thou hast breath!

HIPPOLYTUS

Lo, I have borne my burden.   This is death. . . .
Quick, Father; lay the mantle on my face.
[THESEUS *covers his face with a mantle and rises.*

THESEUS

Ye bounds of Pallas and of Pelops' race,
What greatness have ye lost!
                          Woe, woe is me!
Thou Cyprian, long shall I remember thee!

82

CHORUS

On all this folk, both low and high,
A grief hath fallen beyond men's fears.
There cometh a throbbing of many tears,
  A sound as of waters falling.
    For when great men die,
A mighty name and a bitter cry
    Rise up from a nation calling.

[*They move into the Castle, carrying the body of* HIPPOLYTUS.

NOTES ON THE HIPPOLYTUS

Prologue.—The Aphrodite of Euripides' actual belief, if one may venture to dogmatise on such a subject, was almost certainly not what we should call a goddess, but rather a Force of Nature, or a Spirit working in the world. To deny her existence you would have to say not merely, "There is no such person," but "There is no such thing;" and such a denial would be a defiance of obvious facts. It is in this sense that it is possible to speak of Hippolytus as "sinning against Aphrodite."

For the purposes of drama, of course, this "thing" must be made into a person, and even represented in human form according to the current conceptions of mythology. And, once personified, she becomes, like most of the Olympians in Euripides, certainly hateful and perhaps definitely evil, though still far removed from the degraded, ultra-feminine goddess of Ovid and the handbooks of mythology. In this prologue she retains much of the impersonal grandeur of a Force of Nature. The words "I grudge it not: no grudge know I, nor hate," are doubtless intended to be true.

P. 13, l. 11, *Pittheus.*—Father of Aethra, who was Theseus' mother. Formerly King of Trozên, now ending his days in a life of meditation.

P. 14, ll. 31 ff., *She built a shrine.*—An obscure passage, in which I follow the suggestion of Dr. Verrall (*Class. Rev.* xv. 449). Euripides is evidently giving an account of the origin of a sanctuary of Aphrodite Pandêmos on the Acropolis, which in his day was known as 'Αφροδίτη ἐπὶ 'Ιππολύτῳ, i.e. (as at least, he imagined) "Aphrodite for Hippolytus," or "with a view to Hippolytus." Phaedra,

84

he says, built this shrine *because of*, *thinking of*, Hippolytus
—i.e. seeking to exorcise her passion for him, and to fix her
errant love at home as she fixed the shrine in the rock. She
perhaps—so Dr. Verrall suggests—called it Aphrodite
Endêmos, " Love-at-home " or " in-the-land." When her
plan failed, and it appeared that Love will not be fixed
down in one place, the name was changed to Pandêmos,
" of-all-lands." Of course it is not certain, nor even very
probable, that either Πάνδημος or ἐπὶ Ἱππολύτῳ originally
bore the meaning that Euripides and his contemporaries
attached to them. Ἐπὶ Ἱππολύτῳ, for instance, is quite
likely, in its original form, to have meant " the shrine at the
place where horses are unyoked."

P. 15, l. 73, *From a green and virgin meadow.*—There are
long discussions in the ancient Greek commentators, whether
this meadow is real or allegorical. Is it only the garland
of his adoration from the meadow of his virgin soul? " It
seems odd," says one of them, " to have a meadow which
you are not allowed to enter until you can show that your
good qualities do not come from education! " Doubtless it
is a real sacred meadow.

P. 17, ll. 99, 103.—In two lines, " Then why wilt
thou be proud? " and " Clean? Nay, proud," I follow my
own published text, reading σεμνός for σεμνὴν and σεμνή.

P. 19, l. 121, *Of Ocean's tribe.*—The river Ocean was,
by some accounts, the father of all fresh and pure water.

P. 19, ll. 142, 143, *Hecate . . . Pan . . . the Corybantes.*
—These powers all produced seizures, terrors, and ecstasies.
Dictynna (often a mere alternative name for Artemis) was,
strictly speaking, a Cretan sea-goddess—cf. δίκτυον, " a
net "—a hunter of the sea as Artemis is a hunter of the land.
(She is identified with Artemis on p. 67.) She can catch

Phaedra in Limna, the "Mere" in the neighbourhood of Trozên, because Limna is a dried-up lagoon that was once part of the sea, and therefore belongs to the sea powers.

P. 20, l. 151, *Erechtheus.*—An old king of Athens.

P. 21, ll. 193, 194, *This nameless and shining thing.*— Reading τοῦ δ' ὅτι τοῦτο στίλβει . . . δυσέρωτες.

P. 23, l. 228, *The Sea-lorn Mere.*—The dried lagoon, Limna, near Trozên, used for chariot races. The "unseaswept sands," just below, are the same.

P. 24, ll. 264, 265.—"Thorough" and "Naught too much" were mottoes of two of the legendary Seven Wise Men.

P. 25, l. 281, *Has been abroad.*—Apparently to an oracle (see below). Perhaps there was a definite tradition saying where he had gone and why, but if so, it is lost. A modern playwright would, of course, fill in these details, for the sake of verisimilitude; the ancient playwright intentionally omits them as irrelevant, just as he omits to give proper names to his Nurses, Messengers, and Leaders of the Chorus.

P. 28, l. 325, *What wouldst thou? Force me.*—It was of the nature of sin to reject a suppliant, i.e. a person who threw himself entirely upon your mercy, and implored you. The repugnance that an ordinary person has to such a rejection was felt by the Greeks in a religious way. The ultimate sanction, if you did harden your heart, would be twofold: first, the gods would have a natural repulsion against one who formally and knowingly refused to be merciful; secondly, the suppliant might do what the Nurse threatens to do here, and stay immovable till he died of

86

hunger or exposure—and his death would lie at the door of his rejector!

P. 29, ll. 337–341, *Mother, poor Mother, that didst love so sore.*—Phaedra thinks of the general wreck of her house through love. Her mother, Pasiphaê, wife of Minos, loved the pirate or adventurer Tauros (" The Bull "), was cast into prison by her husband, and there starved herself to death. Her sister, Ariadnê, had loved Theseus; he saved her from her father's vengeance, but by command of the gods left her on the lonely island of Naxos, where the god Dionysus came and carried her away. (In the original myth Tauros was the Cretan Bull God.)

P. 32, l. 372, *The Isle of awful Love.*—Crete, because of Pasiphaê, Ariadnê, Aëropê, the wife of Thyestes, and other heroines of terrible love-stories.

P. 32, l. 373, *O Women, dwellers in this portal seat.*— This wonderful passage is very characteristic of Euripides— a subtle and beautiful study of character expressed in a formal, self-analysing speech. The " delights " that have tempted and undone her are, first, the pleasure of long talks —with Hippolytus, or about him; next, the pleasure of losing herself in dreams; and thirdly, in some sense not precisely explained, but surely not difficult to understand, a feeling of shame or cowardice. She feels that if only she had had more courage all might have been well! Why this " shame," this yielding to fear, strikes her at this moment as a " delight," is not explained; but it does not seem to me unnatural.

P. 34, l. 433, *Mistress, a sharp, swift terror,* etc.—This speech of the Nurse, so beautiful and so full of sophistries, is typically the kind of thing that caused Euripides to be accused of immoral writing.

87

P. 37, l. 478, *Love-philtres.*—The situation at the end of this scene seems to be this: The Nurse goes in to prepare a magic charm *which shall cure Phaedra of her love,* but mentions that, in order to prepare it, she must get something belonging to Hippolytus to weave into the charm. (Either a material object to be actually woven into the charm, or a word, to be ceremonially caught and woven in—a common device in magic.) Phaedra suspects that she means to speak to Hippolytus, and the Nurse's next words rather confirm her suspicions; but, broken and weary as she is, she has not strength or keenness of mind enough to make sure and to prevent her doing so. A large part of her nature, no doubt, longs to have Hippolytus told, and succeeds at this critical moment in lulling to sleep her exhausted will and conscience.

P. 39, ll. 545–564, *Chorus.*—The second strophe and antistrophe ("On Oechalian hills, etc."), are rather obscure. The connection of thought is: "Think of the terrible things that have befallen through love! How Iolê, daughter of Eurytus, suffered, when the angry love of Heracles made him burn her father's house in Oechalia, and carry her off amid flames and blood. And how Semelê, the mother of Bacchus, suffered in Thebes by the waters of Dircê, when Zeus came to her in a blaze of lightning, and his love was her death."

P. 43, l. 612, *'Twas but my tongue, 'twas not my soul that swore.*—A line constantly misrepresented and attacked (see on *Frogs,* l. 101, p. 112). In reality Hippolytus faces death rather than break the oath that he was trapped into.

P. 43, l. 616, *O God, why hast thou made this gleaming snare.* ·The fury of this speech, while not unnatural to the youthful saintliness of Hippolytus, is intentionally made

88

bitter and offensive by the playwright, so as to throw our sympathies for the time entirely on the side of Phaedra. We hate Hippolytus, and can for the moment sympathise with, or at least understand, her terrible act of blind self-preservation and revenge.

P. 46, l. 690, *He speeds to abase me to the King.*—He had definitely said that he would not do so; but she felt his hatred, she had no reason to trust him, she had just been betrayed by one much closer to her, and probably she had hardly even noticed the actual words in his torrent of rage.

P. 47, l. 712, *Know naught and speak of naught.*—This oath of the Chorus is important for the sequel of the play. It prevents them from saving Hippolytus.

P. 48, l. 732, *Could I take me to some cavern for mine hiding.*—This lovely song seems to me a good instance of the artistic value of the Greek chorus. The last scene has been tragic to the point of painfulness; the one thing that can heal the pain without spoiling the interest is an outburst of pure poetry. And the sentiment of this song, the longing to escape to a realm, if not of happiness, at least of beautiful sadness, is so magically right.

Phaëthon, who tried to drive the chariot of the Sun and fell, was buried by the river Eridanus (afterwards identified with the Po). His sisters wept over his grave, and their tears turned to drops of amber.

P. 48, l. 742, *The apple-tree, the singing and the gold.*— The Garden of the Hesperides, or Daughters of the Sunset, was in the West, near the Pillars of Heracles, which marked the utmost limit to which man might travel. The apple-tree bore golden apples, and it was here that Zeus walked in the garden and first met his bride, Hera.

89

P. 49, l. 756, *Sure some spell upon either hand.*—A curse or spell must have come with her from Crete. It was difficult for a curse to come from one country to another. Exactly like infection, it had to be somehow carried. The women suggest that it came with Phaedra in the ship, and then, when the ship was moored in Munychia, the old harbour of Athens, it crawled up the cables to the shore.

P. 51, l. 803, *A fit of the old cold anguish?*—It is characteristic of Euripides to throw these sudden lights back on the history of his characters. We never knew before (except perhaps from the Prologue) that Phaedra had had these fits of "cold anguish," or that Theseus had noticed them. Cf. p. 65, where for the first time we have a reference to Theseus' own turbulent youth, and his crime against the Amazon, Hippolytus' mother. And p. 59, where we first hear that Hippolytus fasted and followed Orphic rites.

P. 51, l. 804, *But now arrived we be.*—A lie, to make the avoidance of explanations easier.

Pp. 52 f., ll. 817–851.—The laments of Theseus, though they cannot compensate for the drop of dramatic interest after Phaedra's death, are full of beauty and also of character. They bring out clearly the passionateness of the old hero, and also the way in which he only gradually, and then with increasing emotion, realises his loss.

P. 60, l. 977.—Sinis was a robber slain by Theseus at the Isthmus of Corinth. He tied his victims to the tops of pine-trees, which he had bent to the ground, and, according to Hyginus, sent them flying in the air so that they fell and were killed; as Pausanias rather more intelligibly puts it, he tied them between two pines, which he had bent together, and then let the pines spring back and rack the men asunder. Skiron was another robber in the same neighbourhood; he made travellers wash his feet on the top of a cliff—the Skironian Rock (cf. p. 71)—and then kicked them into the sea.

Pp. 60–62, ll. 983 ff., Hippolytus' speech.—The ineffectiveness of this speech is, of course, intentional on the poet's part. The one effective answer for Hippolytus would be to break his oath and tell the whole truth. As it is, he can do nothing but appeal to his known character, and plead passionately against all the inferences that his father has drawn as to his general hypocrisy.

P. 62, l. 1036, *It is enough.*—The Chorus, debarred from announcing the truth, catch at any straws that tell in favour of the truth.

P. 62, l. 1041, *Father, 'tis thy mood that makes me marvel.* —He means, I think, to make Theseus realise that the charge is flatly incredible. "You yourself do not believe that I have done such a thing! I know, and you know, that you do not believe it. If you did, you would kill me on the spot, not go on talking like this."

P. 63, l. 1057, *No prophet's lot.*—A prophet spoke from some "sign" or "lot" which he interpreted. This might be an actual "lot," drawn or cast; or by extension, any other sign, from the flesh of a victim or from the flight of birds.

P. 68, l. 1142, *And I, even I,* etc.—The song of this maiden may have given Racine the hint of his additional character, Aricie, the princess whom his Hippolyte loves.

P. 70, l. 1195, *And down the road we henchmen followed.* —They walked or ran beside the chariot, accompanying their master to the frontier. Ancient chariots, when used for travelling, went slowly.

K*

91

P. 78, l. 1391, *O breath of heavenly fragrance*, etc.—This and the next line make one doubt whether Artemis was supposed to be visible, or only present as a voice. Cf. p. 16, l. 86, " Though none may see thine eyes."

P. 80, l. 1420, *My hand shall win its vengeance.*—By causing the death of Adônis, whom Aphrodite loved. It is noteworthy how Euripides' latent hatred of the orthodox Olympian gods breaks out even in this passage, otherwise so exquisitely beautiful. The human beings are full of love and mutual forgiveness. The goddess, radiantly lovely as she is and pure with the purity of dawn, still thinks of revenge, and—as appears at her departure—is, in some profoundly tragic sense, unloving: a being to be adored, not to love back. The last consolation of Hippolytus is the thought of his perfect devotion to one who in the nature of things can care for him only a little: " I have obeyed Her all my days."

In the original edition this vase was represented. Hence this reference.

This last scene is one of those passages which show the ultimate falseness of the distinction between Classical and Romantic. The highest poetry has the beauty of both.

EURIPIDES

ELECTRA

Translated into English rhyming verse
with explanatory notes

by

GILBERT MURRAY

O.M., D.C.L.

*Formerly Regius Professor of Greek
in the
University of Oxford*

London

GEORGE ALLEN & UNWIN LTD

INTRODUCTION[1]

THE *Electra* of Euripides has the distinction of being,
perhaps, the best abused, and, one might add, not the best
understood, of ancient tragedies. " A singular monument of
poetical, or rather unpoetical perversity; " " the very worst
of all his pieces; " are, for instance, the phrases applied to it
by Schlegel. Considering that he judged it by the standards
of conventional classicism, he could scarcely have arrived at
any different conclusion. For it is essentially, and perhaps
consciously, a protest against those standards. So, indeed,
is the tragedy of *The Trojan Women;* but on very different
lines. The *Electra* has none of the imaginative splendour,
the vastness, the intense poetry, of that wonderful work. It
is a close-knit, powerful, well-constructed play, as realistic
as the tragic conventions will allow, intellectual and rebel-
lious. Its psychology reminds one of Browning, or even
of Ibsen.

To a fifth-century Greek all history came in the form of
legend; and no less than three extant tragedies, Aeschylus'
Libation-Bearers (456 B.C.), Euripides' *Electra* (413 B.C.),
and Sophocles' *Electra* (date unknown : but perhaps the latest
of the three) are based on the particular piece of legend or
history now before us. It narrates how the son and daughter
of the murdered king, Agamemnon, slew, in due course of
revenge, and by Apollo's express command, their guilty
mother and her paramour.

Homer had long since told the story, as he tells so many,
simply and grandly, without moral questioning and without
intensity. The atmosphere is heroic. It is all a blood-feud
between chieftains, in which Orestes, after seven years,

[1] Most of this Introduction is reprinted, by the kind permission of
the Editors, from an article in the *Independent Review,* Vol. I. No. 4.

5

succeeds in slaying his foe Aegisthus, who had killed his father. He probably killed his mother also; but we are not directly told so. His sister may have helped him, and he may possibly have gone mad afterwards; but these painful issues are kept determinedly in the shade.

Somewhat surprisingly, Sophocles, although by his time Electra and Clytemnestra had become leading figures in the story and the mother-murder its essential climax, preserves a very similar atmosphere. His tragedy is enthusiastically praised by Schlegel for " the celestial purity, the fresh breath of life and youth, that is diffused over so dreadful a subject." " Everything dark and ominous is avoided. Orestes enjoys the fulness of health and strength. He is beset neither with doubts nor stings of conscience." Especially laudable is the " austerity " with which Aegisthus is driven into the house to receive, according to Schlegel, a specially ignominious death!

This is exaggeration. Still a certain deliberate moral insensitiveness in Sophocles' *Electra* will probably strike most intelligent readers as a little curious, and even, if one may use the word at all in connection with so powerful a play, undramatic. It becomes intelligible as soon as we observe that Sophocles was deliberately seeking what he regarded as an archaic or "Homeric" style (cf. Jebb, Introd. p. xli.); and this archaism, in its turn, seems to me best explained as a conscious reaction against Euripides' searching and unconventional treatment of the same subject (cf. Wilamowitz in *Hermes*, xviii. pp. 214 ff.). In the result Sophocles is not only more " classical " than Euripides; he is more primitive by far than Aeschylus.

For Aeschylus, though steeped in the glory of the world of legend, would not lightly accept its judgment upon religious and moral questions, and above all would not, in that region, play at make-believe. He would not elude the

6

horror of this story by simply not mentioning it, like Homer, or by pretending that an evil act was a good one, like Sophocles. He faces the horror; realises it; and tries to surmount it on the sweep of a great wave of religious emotion. The mother-murder, even if done by a god's command, is a sin; a sin to be expiated by unfathomable suffering. Yet, since the god cannot have commanded evil, it is a duty also. It is a sin that *must* be committed.

Euripides, here as often, represents intellectually the thought of Aeschylus carried a step further. He faced the problem just as Aeschylus did, and as Sophocles did not. But the solution offered by Aeschylus did not satisfy him. It cannot, in its actual details, satisfy any one. To him the mother-murder—like most acts of revenge, but more than most—was a sin and a horror. Therefore it should not have been committed; and the god who enjoined it *did* command evil, as he had done in a hundred other cases! He is no god of light; he is only a demon of old superstition, acting, among other influences, upon a sore-beset man, and driving him towards a miscalled duty, the horror of which, when done, will unseat his reason.

But another problem interests Euripides even more than this. What kind of man was it—above all, what kind of woman can it have been—who would do this deed of mother-murder, not in sudden fury but deliberately, as an act of "justice," after many years? A "sympathetic" hero and heroine are out of the question; and Euripides does not deal in stage villains. He seeks real people. And few attentive readers of this play can doubt that he has found them.

The son is an exile, bred in the desperate hopes and wild schemes of exile; he is a prince without a kingdom, always dreaming of his wrongs and his restoration; and driven by the old savage doctrine, which an oracle has confirmed, of the duty and manliness of revenge. He is, as was shown

7

by his later history, a man subject to overpowering impulses and to fits of will-less brooding. Lastly, he is very young, and is swept away by his sister's intenser nature.

That sister is the central figure of the tragedy. A woman shattered in childhood by the shock of an experience too terrible for a girl to bear; a poisoned and a haunted woman, eating her heart in ceaseless broodings of hate and love, alike unsatisfied—hate against her mother and step-father, love for her dead father and her brother in exile; a woman who has known luxury and state, and cares much for them; who is intolerant of poverty, and who feels her youth passing away. And meantime there is her name, on which all legend, if I am not mistaken, insists; she is *A-lektra*, "the Unmated."

There is, perhaps, no woman's character in the range of Greek tragedy so profoundly studied. Not Aeschylus' Clytemnestra, not Phaedra nor Medea. One's thoughts can only wander towards two great heroines of "lost" plays, Althaea in the *Meleager*, and Stheneboea in the *Bellerophon*.

G. M.

8

CHARACTERS IN THE PLAY

Clytemnestra, *Queen of Argos and Mycenae; widow of Agamemnon.*

Electra, *daughter of Agamemnon and Clytemnestra.*

Orestes, *son of Agamemnon and Clytemnestra, now in banishment.*

A Peasant, *husband of Electra.*

An Old Man, *formerly servant to Agamemnon.*

Pylades, *son of Strophios, King of Phocis; friend to Orestes.*

Aegisthus, *usurping King of Argos and Mycenae, now husband of Clytemnestra.*

The Heroes Castor and Polydeuces.

Chorus of Argive Women, with their Leader.

Followers of Orestes; Handmaids of Clytemnestra.

The Scene is laid in the mountains of Argos. The play was first produced between the years 414 and 412 B.C.

ELECTRA

*The scene represents a hut on a desolate mountain side; the
river Inachus is visible in the distance. The time is the
dusk of early dawn, before sunrise. The* PEASANT *is discovered in front of the hut.*

PEASANT

Old gleam on the face of the world, I give thee hail,
River of Argos land, where sail on sail
The long ships met, a thousand, near and far,
When Agamemnon walked the seas in war;
Who smote King Priam in the dust, and burned
The storied streets of Ilion, and returned
Above all conquerors, heaping tower and fane
Of Argos high with spoils of Eastern slain.
  So in far lands he prospered; and at home
His own wife trapped and slew him. 'Twas the doom
Aegisthus wrought, son of his father's foe.
  Gone is that King, and the old spear laid low
That Tantalus wielded when the world was young.
Aegisthus hath his queen, and reigns among
His people. And the children here alone,
Orestes and Electra, buds unblown
Of man and womanhood when forth to Troy
He shook his sail and left them—lo, the boy
Orestes, ere Aegisthus' hand could fall,
Was stolen from Argos—borne by one old thrall,
Who served his father's boyhood, over seas
Far off, and laid upon King Strophios' knees
In Phocis, for the old king's sake. But here
The maid Electra waited, year by year,

11

Alone, till the warm days of womanhood
Drew nigh and suitors came of gentle blood
In Hellas.   Then Aegisthus was in fear
Lest she be wed in some great house, and bear
A son to avenge her father.   Close he wrought
Her prison in his house, and gave her not
To any wooer.   Then, since even this
Was full of peril, and the secret kiss
Of some bold prince might find her yet, and rend
Her prison walls, Aegisthus at the end
Would slay her.   Then her mother, she so wild
Aforetime, pled with him and saved her child.
Her heart had still an answer for her lord
Murdered, but if the child's blood spoke, what word
Could meet the hate thereof?   After that day
Aegisthus thus decreed: whoso should slay
The old king's wandering son, should win rich meed
Of gold; and for Electra, she must wed
With me, not base of blood—in that I stand
True Mycenaean—but in gold and land
Most poor, which maketh highest birth as naught.
So from a powerless husband shall be wrought
A powerless peril.   Had some man of might
Possessed her, he had called perchance to light
Her father's blood, and unknown vengeances
Risen on Aegisthus yet.
                         Aye, mine she is:
But never yet these arms—the Cyprian knows
My truth!—have clasped her body, and she goes
A virgin still.   Myself would hold it shame
To abase this daughter of a royal name.
I am too lowly to love violence.   Yea,
Orestes too doth move me, far away,

12

Mine unknown brother! Will he ever now
Come back and see his sister bowed so low?
  Doth any deem me fool, to hold a fair
Maid in my room and seek no joy, but spare
Her maidenhood? If any such there be,
Let him but look within. The fool is he
In gentle things, weighing the more and less
Of love by his own heart's untenderness.

[*As he ceases* ELECTRA *comes out of the hut. She is in mourning garb and carries a large pitcher on her head. She speaks without observing the* PEASANT'S *presence.*

ELECTRA

Dark shepherdess of many a golden star,
Dost see me, Mother Night? And how this jar
Hath worn my earth-bowed head, as forth and fro
For water to the hillward springs I go?
Not for mere stress of need, but purpose set,
That never day nor night God may forget
Aegisthus' sin: aye, and perchance a cry
Cast forth to the waste shining of the sky
May find my father's ear. . . . The woman bred
Of Tyndareus, my mother—on her head
Be curses!—from my house hath outcast me;
She hath borne children to our enemy;
She hath made me naught, she hath made Orestes naught. . . .

[*As the bitterness of her tone increases, the* PEASANT *comes forward.*

PEASANT

What wouldst thou now, my sad one, ever fraught
With toil to lighten my toil? And so soft
Thy nurture was! Have I not chid thee oft,
And thou wilt cease not, serving without end?

13

ELECTRA (*turning to him with impulsive affection*)
O friend, my friend, as God might be my friend,
Thou only hast not trampled on my tears.
Life scarce can be so hard, 'mid many fears
And many shames, when mortal heart can find
Somewhere one healing touch, as my sick mind
Finds thee. . . . And should I wait thy word, to endure
A little for thine easing, yea, or pour
My strength out in thy toiling fellowship?
Thou hast enough with fields and kine to keep;
'Tis mine to make all bright within the door.
'Tis joy to him that toils, when toil is o'er
To find home waiting, full of happy things.

PEASANT

If so it please thee, go thy way. The springs
Are not far off. And I before the morn
Must drive my team afield, and sow the corn
In the hollows.—Not a thousand prayers can gain
A man's bare bread, save an he work amain.
[ELECTRA *and the* PEASANT *depart on their several ways.*
After a few moments there enter stealthily two armed men,
ORESTES *and* PYLADES.

ORESTES

Thou art the first that I have known in deed
True and my friend, and shelterer of my need.
Thou only, Pylades, of all that knew,
Hast held Orestes of some worth, all through
These years of helplessness, wherein I lie
Downtrodden by the murderer—yea, and by
The murderess, my mother! . . . I am come,
Fresh from the cleansing of Apollo, home

14

To Argos—and my coming no man yet
Knoweth—to pay the bloody twain their debt
Of blood. This very night I crept alone
To my dead father's grave, and poured thereon
My heart's first tears and tresses of my head
New-shorn, and o'er the barrow of the dead
Slew a black lamb, unknown of them that reign
In this unhappy land. . . . I am not fain
To pass the city gates, but hold me here
Hard on the borders. So my road is clear
To fly if men look close and watch my way;
If not, to seek my sister. For men say
She dwelleth in these hills, no more a maid
But wedded. I must find her house, for aid
To guide our work, and learn what hath betid
Of late in Argos.—Ha, the radiant lid
Of Dawn's eye lifteth! Come, friend; leave we now
This trodden path. Some worker of the plough,
Or serving damsel at her early task
Will presently come by, whom we may ask
If here my sister dwells. But soft! Even now
I see some bondmaid there, her death-shorn brow
Bending beneath its freight of well-water.
Lie close until she pass; then question her.
A slave might help us well, or speak some sign
Of import to this work of mine and thine.
[*The two men retire into ambush.* Electra *enters, returning
from the well.*

ELECTRA

Onward, O labouring tread,
　　As on move the years;
Onward amid thy tears,
　　O happier dead!

15

Let me remember. I am she,   [*Strophe* 1.
Agamemnon's child, and the mother of me
Clytemnestra, the evil Queen,
Helen's sister. And folk, I ween,
That pass in the streets call yet my name
Electra. . . . God protect my shame!
　　For toil, toil is a weary thing,
　　　And life is heavy about my head;
　　And thou far off, O Father and King,
　　　In the lost lands of the dead.
A bloody twain made these things be;
One was thy bitterest enemy,
And one the wife that lay by thee.

Brother, brother, on some far shore   [*Antistrophe* 1.
Hast thou a city, is there a door
That knows thy footfall, Wandering One?
Who left me, left me, when all our pain
Was bitter about us, a father slain,
And a girl that wept in her room alone.
　　Thou couldst break me this bondage sore,
　　　Only thou, who art far away,
　　Loose our father, and wake once more. . . .
　　　Zeus, Zeus, dost hear me pray? . . .
The sleeping blood and the shame and the doom!
O feet that rest not, over the foam
Of distant seas, come home, come home!

What boots this cruse that I carry?   [*Strophe* 2.
　　O, set free my brow!
For the gathered tears that tarry
　　Through the day and the dark till now,
Now in the dawn are free,
　　Father, and flow beneath

16

The floor of the world, to be
    As a song in the house of Death.
From the rising up of the day
They guide my heart alway,
The silent tears unshed,
And my body mourns for the dead;
    My cheeks bleed silently,
        And these bruisèd temples keep
    Their pain, remembering thee
        And thy bloody sleep.

Be rent, O hair of mine head!

As a swan crying alone
    Where the river windeth cold,
For a loved, for a silent one,
    Whom the toils of the fowler hold,
I cry, Father, to thee,
O slain in misery!

The water, the wan water,   [*Antistrophe* 2.
    Lapped him, and his head
Drooped in the bed of slaughter
    Low, as one wearièd;
Woe for the edgèd axe,
    And woe for the heart of hate,
Houndlike about thy tracks,
    O conqueror desolate,
From Troy over land and sea,
Till a wife stood waiting thee;
Not with crowns did she stand,
Nor flowers of peace in her hand;
With Aegisthus' dagger drawn
    For her hire she strove,

17

Through shame and through blood alone;
And won her a traitor's love.
[As she ceases there enters from right and left the CHORUS,
consisting of women of Argos, young and old, in festal dress.

CHORUS
Some Women

Child of the mighty dead,   [*Strophe*
  Electra, lo, my way
To thee in the dawn hath sped,
  And the cot on the mountain grey,
  For the Watcher hath cried this day:
He of the ancient folk,
  The walker of waste and hill,
Who drinketh the milk of the flock;
  And he told of Hera's will;
For the morrow's morrow now
  They cry her festival,
And before her throne shall bow
  Our damsels all.

ELECTRA

Not unto joy, nor sweet
  Music, nor shining of gold,
The wings of my spirit beat.
  Let the brides of Argos hold
  Their dance in the night, as of old;
I lead no dance; I mark
  No beat as the dancers sway;
With tears I dwell in the dark,
  And my thought is of tears alway,
  To the going down of the day.
Look on my wasted hair
And raiment. . . . This that I bear,

18

Is it meet for the King my sire,
  And her whom the King begot?
For Troy, that was burned with fire
  And forgetteth not?

CHORUS
Other Women

Hera is great!—Ah, come,   [*Antistrophe*
  Be kind; and my hand shall bring
Fair raiment, work of the loom,
  And many a golden thing,
  For joyous robe-wearing.
Deemest thou this thy woe
  Shall rise unto God as prayer,
Or bend thine haters low?
  Doth God for thy pain have care?
Not tears for the dead nor sighs,
  But worship and joy divine
Shall win thee peace in thy skies.
  O daughter mine!

ELECTRA

No care cometh to God
  For the voice of the helpless; none
For the crying of ancient blood.
  Alas for him that is gone,
  And for thee, O wandering one,
That now, methinks, in a land
  Of the stranger must toil for hire,
And stand where the poor men stand,
  A-cold by another's fire,
  O son of the mighty sire:
While I in a beggar's cot
On the wrecked hills, changing not,

19

Starve in my soul for food;
But our mother lieth wed
In another's arms, and blood
Is about her bed.

LEADER

On all of Greece she wrought great jeopardy,
Thy mother's sister, Helen—and on thee.
[ORESTES *and* PYLADES *move out from their concealment;*
ORESTES *comes forward:* PYLADES *beckons to two* ARMED
SERVANTS *and stays with them in the background.*

ELECTRA

Woe's me! No more of wailing! Women, flee!
Strange armèd men beside the dwelling there
Lie ambushed! They are rising from their lair.
Back by the road, all you. I will essay
The house; and may our good feet save us!

ORESTES (*between* ELECTRA *and the hut*)
Stay,
Unhappy woman! Never fear my steel.

ELECTRA (*in utter panic*)
Apollo help us! Mercy! See, I kneel;
Slay me not.

ORESTES
Others I have yet to slay
Less dear than thou.

ELECTRA
Go from me! Wouldst thou lay
Hand on a body that is not for thee?

20

302

ORESTES

None is there I would touch more righteously.

ELECTRA

Why lurk'st thou by my house?   And why a sword?

ORESTES

Stay.   Listen!   Thou wilt not gainsay my word.

ELECTRA

There—I am still.   Do what thou wilt with me.
Thou art too strong.
ORESTES
           A word I bear to thee. . .
Word of thy brother.
ELECTRA
           Oh, friend!   More than friend!
Living or dead?
ORESTES
           He lives; so let me send
My comfort foremost, ere the rest be heard.

ELECTRA

God love thee for the sweetness of thy word!

ORESTES

God love the twain of us, both thee and me.

ELECTRA

He lives!   Poor brother!   In what land weareth he
His exile?

21

303

Orestes

Not one region nor one lot
His wasted life hath trod.

Electra

He lacketh not
For bread?

Orestes

Bread hath he; but a man is weak
In exile.

Electra

What charge laid he on thee? Speak.

Orestes

To learn if thou still live, and how the storm,
Living, hath struck thee.

Electra

That thou seest; this form
Wasted . . .

Orestes

Yea, riven with the fire o' woe.
I sigh to look on thee.

Electra

My face; and, lo,
My temples of their ancient glory shorn.

Orestes

Methinks thy brother haunts thee, being forlorn;
Aye, and perchance thy father, whom they slew . . .

22

ELECTRA

What should be nearer to me than those two?

ORESTES

And what to him, thy brother, half so dear
As thou?

ELECTRA

His is a distant love, not near
At need.

ORESTES

But why this dwelling place, this life
Of loneliness?

ELECTRA (*with sudden bitterness*)

Stranger, I am a wife. . . .
O better dead!

ORESTES

That seals thy brother's doom!
What Prince of Argos . . .?

ELECTRA

Not the man to whom
My father thought to give me.

ORESTES

Speak; that I
May tell thy brother all.

ELECTRA

'Tis there, hard by,
His dwelling, where I live, far from men's eyes.

23

ORESTES

Some ditcher's cot, or cowherd's, by its guise!

ELECTRA (*struck with shame for her ingratitude*)
A poor man; but true-hearted, and to me
God-fearing.

ORESTES
How? What fear of God hath he?

ELECTRA
He hath never held my body to his own.

ORESTES
Hath he some vow to keep! Or is it done
To scorn thee?

ELECTRA
Nay; he only scorns to sin
Against my father's greatness.

ORESTES
But to win
A princess! Doth his heart not leap for pride?

ELECTRA
He honoureth not the hand that gave the bride.

ORESTES
I see. He trembles for Orestes' wrath?

ELECTRA
Aye, that would move him. But beside, he hath
A gentle heart.

24

ORESTES
Strange! A good man. . . . I swear
He well shall be requited.

ELECTRA
Whensoe'er
Our wanderer comes again!

ORESTES
Thy mother stays
Unmoved 'mid all thy wrong?

ELECTRA
A lover weighs
More than a child in any woman's heart.

ORESTES
But what end seeks Aegisthus, by such art
Of shame?
ELECTRA
To make mine unborn children low
And weak, even as my husband.

ORESTES
Lest there grow
From t h e e the avenger?

ELECTRA
Such his purpose is:
For which may I requite him!

ORESTES
And of this
Thy virgin life—Aegisthus knows it?

L   25

ELECTRA

Nay,
We speak it not. It cometh not his way.

ORESTES

These women hear us. Are they friends to thee?

ELECTRA

Aye, friends and true. They will keep faithfully
All words of mine and thine.

ORESTES (*trying her*)

Thou art well stayed
With friends. And could Orestes give thee aid
In aught, if e'er . . .

ELECTRA

Shame on thee! Seest thou not?
Is it not time?

ORESTES (*catching her excitement*)

How time? And if he sought
To slay, how should he come at his desire?

ELECTRA

By daring, as they dared who slew his sire!

ORESTES

Wouldst thou dare with him, if he came, thou too,
To slay h e r?

ELECTRA

Yes; with the same axe that slew
My father!

26

ORESTES

　　　'Tis thy message?　And thy mood
Unchanging?

ELECTRA

　　　Let me shed my mother's blood,
And I die happy.

ORESTES

　　　God! . . . I would that now
Orestes heard thee here.

ELECTRA

　　　Yet, wottest thou,
Though here I saw him, I should know him not.

ORESTES

Surely.　Ye both were children, when they wrought
Your parting.

ELECTRA

　　　One alone in all this land
Would know his face.

ORESTES

　　　The thrall, methinks, whose hand
Stole him from death—or so the story ran?

ELECTRA

He taught my father, too, an old old man
Of other days than these.

ORESTES

　　　Thy father's grave . . .
He had due rites and tendance?

27

ELECTRA

What chance gave,
My father had, cast out to rot in the sun.

ORESTES

God, 'tis too much! . . . To hear of such things done
Even to a stranger, stings a man . . . But speak,
Tell of thy life, that I may know and seek
Thy brother with a tale that must be heard
Howe'er it sicken. If mine eyes be blurred,
Remember, 'tis the fool that feels not. Aye,
Wisdom is full of pity; and thereby
Men pay for too much wisdom with much pain.

LEADER

My heart is moved as this man's. I would fain
Learn all thy tale. Here dwelling on the hills
Little I know of Argos and its ills.

ELECTRA

If I must speak—and at love's call, God knows,
I fear not—I will tell thee all; my woes,
My father's woes, and—O, since thou hast stirred
This storm of speech, thou bear him this my word—
His woes and shame! Tell of this narrow cloak
In the wind; this grime and reek of toil, that choke
My breathing; this low roof that bows my head
After a king's. This raiment . . . thread by thread,
'Tis I must weave it, or go bare—must bring,
Myself, each jar of water from the spring,
No holy day for me, no festival,
No dance upon the green! From all, from all
I am cut off. No portion hath my life
'Mid wives of Argos, being no true wife;

28

No portion where the maidens throng to praise
Castor—my Castor, whom in ancient days,
Ere he passed from us and men worshipped him,
They named my bridegroom!—
                              And she, s h e ! . . . The grim
Troy spoils gleam round her throne, and by each hand
Queens of the East, my father's prisoners, stand,
A cloud of Orient webs and tangling gold.
And there upon the floor, the blood, the old
Black blood, yet crawls and cankers, like a rot
In the stone! And on our father's chariot
The murderer's foot stands glorying, and the red
False hand uplifts that ancient staff, that led
The armies of the world! . . . Aye, tell him how
The grave of Agamemnon, even now,
Lacketh the common honour of the dead;
A desert barrow, where no tears are shed,
No tresses hung, no gift, no myrtle spray.
And when the wine is in him, so men say,
Our mother's mighty master leaps thereon,
Spurning the slab, or pelteth stone on stone,
Flouting the lone dead and the twain that live:
"Where is thy son Orestes? Doth he give
Thy tomb good tendance? Or is all forgot?"
So is he scorned because he cometh not. . . .

   O Stranger, on my knees I charge thee, tell
This tale, not mine, but of dumb wrongs that swell
Crowding—and I the trumpet of their pain,
This tongue, these arms, this bitter burning brain;
These dead shorn locks, and he for whom they died!
His father slew Troy's thousands in their pride:
He hath but one to kill. . . . O God, but one!
Is he a man, and Agamemnon's son?

29

LEADER
But hold: is this thy husband from the plain,
His labour ended, hasting home again?
[*Enter the* PEASANT.

PEASANT
Ha, who be these? Strange men in arms before
My house! What would they at this lonely door?
Seek they for me?—Strange gallants should not stay
A woman's goings.

ELECTRA
Friend and helper!—Nay,
Think not of any evil. These men be
Friends of Orestes, charged with words for me! . . .
Strangers, forgive his speech.

PEASANT
What word have they
Of him? At least he lives and sees the day?

ELECTRA
So fares their tale—and sure I doubt it not.

PEASANT
And ye two still are living in his thought,
Thou and his father?

ELECTRA
In his dreams we live.
An exile hath small power.

PEASANT
And did he give
Some privy message?

30

ELECTRA
                  None: they come as spies
For news of me.
                  PEASANT
                  Thine outward news their eyes
Can see; the rest, methinks, thyself will tell.

ELECTRA
They have seen all, heard all. I trust them well.

PEASANT
Why were our doors not open long ago?—
Be welcome, strangers both, and pass below
My lintel. In return for your glad words
Be sure all greeting that mine house affords
Is yours.—Ye followers, bear in their gear!—
Gainsay me not; for his sake are ye dear
That sent you to our house; and though my part
In life be low, I am no churl at heart.
[*The* PEASANT *goes to the* ARMED SERVANTS *at the back,*
 o help them with the baggage.

ORESTES (*aside to* ELECTRA)
Is this the man that shields thy maidenhood
Unknown, and will not wrong thy father's blood?

ELECTRA
He is called my husband. 'Tis for him I toil.

ORESTES
How dark lies honour hid! And what turmoil
In all things human: sons of mighty men
Fallen to naught, and from ill seed again

31

Good fruit: yea, famine in the rich man's scroll
Writ deep, and in poor flesh a lordly soul!
As, lo, this man, not great in Argos, not
With pride of house uplifted, in a lot
Of unmarked life hath shown a prince's grace.
[*To the* PEASANT, *who has returned.*
All that is here of Agamemnon's race,
And all that lacketh yet, from whom we come,
Do thank thee, and the welcome of thy home
Accept with gladness.—Ho, men; hasten ye
Within!—This open-hearted poverty
Is blither to my sense than feasts of gold.

Lady, thine husband's welcome makes me bold;
Yet would thou hadst thy brother, before all
Confessed, to greet us in a prince's hall!
Which may be, even yet. Apollo spake
The word; and surely, though small store I make
Of man's divining, God will fail us not.
[ORESTES *and* PYLADES *go in, following the* SERVANTS.

LEADER

O never was the heart of hope so hot
Within me. How? So moveless in time past,
Hath Fortune girded up her lóins at last?

ELECTRA

Now know'st thou not thine own ill furniture,
To bid these strangers in, to whom for sure
Our best were hardship, men of gentle breed?

PEASANT

Nay, if the men be gentle, as indeed
I deem them, they will take good cheer or ill
With even kindness.

32

314 ————————————————————

ELECTRA

     'Twas ill done; but still—
Go, since so poor thou art, to that old friend
Who reared my father. At the realm's last end
He dwells, where Tanaos river foams between
Argos and Sparta. Long time hath he been
An exile 'mid his flocks. Tell him what thing
Hath chanced on me, and bid him haste and bring
Meat for the strangers' tending.—Glad, I trow,
That old man's heart will be, and many a vow
Will lift to God, to learn the child he stole
From death yet breathes.—I will not ask a dole
From home; how should my mother help me? Nay.
I pity him that seeks that door, to say
Orestes liveth!

PEASANT

    Wilt thou have it so?
I will take word to the old man. But go
Quickly within, and whatso there thou find
Set out for them. A woman, if her mind
So turn, can light on many a pleasant thing
To fill her board. And surely plenishing
We have for this one day.—'Tis in such shifts
As these I care for riches, to make gifts
To friends, or lead a sick man back to health
With ease and plenty. Else small aid is wealth
For daily gladness; once a man be done
With hunger, rich and poor are all as one.

[*The* PEASANT *goes off to the left;* ELECTRA *goes into the house.*

L*   33

CHORUS

Oh, for the ships of Troy, the beat   [*Strophe* 1.
    Of oars that shimmered
Innumerable, and dancing feet
    Of Nereids glimmered;
And dolphins, drunken with the lyre,
Across the dark blue prows, like fire,
    Did bound and quiver,
To cleave the way for Thetis' son,
Fleet-in-the-wind Achilles, on
To war, to war, till Troy be won
    Beside the reedy river.

Up from Eubœa's caverns came   [*Antistrophe* 1.
    The Nereids, bearing
Gold armour from the Lords of Flame,
    Wrought for his wearing:
Long sought those daughters of the deep,
Up Pelion's glen, up Ossa's steep
    Forest enchanted,
Where Peleus reared alone, afar,
His lost sea-maiden's child, the star
Of Hellas, and swift help of war
    When weary armies panted.

There came a man from Troy, and told   [*Strophe* 2.
    Here in the haven,
How, orb on orb, to strike with cold
The Trojan, o'er that targe of gold,
    Dread shapes were graven.
All round the level rim thereof
Perseus, on wingèd feet, above
    The long seas hied him;

34

The Gorgon's wild and bleeding hair
He lifted; and a herald fair,
He of the wilds, whom Maia bare,
    God's Hermes, flew beside him.

[*Antistrophe* 2.

But midmost, where the boss rose higher,
    A sun stood blazing,
And wingèd steeds, and stars in choir,
Hyad and Pleiad, fire on fire,
    For Hector's dazing:
Across the golden helm, each way,
Two taloned Sphinxes held their prey,
    Song-drawn to slaughter:
And round the breastplate ramping came
A mingled breed of lion and flame,
Hot-eyed to tear that steed of fame
    That found Pirênê's water.

The red red sword with steeds four-yoked   [*Epode.*
    Black-maned, was graven,
That laboured, and the hot dust smoked
    Cloudwise to heaven.
Thou Tyndarid woman! Fair and tall
Those warriors were, and o'er them all
    One king great-hearted,
Whom thou and thy false love did slay:
Therefore the tribes of Heaven one day
For these thy dead shall send on thee
An iron death: yea, men shall see
The white throat drawn, and blood's red spray,
    And lips in terror parted.
[*As they cease, there enters from the left a very old man,
bearing a lamb, a wineskin, and a wallet.*

35

OLD MAN

Where is my little Princess? Ah, not now;
But still my queen, who tended long ago
The lad that was her father. . . . How steep-set
These last steps to her porch! But faint not yet:
Onward, ye failing knees and back with pain
Bowed, till we look on that dear face again.
[*Enter* ELECTRA.
Ah, daughter, is it thou?—Lo, here I am,
With gifts from all my store; this suckling lamb
Fresh from the ewe, green crowns for joyfulness,
And creamy things new-curdled from the press.
And this long-storèd juice of vintages
Forgotten, cased in fragrance: scant it is,
But passing sweet to mingle nectar-wise
With feebler wine.—Go, bear them in; mine eyes . . .
Where is my cloak?—They are all blurred with tears.

ELECTRA

What ails thine eyes, old friend? After these years
Doth my low plight still stir thy memories?
Or think'st thou of Orestes, where he lies
In exile, and my father? Aye, long love
Thou gavest him, and seest the fruit thereof
Wasted, for thee and all who love thee!

OLD MAN

All

Wasted! And yet 'tis that lost hope withal
I cannot brook. But now I turned aside
To see my master's grave. All, far and wide,
Was silence; so I bent these knees of mine
And wept and poured drink-offerings from the wine

36

318

I bear the strangers, and about the stone
Laid myrtle sprays. And, child, I saw thereon
Just at the censer slain, a fleecèd ewe,
Deep black, in sacrifice: the blood was new
About it: and a tress of bright brown hair
Shorn as in mourning, close. Long stood I there
And wondered, of all men what man had gone
In mourning to that grave.—My child, 'tis none
In Argos. Did there come . . . Nay, mark me now . . .
Thy brother in the dark, last night, to bow
His head before that unadorèd tomb?

  O come, and mark the colour of it. Come
And lay thine own hair by that mourner's tress!
A hundred little things make likenesses
In brethren born, and show the father's blood.

ELECTRA (*trying to mask her excitement and resist the contagion
of his*)

Old heart, old heart, is this a wise man's mood? . . .
O, not in darkness, not in fear of men,
Shall Argos find him, when he comes again,
Mine own undaunted . . . Nay, and if it were,
What likeness could there be? My brother's hair
Is as a prince's and a rover's, strong
With sunlight and with strife: not like the long
Locks that a woman combs. . . . And many a head
Hath this same semblance, wing for wing, tho' bred
Of blood not ours. . . . 'Tis hopeless. Peace, old man.

OLD MAN

The footprints! Set thy foot by his, and scan
The track of frame and muscles, how they fit!

37

ELECTRA

That ground will take no footprint! All of it
Is bitter stone. . . . It hath? . . . And who hath said
There should be likeness in a brother's tread
And sister's? His is stronger every way.

OLD MAN

But hast thou nothing . . .? If he came this day
And sought to show thee, is there no one sign
Whereby to know him? . . . Stay; the robe was thine,
Work of thy loom, wherein I wrapt him o'er
That night, and stole him through the murderers' door.

ELECTRA

Thou knowest, when Orestes was cast out
I was a child. . . . If I did weave some clout
Of raiment, would he keep the vesture now
He wore in childhood? Should my weaving grow
As his limbs grew? . . . 'Tis lost long since. No more!
Oh, either 'twas some stranger passed, and shore
His locks for very ruth before that tomb:
Or, if he found perchance, to seek his home,
Some spy . . .

OLD MAN

The strangers! Where are they? I fain
Would see them, aye, and bid them answer plain . . .

ELECTRA

Here at the door! How swift upon the thought!
Enter ORESTES *and* PYLADES

38

Old Man

High-born: albeit for that I trust them not.
The highest oft are false. . . . Howe'er it be,
[*Approaching them.*
I bid the strangers hail!

Orestes

All hail to thee,
Greybeard!—Prithee, what man of all the King
Trusted of old, is now this broken thing?

Electra

'Tis he that trained my father's boyhood.

Orestes

How?
And stole from death thy brother? Sayest thou?

Electra

This man was his deliverer, if it be
Deliverance.

Orestes

How his old eye pierceth me,
As one that testeth silver and alloy!
Sees he some likeness here?

Electra

Perchance 'tis joy,
To see Orestes' comrade, that he feels.

Orestes

None dearer.—But what ails the man? He reels
Dizzily back.

39

ELECTRA

I marvel. I can say
No more.

OLD MAN (*in a broken voice*)
Electra, mistress, daughter, pray!
Pray unto God!

ELECTRA

Of all the things I crave,
The thousand things, or all that others have,
What should I pray for?

OLD MAN

Pray thine arms may hold
At last this treasure-dream of more than gold
God shows us!

ELECTRA
God, I pray thee! . . . Wouldst thou more?

OLD MAN

Gaze now upon this man, and bow before
Thy dearest upon earth!

ELECTRA

I gaze on t h e e!
Oh, hath time made thee mad?

OLD MAN

Mad, that I see
Thy brother?

ELECTRA

My . . . I know not what thou say'st:
I looked not for it . . .

40

OLD MAN
　　　　　I tell thee, here confessed
Standeth Orestes, Agamemnon's son!

ELECTRA
A sign before I trust thee! Oh, but one!
How dost thou know . . .?

OLD MAN
　　　　　　There, by his brow, I see
The scar he made, that day he ran with thee
Chasing thy fawn, and fell.

ELECTRA (*in a dull voice*)
　　　　　A scar? 'Tis so.
I see a scar.

OLD MAN
　　And fearest still to throw
Thine arms round him thou lovest?

ELECTRA
　　　　　O, no more!
Thy sign hath conquered me. . . . (*throwing herself into*
　ORESTES' *arms*). At last, at last!
Thy face like light! And do I hold thee fast,
Unhoped for?

ORESTES
　　Yea, at last! And I hold thee.

ELECTRA
I never knew . . .

ORESTES
　　I dreamed not.

41

ELECTRA

Is it he,

Orestes?

ORESTES

Thy defender, yea, alone
To fight the world! Lo, this day have I thrown
A net, which once unbroken from the sea
Drawn home, shall . . . Oh, and it must surely be!
Else men shall know there is no God, no light
In Heaven, if wrong to the end shall conquer right.

CHORUS

Comest thou, comest thou now,
Chained by the years and slow,
    O Day long sought?
A light on the mountains cold
Is lit, yea, a fire burneth.
'Tis the light of one that turneth
From roamings manifold,
Back out of exile old
    To the house that knew him not.

Some spirit hath turned our way,
    Victory visible,
Walking at thy right hand,
Belovèd; O lift this day
Thine arms, thy voice, as a spell;
And pray for thy brother, pray,
Threading the perilous land,
    That all be well!

ORESTES

Enough; this dear delight is mine at last
Of thine embracing; and the hour comes fast

42

When we shall stand again as now we stand,
And stint not.—Stay, Old Man: thou, being at hand
At the edge of time, advise me, by what way
Best to requite my father's murderers.   Say,
Have I in Argos any still to trust;
Or is the love, once borne me, trod in dust,
Even as my fortunes are?   Whom shall I seek?
By day or night?   And whither turn, to wreak
My will on them that hate us?   Say.

Old Man

　　　　　　　　　　　　　　　My son,
In thine adversity, there is not one
Will call thee friend.   Nay, that were treasure-trove,
A friend to share, not faltering from love,
Fair days and foul the same.   Thy name is gone
Forth to all Argos, as a thing o'erthrown
And dead.   Thou hast not left one spark to glow
With hope in one friend's heart!   Hear all, and know:
Thou hast God's fortune and thine own right hand,
Naught else, to conquer back thy fatherland.

Orestes

The deed, the deed!   What must we do?

Old Man

　　　　　　　　　　　　　　Strike down
Aegisthus . . . and thy mother.

Orestes

　　　　　　　　　　'Tis the crown
My race is run for.   But how find him?

43

OLD MAN

Not

Within the city walls, however hot
Thy spirit.

ORESTES

Ha! With watchers doth he go
Begirt, and mailèd pikemen?

OLD MAN

Even so:
He lives in fear of thee, and night nor day
Hath slumber.

ORESTES

That way barred!—'Tis thine to say
What next remains.

OLD MAN

I will; and thou give ear.
A thought has found me!

ORESTES

All good thoughts be near,
For thee to speak and me to understand!

OLD MAN

But now I saw Aegisthus, close at hand
As here I journeyed.

ORESTES

That good word shall trace
My path for me! Thou saw'st him? In what place?

OLD MAN

Out on the pastures where his horses stray.

44

ORESTES

What did he there so far?—A gleam of day
Crosseth our darkness.

OLD MAN

'Twas a feast, methought,
Of worship to the wild-wood nymphs he wrought.

ORESTES

The watchers of men's birth.   Is there a son
New born to him, or doth he pray for one
That cometh?   [Movement of ELECTRA.

OLD MAN

More I know not; he had there
A wreathèd ox, as for some weighty prayer.

ORESTES

What force was with him?   Not his serfs alone?

OLD MAN

No Argive lord was there; none but his own
Household.

ORESTES

Not any that might know my race,
Or guess?

OLD MAN

Thralls, thralls; who ne'er have seen thy face.

ORESTES

Once I prevail, the thralls will welcome me!

OLD MAN

The slaves' way, that; and no ill thing for thee!

45

ORESTES

How can I once come near him?

OLD MAN

                              Walk thy ways
Hard by, where he may see thee, ere he slays
His sacrifice.

ORESTES

How? Is the road so nigh?

OLD MAN

He cannot choose but see thee, passing by,
And bid thee stay to share the beast they kill.

ORESTES

A bitter fellow-feaster, if God will!

OLD MAN

And then . . . then swift be heart and brain, to see
God's chances!

ORESTES

                Aye, Well hast thou counselled me.
But . . . where is s h e?

OLD MAN

                          In Argos now, I guess;
But goes to join her husband, ere the press
Of the feast.

ORESTES

              Why goeth not my mother straight
Forth at her husband's side?

46

OLD MAN
                              She fain will wait
Until the gathered country-folk be gone.

ORESTES
Enough! She knows what eyes are turned upon
Her passings in the land!

OLD MAN
                    Aye, all men hate
The unholy woman.

ORESTES
                    How then can I set
My snare for wife and husband in one breath?

ELECTRA (*coming forward*)
Hold! It is I must work our mother's death.

ORESTES
If that be done, I think the other deed
Fortune will guide.

ELECTRA
                    This man must help our need,
One friend alone for both.

OLD MAN
                    He will, he will!
Speak on. What cunning hast thou found to fill
Thy purpose?

ELECTRA
                    Get thee forth, Old Man, and quick
Tell Clytemnestra . . . tell her I lie sick,
New-mothered of a man-child.

47

OLD MAN
                              Thou hast borne

A son! But when?

ELECTRA
                              Let this be the tenth morn.
Till then a mother stays in sanctity,
Unseen.

OLD MAN
              And if I tell her, where shall be
The death in this?

ELECTRA
                        That word let her but hear,
Straight she will seek me out!

OLD MAN
                                    The queen! What care
Hath she for thee, or pain of thine?

ELECTRA
                              She will;
And weep my babe's low station!

OLD MAN
                              Thou hast skill
To know her, child; say on.

ELECTRA
                        But bring her here,
Here to my hand; the rest will come.

OLD MAN
                              I swear,
Here at the gate she shall stand palpable!

48

ELECTRA

The gate: the gate that leads to me and Hell.

OLD MAN

Let me but see it, and I die content.

ELECTRA

First, then, my brother: see his steps be bent . . .

OLD MAN

Straight yonder, where Aegisthus makes his prayer!

ELECTRA

Then seek my mother's presence, and declare
My news.
OLD MAN
            Thy very words, child, as tho' spoke
From thine own lips!
ELECTRA
            Brother, thine hour is struck.
Thou standest in the van of war this day.

ORESTES (*rousing himself*)

Aye, I am ready. . . . I will go my way,
If but some man will guide me.

OLD MAN
                        Here am I,
To speed thee to the end, right thankfully.

ORESTES (*turning as he goes and raising his hands to
heaven*)

Zeus of my sires, Zeus of the lost battle,

49

ELECTRA

Have pity; have pity; we have earned it well!

OLD MAN

Pity these twain, of thine own body sprung!

ELECTRA

O Queen o'er Argive altars, Hera high,

ORESTES

Grant us thy strength, if for the right we cry.

OLD MAN

Strength to these twain, to right their father's wrong!

ELECTRA

O Earth, deep Earth, to whom I yearn in vain,

ORESTES

And deeper thou, O father darkly slain,

OLD MAN

Thy children call, who love thee: hearken thou!

ORESTES

Girt with thine own dead armies, wake, O wake!

ELECTRA

With all that died at Ilion for thy sake . . .

OLD MAN

And hate earth's dark defilers; help us now!

50

 ELECTRA

Dost hear us yet, O thou in deadly wrong,
Wronged by my mother?

OLD MAN

                    Child, we stay too long.
He hears; be sure he hears!

ELECTRA

                    And while he hears,
I speak this word for omen in his ears:
"Aegisthus dies, Aegisthus dies." . . . Ah me,
My brother, should it strike not him, but thee,
This wrestling with dark death, behold, I too
Am dead that hour. Think of me as one true,
Not one that lives. I have a sword made keen
For this, and shall strike deep.

                    I will go in
And make all ready. If there come from thee
Good tidings, all my house for ecstasy
Shall cry; and if we hear that thou art dead,
Then comes the other end!—Lo, I have said.

ORESTES

I know all, all.

ELECTRA

                    Then be a man to-day!
[ORESTES *and the* OLD MAN *depart.*
O Women, let your voices from this fray
Flash me a fiery signal, where I sit,
The sword across my knees, expecting it.

51

For never, though they kill me, shall they touch
My living limbs!—I know my way thus much.
[*She goes into the house.*

Chorus

When white-haired folk are met   [*Strophe.*
  In Argos about the fold,
A story lingereth yet,
  A voice of the mountains old,
  That tells of the Lamb of Gold:
A lamb from a mother mild,
  But the gold of it curled and beat;
And Pan, who holdeth the keys of the wild,
  Bore it to Atreus' feet:
His wild reed pipes he blew,
  And the reeds were filled with peace,
And a joy of singing before him flew,
  Over the fiery fleece:
And up on the basèd rock,
  As a herald cries, cried he:
"Gather ye, gather, O Argive folk,
  The King's Sign to see,
The sign of the blest of God,
  For he that hath this, hath all!"
Therefore the dance of praise they trod
  In the Atreïd brethren's hall.

They opened before men's eyes   [*Antistrophe.*
  That which was hid before,
The chambers of sacrifice,
  The dark of the golden door,
  And fires on the altar floor.

52

And bright was every street,
  And the voice of the Muses' tree,
The carven lotus, was lifted sweet;
  When afar and suddenly,
Strange songs, and a voice that grew:
  " Come to your king, ye folk!
Mine, mine, is the Golden Ewe ! "
  'Twas dark Thyestes spoke.
For, lo, when the world was still,
  With his brother's bride he lay,
And won her to work his will,
  And they stole the Lamb away!
Then forth to the folk strode he,
  And called them about his fold,
And showed that Sign of the King to be,
  The fleece and the horns of gold.

Then, then, the world was changed; [*Strophe* 2.
  And the Father, where they ranged,
Shook the golden stars and glowing,
  And the great Sun stood deranged
In the glory of his going.

Lo, from that day forth, the East
  Bears the sunrise on his breast,
And the flaming Day in heaven
  Down the dim ways of the west
Driveth, to be lost at even.

The wet clouds to Northward beat;
  And Lord Ammon's desert seat
Crieth from the South, unslaken,
  For the dews that once were sweet,
For the rain that God hath taken.

53

Tis a rustic tale that old
Shepherds to our fathers told,
And we reck not of their telling;
    Wiser, little faith we hold
That the Sun his golden dwelling

    Turned, and fled across the sky
    For the sins of Man, the cry
Of his ailing tribes assembled
    For some justice ere they die.
Once men heard the tale and trembled,

    Fearing God, O Queen: whom thou
    Hast forgotten, till thy brow
With old blood is dark and daunted.
    And thy brethren, even now,
Walk among the stars, enchanted.

LEADER

Ha, friends, was that a voice? Or some dream sound
Of voices shaketh me, as underground
God's thunder shuddering? Hark, again, and clear!
It swells upon the wind.—Come forth and hear!
Mistress, Electra!
[ELECTRA, *a bare sword in her hand, comes from the house.*

ELECTRA

                Friends! Some news is brought?
How hath the battle ended?

LEADER

                        I know naught.
Crying there seemed as of men massacred!

54

ELECTRA

I heard it too.   Far off, but still I heard.

LEADER

A distant floating voice . . . Ah, plainer now!

ELECTRA

Of Argive anguish!—Brother, is it thou?

LEADER

I know not.   Many confused voices cry . . .

ELECTRA

Death, then for me!   That answer bids me die.

LEADER

Nay, wait!   We know not yet thy fortune.   Wait!

ELECTRA

No messenger from him!—Too late, too late!

LEADER

The message yet will come.   'Tis not a thing
So light of compass, to strike down a king.

Enter a MESSENGER, *running.*
MESSENGER

Victory, Maids of Argos, Victory!
Orestes . . . all that love him, list to me! . . .
Hath conquered!   Agamemnon's murderer lies
Dead!   Oh, give thanks to God with happy cries!

ELECTRA

Who art thou?   I mistrust thee. . . . 'Tis a plot!

55

MESSENGER

Thy brother's man.   Look well.   Dost know me not?

ELECTRA

Friend, friend; my terror made me not to see
Thy visage.   Now I know and welcome thee.
How sayst thou?   He is dead, verily dead,
My father's murderer . . .?

MESSENGER

Shall it be said
Once more?   I know again and yet again
Thy heart would hear.   Aegisthus lieth slain!

ELECTRA

Ye Gods!   And thou, O Right, that seest all,
Art come at last? . . . But speak; how did he fall?
How swooped the wing of death? . . . I crave to hear.

MESSENGER

Forth of this hut we set our faces clear
To the world, and struck the open chariot road;
Then on toward the pasture lands, where stood
The great Lord of Mycenae.   In a set
Garden beside a channelled rivulet,
Culling a myrtle garland for his brow,
He walked: but hailed us as we passed: "How now,
Strangers!   Who are ye?   Of what city sprung,
And whither bound?"   "Thessalians," answered young
Orestes: "to Alpheüs journeying,
With gifts to Olympian Zeus."   Whereat the king:
"This while, beseech you, tarry, and make full
The feast upon my hearth.   We slay a bull

56

Here to the Nymphs.   Set forth at break of day
To-morrow, and 'twill cost you no delay.
But come "—and so he gave his hand, and led
The two men in—" I must not be gainsaid;
Come to the house.   Ho, there; set close at hand
Vats of pure water, that the guests may stand
At the altar's verge, where falls the holy spray."
Then quickly spake Orestes: " By the way
We cleansed us in a torrent stream.   We need
No purifying here.   But if indeed
Strangers may share thy worship, here are we
Ready, O King, and swift to follow thee."
  So spoke they in the midst.   And every thrall
Laid down the spears they served the King withal
And hied him to the work.   Some bore amain
The death-vat, some the corbs of hallowed grain;
Or kindled fire, and round the fire and in
Set cauldrons foaming; and a festal din
Filled all the place.   Then took thy mother's lord
The ritual grains, and o'er the altar poured
Its due, and prayed: " O Nymphs of Rock and Mere,
With many a sacrifice for many a year,
May I and she who waits at home for me,
My Tyndarid Queen, adore you.   May it be
Peace with us always, even as now; and all
Ill to mine enemies"—meaning withal
Thee and Orestes.   Then my master prayed
Against that prayer, but silently, and said
No word, to win once more his fatherland.
Then in the corb Aegisthus set his hand,
Took the straight blade, cut from the proud bull's head
A lock, and laid it where the fire was red;
Then, while the young men held the bull on high,
Slew it with one clean gash; and suddenly

57

Turned on thy brother: "Stranger, every true
Thessalian, so the story goes, can hew
A bull's limbs clean, and tame a mountain steed.
Take up the steel, and show us if indeed
Rumour speak true." Right swift Orestes took
The Dorian blade, back from his shoulder shook
The broochèd mantle, called on Pylades
To aid him, and waved back the thralls. With ease
Heelwise he held the bull, and with one glide
Bared the white limb; then stripped the mighty hide
From off him, swifter than a runner runs
His furlongs, and laid clean the flank. At once
Aegisthus stooped, and lifted up with care
The ominous parts, and gazed. No lobe was there;
But lo, strange caves of gall, and, darkly raised,
The portal vein boded to him that gazed
Fell visitations. Dark as night his brow
Clouded. Then spake Orestes: "Why art thou
Cast down so sudden?" "Guest," he cried, "there be
Treasons from whence I know not, seeking me.
Of all my foes, 'tis Agamemnon's son;
His hate is on my house, like war." "Have done!"
Orestes cried: "thou fear'st an exile's plot,
Lord of a city? Make thy cold heart hot
With meat.—Ho, fling me a Thessalian steel!
This Dorian is too light. I will unseal
The breast of him." He took the heavier blade,
And clave the bone. And there Aegisthus stayed,
The omens in his hand, dividing slow
This sign from that; till, while his head bent low,
Up with a leap thy brother flashed the sword,
Then down upon his neck, and cleft the cord
Of brain and spine. Shuddering the body stood
One instant in an agony of blood,

58

And gasped and fell. The henchmen saw, and straight
Flew to their spears, a host of them to set
Against those twain. But there the twain did stand
Unfaltering, each his iron in his hand,
Edge fronting edge. Till " Hold," Orestes calls:
" I come not as in wrath against these walls
And mine own people. One man righteously
I have slain, who slew my father. It is I,
The wronged Orestes! Hold, and smite me not,
Old housefolk of my father!" When they caught
That name, their lances fell. And one old man,
An ancient in the house, drew nigh to scan
His face, and knew him. Then with one accord
They crowned thy brother's temples, and outpoured
Joy and loud songs. And hither now he fares
To show the head, no Gorgon, that he bears,
But that Aegisthus whom thou hatest! Yea,
Blood against blood, his debt is paid this day.
[*He goes off to meet the others*—ELECTRA *stands as though
stupefied.*

CHORUS

Now, now thou shalt dance in our dances,
    Beloved, as a fawn in the night!
The wind is astir for the glances
    Of thy feet; thou art robed with delight.
He hath conquered, he cometh to free us
    With garlands new-won,
More high than the crowns of Alpheüs,
    Thine own father's son:
    Cry, cry, for the day that is won!

ELECTRA

O Light of the Sun, O chariot wheels of flame,
O Earth and Night, dead Night without a name

59

That held me! Now mine eyes are raised to see
And all the doorways of my soul flung free.
Aegisthus dead! My father's murderer dead!
  What have I still of wreathing for the head
Stored in my chambers? Let it come forth now
To bind my brother's and my conqueror's brow.
[Some garlands are brought out from the house to ELECTRA.

CHORUS
Go, gather thy garlands, and lay them
    As a crown on his brow, many-tressed,
But our feet to the dance shall array them
    'Tis the joy that the Muses have blest.
For our king is returned as from prison,
    The old king, to be master again,
Our belovèd in justice re-risen:
        With guile he hath slain . . .
    But cry, cry in joyance again!
[There enter from the left ORESTES *and* PYLADES, *followed
by some thralls.*

ELECTRA
O conqueror, come! The king that trampled Troy
Knoweth his son Orestes. Come in joy,
Brother, and take to bind thy rippling hair
My crowns! . . . Oh, what are crowns, that runners wear
For some vain race? But thou in battle true
Hast felled our foe Aegisthus, him that slew
By craft thy sire and mine.   *[She crowns* ORESTES.
                        And thou no less,
O friend at need, O reared in righteousness,
Take, Pylades, this chaplet from my hand.
'Twas half thy battle. And may ye two stand
Thus alway, victory-crowned, before my face!
[She crowns PYLADES.

60

342

ORESTES

Electra, first as workers of this grace
Praise thou the Gods, and after, if thou will,
Praise also me, as chosen to fulfil
God's work and Fate's.—Aye, 'tis no more a dream;
In very deed I come from slaying him.
Thou hast the knowledge clear, but lo, I bring
More also. See himself, dead!
[*Attendants bring in the body of* AEGISTHUS *on a bier.*
                          Wouldst thou fling
This lord on the rotting earth for beasts to tear?
Or up, where all the vultures of the air
May glut them, pierce and nail him for a sign
Far off? Work all thy will. Now he is thine.

ELECTRA

It shames me; yet, God knows, I hunger sore—

ORESTES

What wouldst thou? Speak; the old fear nevermore
Need touch thee.

ELECTRA

              To let loose upon the dead
My hate! That deed perchance on mine own head
Would loose a world of hate.

ORESTES

                    No man that lives
Shall scathe thee by one word.

ELECTRA

                    Our city gives
Quick blame; and little love have men for me.

61

ORESTES

If aught thou hast unsaid, sister, be free
And speak. Between this man and us no bar
Cometh nor stint, but the utter rage of war.
[*She goes and stands over the body. A moment's silence.*

ELECTRA

Ah me, what have I? What first flood of hate
To loose upon thee? What last curse to sate
My pain, or river of wild words to flow
Bank-high between? . . . Nothing? . . . And yet I know
There hath not passed one sun, but through the long
Cold dawns, over and over, like a song,
I have said them—words held back, O, some day yet
To flash into thy face, would but the fret
Of ancient fear fall loose and let me free.
And free I am, now; and can pay to thee
At last the weary debt.
                             Oh, thou didst kill
My soul within. Who wrought thee any ill,
That thou shouldst make me fatherless? Aye, me
And this my brother, loveless, solitary?
'Twas thou, didst bend my mother to her shame:
Thy weak hand murdered him who led to fame
The hosts of Hellas—thou, that never crossed
O'erseas to Troy! . . . God help thee, wast thou lost
In blindness, long ago, dreaming, some-wise,
She would be true with thee, whose sin and lies
Thyself had tasted in my father's place?
And then, that thou wert happy, when thy days
Were all one pain? Thou knewest ceaselessly
Her kiss a thing unclean, and she knew thee

62

344 ————————————————————————

A lord so little true, so dearly won!
So lost ye both, being in falseness one,
What fortune else had granted; she thy curse,
Who marred thee as she loved thee, and thou hers . . .
And on thy ways thou heardst men whispering,
" Lo, the Queen's husband yonder "—not " the King."
　　And then the lie of lies that dimmed thy brow,
Vaunting that by thy gold, thy chattels, Thou
Wert Something; which themselves are nothingness,
Shadows, to clasp a moment ere they cease.
The thing thou art, and not the things thou hast,
Abideth, yea, and bindeth to the last
Thy burden on thee: while all else, ill-won
And sin-companioned, like a flower o'erblown,
Flies on the wind away.
　　　　　　　　　　Or didst thou find
In women . . . Women? . . . Nay, peace, peace!　The blind
Could read thee.　Cruel wast thou in thine hour,
Lord of a great king's house, and like a tower
Firm in thy beauty.
[*Starting back with a look of loathing.*
　　　　　　　　　Ah, that girl-like face!
God grant, not that, not that, but some plain grace
Of manhood to the man who brings me love:
A father of straight children, that shall move
Swift on the wings of War.
　　　　　　　　　So, get thee gone!
Naught knowing how the great years, rolling on,
Have laid thee bare, and thy long debt full paid.
　　O vaunt not, if one step be proudly made
In evil, that all Justice is o'ercast:
Vaunt not, ye men of sin, ere at the last
The thin-drawn marge before you glimmereth
Close, and the goal that wheels 'twixt life and death.

63

LEADER

Justice is mighty. Passing dark hath been
His sin: and dark the payment of his sin.

ELECTRA (*with a weary sigh, turning from the body*)
Ah me! Go some of you, bear him from sight,
That when my mother comes, her eyes may light
On nothing, nothing, till she know the sword . . .
[*The body is borne into the hut.* PYLADES *goes with it.*

ORESTES (*looking along the road*)
Stay, 'tis a new thing! We have still a word
To speak . . .
ELECTRA
What? Not a rescue from the town
Thou seest?
ORESTES
'Tis my mother comes: my own
Mother, that bare me. [*He takes off his crown.*

ELECTRA (*springing, as it were, to life again, and moving
where she can see the road*)
Straight into the snare!
Aye, there she cometh.—Welcome in thy rare
Chariot! All welcome in thy brave array!

ORESTES

What would we with our mother? Didst thou say
Kill her?
ELECTRA (*turning on him*)
What? Is it pity? Dost thou fear
To see thy mother's shape?

64

346

ORESTES

> 'Twas she that bare
My body into life. She gave me suck.
How can I strike her?

ELECTRA

> Strike her as she struck
Our father!

ORESTES (*to himself, brooding*)
> Phoebus, God, was all thy mind
Turned unto darkness?

ELECTRA

> If thy God be blind,
Shalt thou have light?

ORESTES (*as before*)
> Thou, thou, didst bid me kill
My mother: which is sin.

ELECTRA

> How brings it ill
To thee, to raise our father from the dust?

ORESTES

I was a clean man once. Shall I be thrust
From men's sight, blotted with her blood?

ELECTRA

> Thy blot
Is black as death if him thou succour not!

65

ORESTES

Who shall do judgment on me, when she dies?

ELECTRA

Who shall do judgment, if thy father lies
Forgotten?

ORESTES *(turning suddenly to* ELECTRA*)*
Stay! How if some fiend of Hell,
Hid in God's likeness, spake that oracle?

ELECTRA

In God's own house? I trow not.

ORESTES

And I trow
It was an evil charge!   [*He moves away from her.*

ELECTRA *(almost despairingly)*
To fail me now!
To fail me now! A coward!—O brother, no!

ORESTES

What shall it be, then? The same stealthy blow . . .

ELECTRA

That slew our father! Courage! thou hast slain
Aegisthus.

ORESTES

Aye. So be it.—I have ta'en
A path of many terrors: and shall do
Deeds horrible. 'Tis God will have it so. . . .
Is this the joy of battle or wild woe?
[*He goes into the house.*

66

LEADER

O Queen o'er Argos thronèd high,
　O Woman, sister of the twain,
　God's Horsemen, stars without a stain,
Whose home is in the deathless sky,
　Whose glory in the stormy main,
Toiling to succour men that die:
Long years above us hast thou been,
　God-like for gold and marvelled power:
　Ah, well may mortal eyes this hour
Observe thy state: All hail, O Queen!

[Enter from the right CLYTEMNESTRA *on a chariot
accompanied by richly dressed Handmaidens.*

CLYTEMNESTRA

Down from the wain, ye dames of Troy, and hold
Mine arm as I dismount. . . .
[Answering ELECTRA'S *thought.*

　　　　　　　　The spoils and gold
Of Ilion I have sent out of my hall
To many shrines. These bondwomen are all
I keep in mine own house . . . Deemst thou the cost
Too rich to pay me for the child I lost—
Fair though they be?

ELECTRA

　　　　Nay, Mother, here am I
Bond likewise, yea, and homeless, to hold high
Thy royal arm!

CLYTEMNESTRA

　　　　Child, the war-slaves are here;
Thou needst not toil.

67

ELECTRA

What was it but the spear
Of war, drove me forth too? Mine enemies
Have sacked my father's house, and, even as these,
Captives and fatherless, made me their prey.

CLYTEMNESTRA

It was thy father cast his child away,
A child he might have loved! . . . Shall I speak out?
(*Controlling herself*) Nay; when a woman once is caught
    about
With evil fame, there riseth in her tongue
A bitter spirit—wrong, I know! Yet, wrong
Or right, I charge ye look on the deeds done;
And if ye needs must hate, when all is known,
Hate on! What profits loathing ere ye know?
    My father gave me to be his. 'Tis so.
But was it his to kill me, or to kill
The babes I bore? Yet, lo, he tricked my will
With fables of Achilles' love: he bore
To Aulis and the dark ship-clutching shore,
He held above the altar-flame, and smote,
Cool as one reaping, through the strainèd throat,
My white Iphigenia. . . . Had it been
To save some falling city, leaguered in
With foemen; to prop up our castle towers,
And rescue other children that were ours,
Giving one life for many, by God's laws
I had forgiven all! Not so. Because
Helen was wanton, and her master knew
No curb for her: for that, for that, he slew
My daughter!—Even then, with all my wrong,
No wild beast yet was in me. Nay, for long,

I never would have killed him.   But he came,
At last, bringing that damsel, with the flame
Of God about her, mad and knowing all:
And set her in my room; and in one wall
Would hold two queens!—O wild are woman's eyes
And hot her heart.   I say not otherwise.
But, being thus wild, if then her master stray
To love far off, and cast his own away,
Shall not her will break prison too, and wend
Somewhere to win some other for a friend?
And then on us the world's curse waxes strong
In righteousness!   The lords of all the wrong
Must hear no curse!—I slew him.   I trod then
The only road: which led me to the men
He hated.   Of the friends of Argos whom
Durst I have sought, to aid me to the doom
I craved?—Speak if thou wouldst, and fear not me,
If yet thou deemst him slain unrighteously.

LEADER

Thy words be just, yet shame their justice brings;
A woman true of heart should bear all things
From him she loves.   And she who feels it not,
I cannot reason of her, nor speak aught.

ELECTRA

Remember, mother, thy last word of grace,
Bidding me speak, and fear not, to thy face.

CLYTEMNESTRA

So said I truly, child, and so say still.

ELECTRA

Wilt softly hear, and after work me ill?

69

CLYTEMNESTRA

Not so, not so. I will but pleasure thee.

ELECTRA

I answer then. And, mother, this shall be
My prayer of opening, where hangs the whole:
Would God that He had made thee clean of soul!
Helen and thou—Oh, face and form were fair,
Meet for men's praise; but sisters twain ye were,
Both things of naught, a stain on Castor's star.
And Helen slew her honour, borne afar
In wilful ravishment: but thou didst slay
The highest man of the world. And now wilt say
'Twas wrought in justice for thy child laid low
At Aulis? . . . Ah, who knows thee as I know?
Thou, thou, who long ere aught of ill was done
Thy child, when Agamemnon scarce was gone,
Sate at the looking-glass, and tress by tress
Didst comb the twinèd gold in loneliness.
When any wife, her lord being far away,
Toils to be fair, Oh, blot her out that day
As false within! What would she with a cheek
So bright in strange men's eyes, unless she seek
Some treason? None but I, thy child, could so
Watch thee in Hellas: none but I could know
Thy face of gladness when our enemies
Were strong, and the swift cloud upon thine eyes
If Troy seemed falling, all thy soul keen-set
Praying that h e might come no more! . . . And yet
It was so easy to be true. A king
Was thine, not feebler, not in anything
Below Aegisthus; one whom Hellas chose
For chief beyond all kings. Aye, and God knows,

70

How sweet a name in Greece, after the sin
Thy sister wrought, lay in thy ways to win.
Ill deeds make fair ones shine, and turn thereto
Men's eyes.—Enough: but say he wronged thee; slew
By craft thy child:—what wrong had I done, what
The babe Orestes? Why didst render not
Back unto us, the children of the dead,
Our father's portion? Must thou heap thy bed
With gold of murdered men, to buy to thee
Thy strange man's arms? Justice! Why is not he
Who cast Orestes out, cast out again?
Not slain for me whom doubly he hath slain,
In living death, more bitter than of old
My sister's? Nay, when all the tale is told
Of blood for blood, what murder shall we make,
I and Orestes, for our father's sake?

CLYTEMNESTRA

Aye, child; I know thy heart, from long ago.
Thou hast alway loved him best. 'Tis oft-time so:
One is her father's daughter, and one hot
To bear her mother's part. I blame thee not. . . .
Yet think not I am happy, child; nor flown
With pride now, in the deeds my hand hath done . . .
[*Seeing* ELECTRA *unsympathetic, she checks herself.*
  But thou art all untended, comfortless
Of body and wild of raiment; and thy stress
Of travail scarce yet ended! . . . Woe is me!
'Tis all as I have willed it. Bitterly
I wrought against him, to the last blind deep
Of bitterness. . . . Woe's me!

71

ELECTRA

               Fair days to weep,
When help is not! Or stay: though he lie cold
Long since, there lives another of thy fold
Far off; there might be pity for thy son?

CLYTEMNESTRA

I dare not! . . . Yes, I fear him. 'Tis mine own
Life, and not his, comes first. And rumour saith
His heart yet rages for his father's death.

ELECTRA

Why dost thou keep thine husband ever hot
Against me?

CLYTEMNESTRA

        'Tis his mood. And thou art not
So gentle, child!

ELECTRA

       My spirit is too sore!
Howbeit, from this day I will no more
Hate him.

CLYTEMNESTRA (*with a flash of hope*)
        O daughter!—Then, indeed, shall he,
I promise, never more be harsh to thee!

ELECTRA

He lieth in my house, as 'twere his own.
'Tis that hath made him proud.

CLYTEMNESTRA

           Nay, art thou flown
To strife again so quick, child?

72

ELECTRA

Well; I say
No more; long have I feared him, and alway
Shall fear him, even as now!

CLYTEMNESTRA

Nay, daughter, peace!
It bringeth little profit, speech like this . . .
Why didst thou call me hither?

ELECTRA

It reached thee,
My word that a man-child is born to me?
Do thou make offering for me—for the rite
I know not—as is meet on the tenth night.
I cannot; I have borne no child till now.

CLYTEMNESTRA

Who tended thee? 'Tis she should make the vow.

ELECTRA

None tended me. Alone I bare my child.

CLYTEMNESTRA

What, is thy cot so friendless? And this wild
So far from aid?

ELECTRA

Who seeks for friendship sake
A beggar's house?

CLYTEMNESTRA

I will go in, and make
Due worship for thy child, the Peace-bringer.
To all thy need I would be minister.

73

Then to my lord, where by the meadow side
He prays the woodland nymphs.

                  Ye handmaids, guide
My chariot to the stall, and when ye guess
The rite draws near its end, in readiness
Be here again. Then to my lord! . . . I owe
My lord this gladness, too.

[*The Attendants depart;* CLYTEMNESTRA, *left alone, proceeds
  to enter the house.*

ELECTRA
             Welcome below
My narrow roof! But have a care withal,
A grime of smoke lies deep upon the wall.
Soil not thy robe! . . .

            Not far now shall it be,
The sacrifice God asks of me and thee.
The bread of Death is broken, and the knife
Lifted again that drank the Wild Bull's life:
And on his breast . . . Ha, Mother, hast slept well
Aforetime? Thou shalt lie with him in Hell.
That grace I give to cheer thee on thy road;
Give thou to me—peace from my father's blood!

[*She follows her mother into the house.*

CHORUS
Lo, the returns of wrong.
  The wind as a changèd thing
Whispereth overhead
Of one that of old lay dead
In the water lapping long:
  My King, O my King!

A cry in the rafters then
  Rang, and the marble dome:

74

" Mercy of God, not thou
" Woman! To slay me now,
" After the harvests ten
    " Now, at the last, come home!"

Oh, Fate shall turn as the tide,
    Turn, with a doom of tears
For the flying heart too fond;
A doom for the broken bond.
She hailed him there in his pride,
    Home from the perilous years.

In the heart of his wallèd lands,
    In the Giants' cloud-capt ring;
Herself, none other, laid
The hone to the axe's blade;
She lifted it in her hands,
    The woman, and slew her king.

Woe upon spouse and spouse,
    Whatso of evil sway
Held her in that distress!
Even as a lioness
Breaketh the woodland boughs
    Starving, she wrought her way.

                VOICE OF CLYTEMNESTRA
O Children, Children; in the name of God,
    Slay not your mother!

                    A WOMAN
                        Did ye hear a cry
Under the rafters?

                        75

                                                    357

ANOTHER

I weep too, yea, I;
Down on the mother's heart the child hath trod!
[*A death-cry from within.*

ANOTHER

God bringeth Justice in his own slow tide.
   Aye, cruel is thy doom; but thy deeds done
   Evil, thou piteous woman, and on one
      Whose sleep was by thy side!
[*The door bursts open, and* ORESTES *and* ELECTRA *come forth
in disorder. Attendants bring out the bodies of* CLYTEM-
NESTRA *and* AEGISTHUS.

LEADER

Lo, yonder, in their mother's new-spilt gore
Red-garmented and ghastly, from the door
They reel. . . . O horrible! Was it agony
Like this, she boded in her last wild cry?
There lives no seed of man calamitous,
Nor hath lived, like this seed of Tantalus.

ORESTES

O Dark of the Earth, O God,
   Thou to whom all is plain;
Look on my sin, my blood,
   This horror of dead things twain:
Gathered as one they lie
Slain; and the slayer was I,
   I, to pay for my pain!

ELECTRA

Let tear rain upon tear,
   Brother: but mine is the blame.

76

A fire stood over her,
　And out of the fire I came,
I, in my misery. . . .
And I was the child at her knee.
　'Mother' I named her name.

Chorus

Alas for Fate, for the Fate of thee,
O Mother, Mother of Misery:
And Misery, lo, hath turned again,
To slay thee, Misery and more,
Even in the fruit thy body bore.
Yet hast thou Justice, Justice plain,
　For a sire's blood spilt of yore!

Orestes

Apollo, alas for the hymn
　Thou sangest, as hope in mine ear!
The Song was of Justice dim,
　But the Deed is anguish clear;
And the Gift, long nights of fear,
　Of blood and of wandering,
　Where cometh no Greek thing.
Nor sight, nor sound on the air.
Yea, and beyond, beyond,
　Roaming—what rest is there?
Who shall break bread with me?
Who, that is clean, shall see
And hate not the blood-red hand,
　His mother's murderer?

Electra

And I? What clime shall hold
　My evil, or roof it above?

77

I cried for dancing of old,
   I cried in my heart for love:
What dancing waiteth me now?
What love that shall kiss my brow
   Nor blench at the brand thereof?

CHORUS

Back, back, in the wind and rain
Thy driven spirit wheeleth again.
Now is thine heart made clean within
That was dark of old and murder-fraught.
But, lo, thy brother; what hast thou wrought . . .
Yea, though I love thee . . . what woe, what sin,
   On him, who willed it not!

ORESTES

Saw'st thou her raiment there,
   Sister, there in the blood?
   She drew it back as she stood,
She opened her bosom bare,
   She bent her knees to the earth,
   The knees that bent in my birth . . .
And I . . . Oh, her hair, her hair . . .
[*He breaks into inarticulate weeping.*

CHORUS

Oh, thou didst walk in agony,
Hearing thy mother's cry, the cry
Of wordless wailing, well know I.

ELECTRA

She stretched her hand to my cheek,
   And there brake from her lips a moan;
   "Mercy, my child, my own!"

78

Her hand clung to my cheek;
Clung, and my arm was weak;
   And the sword fell and was gone.

CHORUS

Unhappy woman, could thine eye
Look on the blood, and see her lie,
Thy mother, where she turned to die?

ORESTES

I lifted over mine eyes
   My mantle: blinded I smote,
As one smiteth a sacrifice;
   And the sword found her throat.

ELECTRA

I gave thee the sign and the word;
I touched with mine hand thy sword.

LEADER

Dire is the grief ye have wrought.

ORESTES

Sister, touch her again:
   Oh, veil the body of her;
   Shed on her raiment fair,
And close that death-red stain.
   —Mother! And didst thou bear,
Bear in thy bitter pain,
      To life, thy murderer?

[*The two kneel over the body of* CLYTEMNESTRA, *and cover
her with raiment.*

79

ELECTRA

On her that I loved of yore,
　　Robe upon robe I cast:
On her that I hated sore.

CHORUS

O House that hath hated sore,
　　Behold thy peace at the last!

LEADER

Ha, see: above the roof-tree high
　　There shineth . . . Is some spirit there
　　Of earth or heaven? That thin air
Was never trod by things that die!
　　What bodes it now that forth they fare,
　　To men revealèd visibly?

[*There appears in the air a vision of* CASTOR *and* POLY-
DEUCES. *The mortals kneel or veil their faces.*

CASTOR

Thou Agamemnon's Son, give ear! 'Tis we,
Castor and Polydeuces, call to thee,
God's Horsemen and thy mother's brethren twain.
An Argive ship, spent with the toiling main,
We bore but now to peace, and, here withal
Being come, have seen thy mother's bloody fall,
Our sister's. Righteous is her doom this day,
But not thy deed. And Phoebus, Phoebus . . . Nay;
He is my lord; therefore I hold my peace.
Yet though in light he dwell, no light was this
He showed to thee, but darkness! Which do thou
Endure, as man must, chafing not. And now
Fare forth where Zeus and Fate have laid thy life.
　　The maid Electra thou shalt give for wife

80

To Pylades; then turn thy head and flee
From Argos' land. 'Tis never more for thee
To tread this earth where thy dead mother lies.
And, lo, in the air her Spirits, bloodhound eyes,
Most horrible yet Godlike, hard at heel
Following shall scourge thee as a burning wheel,
Speed-maddened. Seek thou straight Athena's land,
And round her awful image clasp thine hand,
Praying: and she will fence them back, though hot
With flickering serpents, that they touch thee not,
Holding above thy brow her gorgon shield.
   There is a hill in Athens, Ares' field,
Where first for that first death by Ares done
On Halirrhothius, Poseidon's son,
Who wronged his daughter, the great Gods of yore
Held judgment: and true judgments evermore
Flow from that Hill, trusted of man and God.
There shalt thou stand arraignèd of this blood;
And of those judges half shall lay on thee
Death, and half pardon; so shalt thou go free.
For Phoebus in that hour, who bade thee shed
Thy mother's blood, shall take on his own head
The stain thereof. And ever from that strife
The law shall hold, that when, for death or life
Of one pursued, men's voices equal stand,
Then Mercy conquereth.—But for thee, the band
Of Spirits dread, down, down, in very wrath,
Shall sink beside that Hill, making their path
Through a dim chasm, the which shall aye be trod
By reverent feet, where men may speak with God.
But thou forgotten and far off shalt dwell,
By great Alpheüs' waters, in a dell
Of Arcady, where that gray Wolf-God's wall
Stands holy. And thy dwelling men shall call

81

Orestes' Town. So much to thee be spoke.
But this dead man, Aegisthus, all the folk
Shall bear to burial in a high green grave
Of Argos. For thy mother, she shall have
Her tomb from Menelaus, who hath come
This day, at last, to Argos, bearing home
Helen. From Egypt comes she, and the hall
Of Proteus, and in Troy hath ne'er at all
Set foot. 'Twas but a wraith of Helen, sent
By Zeus to make much wrath and ravishment.

So forth for home, bearing the virgin bride,
Let Pylades make speed, and lead beside
Thy once-named brother, and with golden store
Stablish his house far off on Phocis' shore.

Up, gird thee now to the steep Isthmian way,
Seeking Athena's blessèd rock; one day,
Thy doom of blood fulfilled and this long stress
Of penance past, thou shalt have happiness.

LEADER (*looking up*)

Is it for us, O Seed of Zeus,
　　To speak and hear your words again?
CASTOR.　　Speak: of this blood ye bear no stain.
ELECTRA. I also, sons of Tyndareus,

My kinsmen; may my word be said?
CASTOR.　　Speak: on Apollo's head we lay
　　The bloody doings of this day.
LEADER. Ye Gods, ye brethren of the dead,

Why held ye not the deathly herd
　　Of Furies back from off this home?

82

CASTOR.   There came but that which needs must come
              By ancient Fate and that dark word
              That rang from Phoebus in his mood.

ELECTRA.   And what should Phoebus seek with me,
              Or all God's oracles that be,
              That I must bear my mother's blood?

CASTOR.   Thy hand was as thy brother's hand,
              Thy doom shall be as his.   One stain,
              From dim forefathers on the twain
              Lighting, hath sapped your hearts as sand.

ORESTES.   After so long, sister, to see
(who has never   And hold thee, and then part, then part,
raised his head
nor spoken to   By all that chained thee to my heart
the Gods).   Forsaken, and forsaking thee!

CASTOR.   Husband and house are hers.   She bears
              No bitter judgment, save to go
              Exiled from Argos.

ELECTRA.   And what woe,
              What tears are like an exile's tears?

ORESTES.   Exiled and more am I; impure,
              A murderer in a stranger's hand!

CASTOR.   Fear not.   There dwells in Pallas' land
              All holiness.   Till then endure!

[ORESTES *and* ELECTRA *embrace.*

ORESTES.   Aye, closer; clasp my body well,
              And let thy sorrow loose, and shed,
              As o'er the grave of one new dead,
              Dead evermore, thy last farewell!

[*A sound of weeping.*

CASTOR.   Alas, what would ye? For that cry
          Ourselves and all the sons of heaven
          Have pity. Yea, our peace is riven
          By the strange pain of these that die.

ORESTES. No more to see thee! ELECTRA. Nor thy
               breath
          Be near my face! ORESTES. Ah, so it ends.
ELECTRA.   Farewell, dear Argos. All ye friends,
          Farewell! ORESTES. O faithful unto death,
          Thou goest? ELECTRA. Aye, I pass from you,
          Soft-eyed at last. ORESTES. Go, Pylades,
          And God go with you! Take in peace
          Thy bride Electra, and be true.
[ELECTRA *and* PYLADES *depart to the left.*

CASTOR

          Their troth shall fill their hearts.—But on:
          Dread feet are near thee, hounds of prey,
          Snake-handed, midnight-visaged, yea,
          And bitter pains their fruit! Begone!
[ORESTES *departs to the right.*

          But hark, the far Sicilian sea
          Calls, and a noise of men and ships
          That labour sunken to the lips
          In bitter billows; forth go we,

          Through the long leagues of fiery blue,
          With saving; not to souls unshriven;
          But whoso in his life hath striven
          To love things holy and be true,

84

Through toil and storm we guard him; we
Save, and he shall not die!—Therefore,
Oh, praise the lying man no more,
Nor with oath-breakers sail the sea:
Farewell, ye walkers on the shore
Of death!   A God hath counselled ye.

[CASTOR *and* POLYDEUCES *disappear.*

CHORUS

Farewell, farewell!—But he who can so fare,
And stumbleth not on mischief anywhere,
Blessèd on earth is he!

85

367

NOTES TO THE ELECTRA

THE chief characters in the play belong to one family, as is shown by the two genealogies:—

I.

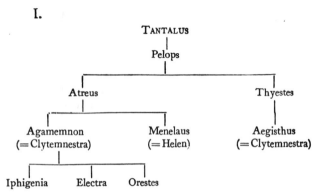

(Also, a sister of Agamemnon, name variously given, married Strophios, and was the mother of Pylades.)

II.

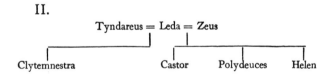

P. 11, l. 10, *Son of his father's foe.*—Both foe and brother. Atreus and Thyestes became enemies after the theft of the Golden Lamb. See pp. 52 ff.

P. 12, l. 34, *Must wed with me.*—In Aeschylus and Sophocles Electra is unmarried. This story of her peasant husband is found only in Euripides, but is not likely to have been wantonly invented by him. It was no doubt an existing legend—an ὦν λόγος, to use the phrase attributed

86

to Euripides in the *Frogs* (l. 1052). He may have chosen to adopt it for several reasons. First, to marry Electra to a peasant was a likely step for Aegisthus to take, since any child born to her afterwards would bear a stigma, calculated to damage him fatally as a pretender to the throne. Again, it seemed to explain the name "A-lektra" (as if from λεκτρὸν, "bed;" cf. Schol. *Orestes*, 71, Soph. *El.* 962, *Ant.* 917) more pointedly than the commoner version. And it helps in the working out of Electra's character (cf. pp. 19, 23, etc.). Also it gives an opportunity of introducing the fine character of the peasant. He is an *Αὐτουργός*, literally "self-worker," a man who works his own land, far from the city, neither a slave nor a slave-master; "the men," as Euripides says in the *Orestes* (920), "who alone save a nation." (Cf. *Bac.*, p. 115 foot, and below, p. 31, ll.367–390.) As Euripides became more and more alienated from the town democracy he tended, like Tolstoy and others, to idealise the workers of the soil.

P. 13, l. 62, *Children to our enemy.*—Cf. 626. Soph. *El.* 589. They do not seem to be in existence at the time of the play.

Pp. 13–14.—Electra's first two speeches are admirable as expositions of her character—the morbid nursing of hatred as a duty, the deliberate posing, the impulsiveness, the quick response to kindness.

P. 14, l. 82, *Pylades.*—Pylades is a *persona muta* both here and in Sophocles' *Electra*, a fixed traditional figure, possessing no quality but devotion to Orestes. In Aeschylus' *Libation-Bearers* he speaks only once, with tremendous effect, at the crisis of the play, to rebuke Orestes when his heart fails him. In the *Iphigenia in Tauris*, however, and still more in the *Orestes*, he is a fully studied character.

P. 17, l. 151, *A swan crying alone.*—Cf. *Bacchae*, l. 1365, " As yearns the milk-white swan when old swans die."

P. 18, ll. 169 ff., *The Watcher hath cried this day.*—Hera was an old " Pelasgian " goddess, whose worship was kept in part a mystery from the invading Achaeans or Dorians. There seems to have been a priest born " of the ancient folk," i.e. a Pelasgian or aboriginal Mycenaean, who, by some secret lore—probably some ancient and superseded method of calculating the year—knew when Hera's festival was due, and walked round the country three days before-hand to announce it. He drank " the milk of the flock " and avoided wine, either from some religious taboo, or because he represented the religion of the milk-drinking mountain shepherds.

P. 20, ll. 220 ff.—Observe Electra's cowardice when surprised; contrast her courage, p. 51, when sending Orestes off, and again her quick drop to despair when the news does not come soon enough.

P. 23, ll. 247 ff., *I am a wife. . . . O better dead!*—Rather ungenerous, when compared with her words on p. 13. (Cf. also her words on pp. 30 and 33.) But she feels this herself, almost immediately. Orestes naturally takes her to mean that her husband is one of Aegisthus' friends. This would have ruined his plot. (Cf. above, p. 15, l. 98.)

P. 29, l. 312, *Castor.*—I know no other mention of Electra's betrothal to Castor. He was her kinsman: see below on l. 990.

Pp. 28–29, ll. 300–337.—In this wonderful outbreak, observe the mixture of all sorts of personal resentments and jealousies with the devotion of the lonely woman to her father and her brother. " So men say," is an interesting touch; perhaps conscience tells her midway that she does not quite believe what she is saying. So is the self-conscious recognition of her "bitter burning brain" that interprets all things in a sort of distortion.—Observe, too, how instinctively she turns to the peasant for sympathy in the strain of her emotion. It is his entrance, perhaps, which prevents Orestes from being swept away and revealing himself. The peasant's courage towards two armed men is striking, as well as his courtesy and his sanity. He is the one character in the play not somehow tainted with blood-madness.

P. 33, ll. 403, 409.—Why does Electra send her husband to the Old Man? Not, I think, really for want of the food. It would have been easier to borrow (p. 19, l. 191) from the Chorus; and, besides, what the peasant says is no doubt true, that, if she liked, she could find "many a pleasant thing" in the house. I think she sends for the Old Man because he is the only person who would know Orestes (p. 27, l. 285). She is already, like the Leader (p. 32, l. 401), excited by hopes which she will not confess. This reading makes the next scene clearer also.

Pp. 34–35, ll. 432–487, *Oh, for the Ships of Troy.*—The two main Choric songs of this play are markedly what Aristotle calls ἐμβόλιμα, "things thrown in." They have no effect upon the action, and form little more than musical "relief." Not that they are positively irrelevant. Agamemnon is in our minds all through the play, and Agamemnon's glory is of course enhanced by the mention of Troy and the praises of his subordinate king, Achilles.

Thetis, the Nereid, or sea-maiden, was won to wife by Peleus. (He wrestled with her on the seashore, and never loosed hold, though she turned into divers strange beings— a lion, and fire, and water, and sea-beasts.) She bore him Achilles, and then, unable permanently to live with a mortal, went back beneath the sea.   When Achilles was about to sail to Troy, she and her sister Nereids brought him divine armour, and guided his ships across the Aegean.   The designs on Achilles' armour, as on Heracles' shield, form a fairly common topic of poetry.

The descriptions of the designs are mostly clear.   Perseus with the Gorgon's head, guided by Hermês; the Sun on a winged chariot, and stars about him; two Sphinxes, holding as victims the men who had failed to answer the riddles which they sang; and, on the breastplate, the Chimaera attacking Bellerophon's winged horse, Pêgasus.   The name Pêgasus suggested to a Greek πηγή, "fountain;" and the great spring of Pirênê, near Corinth, was made by Pêgasus stamping on the rock.

Pp. 36–51.—The Old Man, like other old family servants in Euripides—the extreme case is in the *Ion*—is absolutely and even morbidly devoted to his masters.   Delightful in this first scene, he becomes a little horrible in the next where they plot the murders; not only ferocious himself, but, what seems worse, inclined to pet and enjoy the bloodthirstiness of his "little mistress."

Pp. 36–38, ll. 510–545.—The Signs of Orestes.   This scene, I think, has been greatly misunderstood by critics.   In Aeschylus' *Libation-Bearers*, which deals with the same subject as the *Electra*, the scene is at Agamemnon's tomb.   Orestes lays his tress there in the prologue.   Electra comes bringing libations, sees the hair, compares it with her own, finds that it is similar "wing for wing" (ὁμόπτερος—the same word as here), and guesses that it belongs to Orestes. She then measures the footprints, and finds one that is like her own, one not; evidently Orestes and a fellow-traveller! Orestes enters and announces himself; she refuses to believe, until he shows her a "woven thing," perhaps the robe

90

which he is wearing, which she recognises as the work of her own hand.

The same signs, described in one case by the same peculiar word, occur here. The Old Man mentions one after the other, and Electra refutes or rejects them. It has been thought therefore that this scene was meant as an attack— a very weak and undignified attack—on Euripides' great master. No parallel for such an artistically ruinous proceeding is quoted from any Greek tragedy. And, apart from the improbability *a priori*, I do not think it even possible to read the scene in this sense. To my mind, Electra here rejects the signs not from reason, but from a sort of nervous terror. She dares not believe that Orestes has come; because, if it prove otherwise, the disappointment will be so terrible. As to both signs, the lock of hair and the footprints, her arguments may be good; but observe that she is afraid to make the comparison at all. And as to the footprint, she says there cannot be one, when the Old Man has just seen it! And, anyhow, she will not go to look. Similarly as to the robe, she does her best to deny that she ever wove it, though she and the Old Man both remember it perfectly. She is fighting tremulously, with all her flagging strength, against the thing she longs for. The whole point of the scene requires that one ray of hope after another should be shown to Electra, and that she should passionately, blindly, reject them all. That is what Euripides wanted the signs for.

But why, it may be asked, did he adopt Aeschylus' signs, and even his peculiar word? Because, whatever we say about Aeschylus, these signs were a canonical part of the story by the time Euripides wrote. Every one who knew the story of Orestes' return at all, knew of the hair and the footprint. Aristophanes in the *Clouds* (534 ff.) uses them proverbially, when he speaks of his comedy " recognising its brother's tress." It would have been frivolous to invent new ones. As a matter of fact, it seems certain that the signs are older than Aeschylus; neither they nor the word ὁμόπτερος particularly suit Aeschylus' purpose. (Cf. Dr. Verrall's introduction to the *Libation-Bearers.*) They probably come from the old lyric poet, Stesichorus.

P. 47, l. 652, *New-mothered of a Man-Child.*—Her true Man-Child, the Avenger whom they had sought to rob her of! This pitiless plan was suggested apparently by the sacrifice to the Nymphs (p. 45). "Weep my babe's low station" is of course ironical. The babe would set a seal on Electra's degradation to the peasant class, and so end the blood-feud, as far as she was concerned. Clytemnestra, longing for peace, must rejoice in Electra's degradation. Yet she has motherly feelings too, and in fact hardly knows what to think or do till she can consult Aegisthus (p. 74). Electra, it would seem, actually calculates upon these feelings, while despising them.

P. 49, l. 669, *If but some man will guide me.*—A suggestion of the irresolution or melancholia that beset Orestes afterwards, alternating with furious action. (Cf. Aeschylus' *Libation-Bearers*, Euripides' *Andromache* and *Orestes.*)

P. 49, l. 671, *Zeus of my sires*, etc.—In this invocation, short and comparatively restrained, one can see perhaps an effect of Aeschylus' play. In the *Libation-Bearers* the invocation of Agamemnon comprises 200 lines of extraordinarily eloquent poetry.

P. 52 ff., ll. 699 ff.—The Golden Lamb. The theft of the Golden Lamb is treated as a story of the First Sin, after which all the world was changed and became the poor place that it now is. It was at least the First Sin in the blood-feud of this drama.

92

The story is not explicitly told. Apparently the magic lamb was brought by Pan from the gods, and given to Atreus as a special grace and a sign that he was the true king. His younger brother, Thyestes, helped by Atreus' wife, stole it and claimed to be king himself. So good was turned into evil, and love into hatred, and the stars shaken in their courses.

[It is rather curious that the Lamb should have such a special effect upon the heavens and the weather. It is the same in Plato (*Polit.* 268 ff.), and more definitely so in the treatise *De Astrologia*, attributed to Lucian, which says that the Golden Lamb is the constellation Aries, "The Ram." Hugo Winckler (*Weltanschauung des alten Orients*, pp. 30, 31) suggests that the story is a piece of Babylonian astronomy misunderstood. It seems that the vernal equinox, which is now moving from the Ram into the Fish, was in the ninth and eighth centuries B.C. moving from the Bull into the Ram. Now the Bull, Marduk, was the special god of Babylon, and the time when he yielded his place to the Ram was also, as a matter of fact, the time of the decline of Babylon. The gradual advance of the Ram not only upset the calendar, and made all the seasons wrong; but seemed, since it coincided with the fall of the Great City, to upset the world in general! Of course Euripides probably knew nothing of this. He was apparently attracted to the Golden Lamb merely by the quaint beauty of the story.]

P. 54, l. 746, *Thy brethren even now.*—Castor and Polydeuces, who were received into the stars after their death. See below, on l. 990.

P. 55, l. 757, *That answer bids me die.*—Why? Because Orestes, if he won at all, would win by a surprise attack, and would send news instantly. A prolonged conflict, without a message, would mean that Orestes and Pylades were being overpowered. Of course she is wildly impatient.

P. 55, l. 765, *Who art thou? I mistrust thee.*—Just as she mistrusted the Old Man's signs. See note, p. 90.

P. 56 ff., ll. 774 ff.—Messenger's Speech. This speech, though swift and vivid, is less moving and also less sympathetic than most of the Messengers' Speeches. Less moving, because the slaying of Aegisthus has little moral interest; it is merely a daring and dangerous exploit. Less sympathetic, because even here, in the first and comparatively blameless step of the blood-vengeance, Euripides makes us feel the treacherous side of it. A δολοφονία, a "slaying by guile," even at its best, remains rather an ugly thing.

P. 57, l. 793, *Then quickly spake Orestes.*—If Orestes had washed with Aegisthus, he would have become his *xenos*, or guest, as much as if he had eaten his bread and salt. In that case the slaying would have been definitely a crime, a dishonourable act. Also, Aegisthus would have had the right to ask his name.—The unsuspiciousness of Aegisthus is partly natural; it was not thus, alone and unarmed, that he expected Orestes to stand before him. Partly it seems like a heaven-sent blindness. Even the omens do not warn him, though no doubt in a moment more they would have done so.

P. 60, l. 878, *With guile he hath slain.*—So the MSS. The Chorus have already a faint feeling, quickly suppressed, that there may be another side to Orestes' action. Most editors alter the text to mean " He hath slain these guileful ones."

P. 61, l. 900, *It shames me, yet God knows I hunger sore.*— To treat the dead with respect was one of the special marks of a Greek as opposed to a barbarian. It is possible that the

94

body of Aegisthus might legitimately have been refused burial, or even nailed on a cross as Orestes in a moment of excitement suggests. But to insult him lying dead would be a shock to all Greek feeling. (" Unholy is the voice of loud thanksgiving over slaughtered men," *Odyssey* xxii. 412.) Any excess of this kind, any violence towards the helpless, was apt to rouse " The sleeping wrath of the world." There was a Greek proverb, " Even an injured dog has his Erinys " —i.e. his unseen guardian or avenger. It is interesting, though not surprising, to hear that men had little love for Electra. The wonderful speech that follows, though to a conventional Greek perhaps the most outrageous thing of which she is guilty, shows best the inherent nobility of her character before years of misery had " killed her soul within."

P. 63, ll. 928 f., *Being in falseness one*, etc.—The Greek here is very obscure and almost certainly corrupt.

P. 64, l. 964, *'Tis my mother comes.*—The reaction has already begun in Orestes. In the excitement and danger of killing his enemy he has shown coolness and courage, but now a work lies before him vastly more horrible, a little more treacherous, and with no element of daring to redeem it. Electra, on the other hand, has done nothing yet; she has merely tried, not very successfully, to revile the dead body, and her hate is unsatisfied. Besides, one sees all through the play that Aegisthus was a kind of odious stranger to her; it was the woman, her mother, who came close to her and whom she really hated.

P. 66, l. 979, *Was it some fiend of Hell?*—The likeness to *Hamlet* is obvious. (" The spirit that I have seen May be the Devil." End of Act II.)

P. 66, l. 983, *How shall it be then, the same stealthy blow?* . . .—He means, I think, " the same as that with which I

95

have already murdered an unsuspecting man to-day," but Electra for her own purposes misinterprets him.

P. 67, l. 990, *God's horsemen, stars without a stain.*— Cf. above, ll. 312, 746. Castor and Polydeuces were sons of Zeus and Leda, brothers of Helen, and half-brothers of Clytemnestra, whose father was the mortal Tyndareus. They lived as knights without reproach, and afterwards became stars and demigods. The story is told that originally Castor was mortal and Polydeuces immortal; but when Castor was fatally wounded Polydeuces prayed that he might be allowed to give him half his immortality. The prayer was granted; and the two live as immortals, yet, in some mysterious way, knowing the taste of death. Unlike the common sinners and punishers of the rest of the play, these Heroes find their " glory " in saving men from peril and suffering, especially at sea, where they appear as the globes of light, called St. Elmo's fire, upon masts and yards.

Pp. 67 ff., ll. 998 ff.—Clytemnestra. " And what sort of woman is this doomed and ' evil ' Queen? We know the majestic murderess of Aeschylus, so strong as to be actually beautiful, so fearless and unrepentant that one almost feels her to be right. One can imagine also another figure that would be theatrically effective—a ' sympathetic ' sinner, beautiful and penitent, eager to redeem her sin by self-sacrifice. But Euripides gives us neither. Perhaps he believed in neither. It is a piteous and most real character that we have here, in this sad middle-aged woman, whose first words are an apology; controlling quickly her old fires, anxious to be as little hated as possible. She would even atone, one feels, if there were any safe way of atonement; but the consequences of her old actions are holding her, and she is bound to persist. . . . In her long speech it is scarcely to Electra that she is chiefly speaking; it is to the Chorus,

96

perhaps to her own bondmaids; to any or all of the people whose shrinking so frets her." (*Independent Review, l.c.*)

P. 68, l. 1011, *Cast his child away.*—The Greek fleet assembled for Troy was held by contrary winds at Aulis, in the Straits of Euboea, and the whole expedition was in danger of breaking up. The prophets demanded a human sacrifice, and Agamemnon gave his own daughter, Iphigenia. He induced Clytemnestra to send her to him, by the pretext that Achilles had asked for her in marriage.

P. 69, l. 1046, *Which led me to the men he hated.*—It made Clytemnestra's crime worse, that her accomplice was the blood-foe.

Pp. 69–71.—As elsewhere in Euripides, these two speeches leave the matter undecided. He does not attempt to argue the case out. He gives us a flash of light, as it were, upon Clytemnestra's mind and then upon Electra's. Each believes what she is saying, and neither understands the whole truth. It is clear that Clytemnestra, being left for ten tears utterly alone, and having perhaps something of Helen's temperament about her, naturally fell in love with the Lord of a neighbouring castle; and having once committed herself had no way of saving her life except by killing her husband, and afterwards either killing or keeping strict watch upon Orestes and Electra. Aegisthus, of course, was deliberately plotting to carry out his blood-feud and to win a great kingdom.

P. 75, l. 1156, *For the flying heart too fond.*—The text is doubtful, but this seems to be the literal translation, and the reference to Clytemnestra is intelligible enough.

P. 75, l. 1157, *The giants' cloud-capt ring.*—The great walls of Mycenae, built by the Cyclopes; cf. *Trojan Women,*

97

l. 1088, "Where the towers of the giants shine O'er Argos cloudily."

P. 78, l. 1201, *Back, back in the wind and rain.*—The only explicit moral judgment of the Chorus; cf. note on l. 878.

P. 79, l. 1225, *I touched with mine hand thy sword.*—i.e. Electra dropped her own sword in horror, then in a revulsion of feeling laid her hand upon Orestes' sword—out of generosity, that he might not bear his guilt alone.

P. 80, l. 1241, *An Argive ship.*—This may have been the ship of Menelaus, which was brought to Argos by Castor and Polydeuces, see l. 1278, *Helena* 1663. The ships labouring in the " Sicilian sea " (p. 84, l. 1347) must have suggested to the audience the ships of the great expedition against Sicily, then drawing near to its destruction. The Athenian fleet was destroyed early in September 413 B.C.: this play was probably produced in the spring of the same year, at which time the last reinforcements were being sent out.

P. 80, l. 1249.—Marriage of Pylades and Electra. A good example of the essentially historic nature of Greek tragedy. No one would have invented a marriage between Electra and Pylades for the purposes of this play. It is even a little disturbing. But it is here, because it was a fixed fact in the tradition (cf. *Iphigenia in Tauris*, l. 915 ff.), and could not be ignored. Doubtless there were people living who claimed descent from Pylades and Electra.

P. 81, l. 1253, *Scourge thee as a burning wheel.*—At certain feasts a big wheel soaked in some inflammable resin or tar was set fire to and rolled down a mountain.

P. 81, l. 1258, *There is a hill in Athens.*—The great fame of the Areopagus as a tribunal for manslaying (see Aeschylus'

98

NOTES

Eumenides) cannot have been due merely to its incorrupti-
bility. Hardly any Athenian tribunal was corruptible. But
the Areopagus in very ancient times seems to have superseded
the early systems of "blood-feud" or "blood-debt" by a
humane and rational system of law, taking account of
intention, provocation, and the varying degrees of guilt.
The Erinyes, being the old "Pelasgian" avengers of blood,
now superseded, have their dwelling in a cavern underneath
the Areopagus.

P. 82, ll. 1276 ff.—The graves of Aegisthus and Clytemnestra actually existed in Argos (Paus. ii. 16, 7). They
form, so to speak, the concrete material fact round which the
legend of this play circles (cf. Ridgeway in *Hellenic Journal*,
xxiv. p. xxxix.).

P. 82, l. 1280.—Helen. The story here adumbrated is
taken from Stesichorus, and forms the plot of Euripides'
play *Helena* (cf. Herodotus, ii. 113 ff.).

P. 82, l. 1295, *I also, sons of Tyndareus.*—Observe that
Electra claims the gods as cousins (cf. p. 29, l. 313), addressing
them by the name of their mortal father. The Chorus
has called them "sons of Zeus." In the same spirit she
faces the gods, complains, and even argues, while Orestes
never raises his eyes to them.

P. 82, l. 1300.—Furies: literally Kêres. The death-
spirits that flutter over our heads, as Homer says, "innumerable, whom no man can fly nor hide from."

P. 84, l. 1329, *Yea, our peace is riven by the strange pain
of these that die.*—Cf. the attitude of Artemis at the end of
the *Hippolytus*. Sometimes Euripides introduces gods whose
peace is not riven, but then they are always hateful. (Cf.

99

Aphrodite in the *Hippolytus*, Dionysus in the *Bacchae*, Athena in the *Trojan Women*.)

P. 84, l. 1336, *O faithful unto death.*—This is the last word we hear of Electra, and it is interesting. With all her unlovely qualities it remains true that she was faithful—faithful to the dead and the absent, and to what she looked upon as a fearful duty.

Additional Note on the presence of the Argive women during the plot against the King and Queen. (Cf. especially p. 26, l. 272, "These women hear us.")—It would seem to us almost mad to speak so freely before the women. But one must observe: 1. Stasis, or civil enmity, ran very high in Greece, and these women were of the party that hated Aegisthus. 2. There runs all through Euripides a very strong conception of the cohesiveness of women, their secretiveness, and their faithfulness to one another. Medea, Iphigenia, and Creusa, for instance, trust their women friends with secrets involving life and death, and the secrets are kept. On the other hand, when a man—Xuthus in the *Ion*—tells the Chorus women a secret, they promptly and with great courage betray him. Aristophanes leaves the same impression; and so do many incidents in Greek history. Cf. the murders plotted by the Athenian women (Hdt. v. 87), and both by and against the Lemnian women (Hdt. vi. 138). The subject is a large one, but I would observe: 1. Athenian women were kept as a rule very much together, and apart from men. 2. At the time of the great invasions the women of a community must often have been of different race from the men; and this may have started a tradition of behaviour. 3. Members of a subject (or disaffected) nation have generally this cohesiveness: in Ireland, Poland, and parts of Turkey

100

the details of a political crime will, it is said, be known to a whole country side, but not a whisper come to the authorities.

Of course the mere mechanical fact that the Chorus had to be present on the stage counts for something. It saved the dramatist trouble to make his heroine confide in the Chorus. But I do not think Euripides would have used this situation so often unless it had seemed to him both true to life and dramatically interesting.

101

EURIPIDES

THE BACCHAE

TRANSLATED INTO ENGLISH RHYMING VERSE

WITH EXPLANATORY NOTES BY

GILBERT MURRAY
LL.D., D.Litt.
REGIUS PROFESSOR OF GREEK IN THE
UNIVERSITY OF OXFORD

LONDON: GEORGE ALLEN & UNWIN LTD
NEW YORK: LONGMANS, GREEN & CO

CHARACTERS IN THE PLAY

Dionŷsus, the God : *son of Zeus and of the Theban princess Semelê.*

Cadmus, *formerly King of Thebes, father of Semelê.*

Pentheus, *King of Thebes, son of Echîon, grandson of Cadmus.*

Agâvê, *daughter of Cadmus, mother of Pentheus.*

Teiresias, *an aged Theban prophet.*

A Soldier of Pentheus' Guard.

Two Messengers.

A Chorus of Inspired Damsels, *following Dionysus from the East.*

"*The play was first produced after the death of Euripides by his son, who bore the same name, together with the 'Iphigenîa in Aulis' and the 'Alcmaeon,' probably in the year* 405 b.c."

THE BACCHAE

The background represents the front of the Castle of PENTHEUS, *King of Thebes. At one side is visible the sacred Tomb of Semelê, a little enclosure overgrown with wild vines, with a cleft in the rocky floor of it from which there issues at times steam or smoke. The God* DIONYSUS *is discovered alone.*

DIONYSUS

Behold, God's Son is come unto this land
Of Thebes, even I, Dionysus, whom the brand
Of heaven's hot splendour lit to life, when she
Who bore me, Cadmus' daughter Semelê,
Died here. So, changed in shape from God to man,
I walk again by Dircê's streams and scan
Ismênus' shore. There by the castle side
I see her place, the Tomb of the Lightning's Bride,

7

The wreck of smouldering chambers, and the great
Faint wreaths of fire undying—as the hate
Dies not, that Hera held for Semelê.

Aye, Cadmus hath done well; in purity
He keeps this place apart, inviolate,
His daughter's sanctuary; and I have set
My green and clustered vines to robe it round.

Far now behind me lies the golden ground
Of Lydian and of Phrygian; far away
The wide hot plains where Persian sunbeams play,
The Bactrian war-holds, and the storm-oppressed
Clime of the Mede, and Araby the Blest,
And Asia all, that by the salt sea lies
In proud embattled cities, motley-wise
Of Hellene and Barbarian interwrought;
And now I come to Hellas—having taught
All the world else my dances and my rite
Of mysteries, to show me in men's sight
Manifest God.
                    And first of Hellene lands
I cry this Thebes to waken; set her hands
To clasp my wand, mine ivied javelin,
And round her shoulders hang my wild fawn-skin.
For they have scorned me whom it least beseemed,
Semelê's sisters; mocked my birth, nor deemed
That Dionysus sprang from Dian seed.
My mother sinned, said they; and in her need,
With Cadmus plotting, cloaked her human shame
With the dread name of Zeus; for that the flame
From heaven consumed her, seeing she lied to God.

Thus must they vaunt; and therefore hath my rod
On them first fallen, and stung them forth wild-eyed
From empty chambers; the bare mountain side
Is made their home, and all their hearts are flame.

8

Yea, I have bound upon the necks of them
The harness of my rites.   And with them all
The seed of womankind from hut and hall
Of Thebes, hath this my magic goaded out.
And there, with the old King's daughters, in a rout
Confused, they make their dwelling-place between
The roofless rocks and shadowy pine trees green.
Thus shall this Thebes, how sore soe'er it smart,
Learn and forget not, till she crave her part
In mine adoring; thus must I speak clear
To save my mother's fame, and crown me here
As true God, born by Semelê to Zeus.

Now Cadmus yieldeth up his throne and use
Of royal honour to his daughter's son
Pentheus; who on my body hath begun
A war with God.   He thrusteth me away
From due drink-offering, and, when men pray,
My name entreats not.   Therefore on his own
Head and his people's shall my power be shown.
Then to another land, when all things here
Are well, must I fare onward, making clear
My godhead's might.   But should this Theban town
Essay with wrath and battle to drag down
My maids, lo, in their path myself shall be,
And maniac armies battled after me!
For this I veil my godhead with the wan
Form of the things that die, and walk as Man.

O Brood of Tmolus o'er the wide world flown,
O Lydian band, my chosen and mine own,
Damsels uplifted o'er the orient deep
To wander where I wander, and to sleep
Where I sleep; up, and wake the old sweet sound,
The clang that I and mystic Rhea found,

9

The Timbrel of the Mountain! Gather all
Thebes to your song round Pentheus' royal hall.
I seek my new-made worshippers, to guide
Their dances up Kithaeron's pine-clad side.

[*As he departs, there comes stealing in from the left a band of
fifteen Eastern Women, the light of the sunrise streaming
upon their long white robes and ivy-bound hair. They wear
fawn-skins over the robes, and carry some of them timbrels,
some pipes and other instruments. Many bear the thyrsus,
or sacred Wand, made of reed ringed with ivy. They enter
stealthily till they see that the place is empty, and then begin
their mystic song of worship.*

CHORUS

A Maiden

From Asia, from the dayspring that uprises,
  To Bromios ever glorying we came.
We laboured for our Lord in many guises;
We toiled, but the toil is as the prize is;
  Thou Mystery, we hail thee by thy name!

Another

Who lingers in the road? Who espies us?
  He shall hide him in his house nor be bold.
Let the heart keep silence that defies us;
For I sing this day to Dionysus
  The song that is appointed from of old.

All the Maidens

Oh, blessèd he in all wise,
  Who hath drunk the Living Fountain,
    Whose life no folly staineth,
      And his soul is near to God;

10

Whose sins are lifted, pall-wise,
　　As he worships on the Mountain,
　　And where Cybele ordaineth,
　　Our Mother, he has trod:

　　　　His head with ivy laden
　　　　　And his thyrsus tossing high,
　　　　　For our God he lifts his cry;
　　　" Up, O Bacchae, wife and maiden,
　　　　　Come, O ye Bacchae, come;
　　　Oh, bring the Joy-bestower,
　　　God-seed of God the Sower,
　　　Bring Bromios in his power
　　　　　From Phrygia's mountain dome;
　　　To street and town and tower,
　　　　　Oh, bring ye Bromios home!"

Whom erst in anguish lying
　　For an unborn life's desire,
　　As a dead thing in the Thunder
　　　His mother cast to earth;
For her heart was dying, dying,
　In the white heart of the fire;
　　Till Zeus, the Lord of Wonder,
　　Devised new lairs of birth;

　　　　Yea, his own flesh tore to hide him,
　　　　　And with clasps of bitter gold
　　　　　Did a secret son enfold,
　　　And the Queen knew not beside him;
　　　　　Till the perfect hour was there;
　　　Then a hornèd God was found,
　　　And a God with serpents crowned;

II

And for that are serpents wound
In the wands his maidens bear,
And the songs of serpents sound
In the mazes of their hair.

Some Maidens

All hail, O Thebes, thou nurse of Semelê!
With Semelê's wild ivy crown thy towers;
Oh, burst in bloom of wreathing bryony,
Berries and leaves and flowers;
Uplift the dark divine wand,
The oak-wand and the pine-wand,
And don thy fawn-skin, fringed in purity
With fleecy white, like ours.

Oh, cleanse thee in the wands' waving pride!
Yea, all men shall dance with us and pray,
When Bromios his companies shall guide
Hillward, ever hillward, where they stay,
The flock of the Believing,
The maids from loom and weaving
By the magic of his breath borne away.

Others

Hail thou, O Nurse of Zeus, O Caverned Haunt
Where fierce arms clanged to guard God's cradle
rare,
For thee of old some crested Corybant
First woke in Cretan air
The wild orb of our orgies,
Our Timbrel; and thy gorges
Rang with this strain; and blended Phrygian chant
And sweet keen pipes were there.

12

But the Timbrel, the Timbrel was another's,
  And away to Mother Rhea it must wend;
And to our holy singing from the Mother's
  The mad Satyrs carried it, to blend
      In the dancing and the cheer
      Of our third and perfect Year;
  And it serves Dionysus in the end!

A Maiden

O glad, glad on the mountains
  To swoon in the race outworn,
      When the holy fawn-skin clings,
      And all else sweeps away,
To the joy of the red quick fountains,
  The blood of the hill-goat torn,
      The glory of wild-beast ravenings,
          Where the hill-tops catch the day;
To the Phrygian, Lydian, mountains!
  'Tis Bromios leads the way.

Another Maiden

Then streams the earth with milk, yea, streams
With wine and nectar of the bee,
And through the air dim perfume steams
Of Syrian frankincense; and He,
Our leader, from his thyrsus spray
A torchlight tosses high and higher,
A torchlight like a beacon-fire,
To waken all that faint and stray;
  And sets them leaping as he sings,
  His tresses rippling to the sky,
  And deep beneath the Maenad cry
      His proud voice rings:
      " Come, O ye Bacchae, come ! "

13

All the Maidens

Hither, O fragrant of Tmolus the Golden,
    Come with the voice of timbrel and drum;
Let the cry of your joyance uplift and embolden
    The God of the joy-cry; O Bacchanals, come!
With pealing of pipes and with Phrygian clamour,
    On, where the vision of holiness thrills,
And the music climbs and the maddening glamour,
    With the wild White Maids, to the hills, to the hills!
Oh, then, like a colt as he runs by a river,
    A colt by his dam, when the heart of him sings,
With the keen limbs drawn and the fleet foot a-quiver,
    Away the Bacchanal springs!

[*Enter* TEIRESIAS. *He is an old man and blind, leaning upon
a staff and moving with slow stateliness, though wearing the
Ivy and the Bacchic fawn-skin.*

TEIRESIAS

Ho, there, who keeps the gate?—Go, summon me
Cadmus, Agênor's son, who crossed the sea
From Sidon and upreared this Theban hold.
Go, whosoe'er thou art.   See he be told
Teiresias seeketh him.   Himself will gauge
Mine errand, and the compact, age with age,
I vowed with him, grey hair with snow-white hair,
To deck the new God's thyrsus, and to wear
His fawn-skin, and with ivy crown our brows.

[*Enter* CADMUS *from the Castle.   He is even older than*
TEIRESIAS, *and wears the same attire.*

CADMUS

True friend!   I knew that voice of thine that flows
Like mellow wisdom from a fountain wise.
And, lo, I come prepared, in all the guise

14

And harness of this God.   Are we not told
His is the soul of that dead life of old
That sprang from mine own daughter?   Surely then
Must thou and I with all the strength of men
Exalt him.
                    Where then shall I stand, where tread
The dance and toss this bowed and hoary head?
O friend, in thee is wisdom; guide my grey
And eld-worn steps, eld-worn Teiresias.—Nay;
I am not weak.

[*At the first movement of worship his manner begins to change;
   a mysterious strength and exaltation enter him.*
                    Surely this arm could smite
The wild earth with its thyrsus, day and night,
And faint not!   Sweetly and forgetfully
The dim years fall from off me!

Teiresias
                         As with thee,
With me 'tis likewise.   Light am I and young,
And will essay the dancing and the song.

Cadmus
Quick, then, our chariots to the mountain road.

Teiresias
Nay; to take steeds were to mistrust the God.

Cadmus
So be it.   Mine old arm shall guide thee there.

Teiresias
The God himself shall guide!   Have thou no care.

15

CADMUS

And in all Thebes shall no man dance but we?

TEIRESIAS

Aye, Thebes is blinded.   Thou and I can see.

CADMUS

'Tis weary waiting; hold my hand, friend; so.

TEIRESIAS

Lo, there is mine.   So linkèd let us go.

CADMUS

Shall things of dust the Gods' dark ways despise?

TEIRESIAS

Or prove our wit on Heaven's high mysteries?
Not thou and I!   That heritage sublime
Our sires have left us, wisdom old as time,
No word of man, how deep soe'er his thought
And won of subtlest toil, may bring to naught.

Aye, men will rail that I forget my years.
To dance and wreathe with ivy these white hairs;
What recks it?   Seeing the God no line hath told
To mark what man shall dance, or young or old;
But craves his honours from mortality
All, no man marked apart; and great shall be!

CADMUS (*after looking away toward the Mountain*)
Teiresias, since this light thou canst not read,
I must be seer for thee.   Here comes in speed
Pentheus, Echîon's son, whom I have raised
To rule my people in my stead.—Amazed
He seems.   Stand close, and mark what we shall hear.

16

[*The two stand back, partially concealed, while there enters
in hot haste* PENTHEUS, *followed by a bodyguard. He is
speaking to the* SOLDIER *in command.*

PENTHEUS

Scarce had I crossed our borders, when mine ear
Was caught by this strange rumour, that our own
Wives, our own sisters, from their hearths are flown
To wild and secret rites; and cluster there
High on the shadowy hills, with dance and prayer
To adore this new-made God, this Dionyse,
Whate'er he be!—And in their companies
Deep wine-jars stand, and ever and anon
Away into the loneliness now one
Steals forth, and now a second, maid or dame,
Where love lies waiting, not of God!   The flame,
They say, of Bacchios wraps them.   Bacchios!   Nay,
'Tis more to Aphrodite that they pray.

Howbeit, all that I have found, my men
Hold bound and shackled in our dungeon den;
The rest, I will go hunt them!   Aye, and snare
My birds with nets of iron, to quell their prayer
And mountain song and rites of rascaldom!

They tell me, too, there is a stranger come,
A man of charm and spell, from Lydian seas,
A head all gold and cloudy fragrancies,
A wine-red cheek, and eyes that hold the light
Of the very Cyprian.   Day and livelong night
He haunts amid the damsels, o'er each lip
Dangling his cup of joyance!—Let me grip
Him once, but once, within these walls, right swift
That wand shall cease its music, and that drift
Of tossing curls lie still—when my rude sword
Falls between neck and trunk!   'Tis all his word,

17

This tale of Dionysus; how that same
Babe that was blasted by the lightning flame
With his dead mother, for that mother's lie,
Was re-conceived, born perfect from the thigh
Of Zeus, and now is God! What call ye these?
Dreams? Gibes of the unknown wanderer? Blasphemies
That crave the very gibbet?

                  Stay! God wot,
Here is another marvel! See I not
In motley fawn-skins robed the vision-seer
Teiresias? And my mother's father here—
O depth of scorn!—adoring with the wand
Of Bacchios?—Father!—Nay, mine eyes are fond;
It is not your white heads so fancy-flown!
It cannot be! Cast off that ivy crown,
O mine own mother's sire! Set free that hand
That cowers about its staff.

                'Tis thou hast planned
This work, Teiresias! 'Tis thou must set
Another altar and another yet
Amongst us, watch new birds, and win more hire
Of gold, interpreting new signs of fire!
But for thy silver hairs, I tell thee true,
Thou now wert sitting chained amid thy crew
Of raving damsels, for this evil dream
Thou hast brought us, of new Gods! When once the gleam
Of grapes hath lit a Woman's Festival,
In all their prayers is no more health at all!

LEADER OF THE CHORUS
(the words are not heard by PENTHEUS)
Injurious King, hast thou no care for God,
Nor Cadmus, sower of the Giants' Sod,
Life-spring to great Echîon and to thee?

18

398

TEIRESIAS

Good words, my son, come easily, when he
That speaks is wise, and speaks but for the right.
Else come they never! Swift are thine, and bright
As though with thought, yet have no thought at all.

  Lo, this new God, whom thou dost flout withal,
I cannot speak the greatness wherewith He
In Hellas shall be great! Two spirits there be,
Young Prince, that in man's world are first of worth.
Dêmêtêr one is named; she is the Earth—
Call her which name thou will!—who feeds man's frame
With sustenance of things dry. And that which came
Her work to perfect, second, is the Power
From Semelê born. He found the liquid shower
Hid in the grape. He rests man's spirit dim
From grieving, when the vine exalteth him.
He giveth sleep to sink the fretful day
In cool forgetting. Is there any way
With man's sore heart, save only to forget?

  Yea, being God, the blood of him is set
Before the Gods in sacrifice, that we
For his sake may be blest.—And so, to thee,
That fable shames him, how this God was knit
Into God's flesh? Nay, learn the truth of it,
Cleared from the false.—When from that deadly light
Zeus saved the babe, and up to Olympus' height
Raised him, and Hera's wrath would cast him thence,
Then Zeus devised him a divine defence.
A fragment of the world-encircling fire
He rent apart, and wrought to his desire
Of shape and hue, in the image of the child,
And gave to Hera's rage. And so, beguiled
By change and passing time, this tale was born,
How the babe-god was hidden in the torn

19

Flesh of his sire. He hath no shame thereby.
  A prophet is he likewise. Prophecy
Cleaves to all frenzy, but beyond all else
To frenzy of prayer. Then in us verily dwells
The God himself, and speaks the thing to be.
Yea, and of Ares' realm a part hath he.
When mortal armies, mailèd and arrayed,
Have in strange fear, or ever blade met blade,
Fled maddened, 'tis this God hath palsied them.
Aye, over Delphi's rock-built diadem
Thou yet shalt see him leaping with his train
Of fire across the twin-peaked mountain-plain,
Flaming the darkness with his mystic wand,
And great in Hellas.—List and understand,
King Pentheus! Dream not thou that force is power;
Nor, if thou hast a thought, and that thought sour
And sick, oh, dream not thought is wisdom!—Up,
Receive this God to Thebes; pour forth the cup
Of sacrifice, and pray, and wreathe thy brow.

  Thou fearest for the damsels? Think thee now;
How toucheth this the part of Dionyse
To hold maids pure perforce? In them it lies,
And their own hearts; and in the wildest rite
Cometh no stain to her whose heart is white.

  Nay, mark me! Thou hast thy joy, when the Gate
Stands thronged, and Pentheus' name is lifted great
And high by Thebes in clamour; shall not He
Rejoice in his due meed of majesty?

  Howbeit, this Cadmus whom thou scorn'st and I
Will wear His crown, and tread His dances! Aye,
Our hairs are white, yet shall that dance be trod!
I will not lift mine arm to war with God
For thee nor all thy words. Madness most fell
Is on thee, madness wrought by some dread spell,
But not by spell nor leechcraft to be cured!

20

CHORUS

Grey prophet, worthy of Phoebus is thy word,
And wise in honouring Bromios, our great God

CADMUS

My son, right well Teiresias points thy road.
Oh, make thine habitation here with us,
Not lonely, against men's uses. Hazardous
Is this quick bird-like beating of thy thought
Where no thought dwells.—Grant that this God be naught,
Yet let that Naught be Somewhat in thy mouth;
Lie boldly, and say He Is! So north and south
Shall marvel, how there sprang a thing divine
From Semelê's flesh, and honour all our line.
[*Drawing nearer to* PENTHEUS.

Is there not blood before thine eyes even now?
Our lost Actaeon's blood, whom long ago
His own red hounds through yonder forest dim
Tore unto death, because he vaunted him
Against most holy Artemis? Oh, beware,
And let me wreathe thy temples. Make thy prayer
With us, and bear thee humbly in God's sight.
[*He makes as if to set the wreath on* PENTHEUS' *head.*

PENTHEUS

Down with that hand! Aroint thee to thy rite,
Nor smear on me thy foul contagion!
[*Turning upon* TEIRESIAS.

This
Thy folly's head and prompter shall not miss
The justice that he needs!—Go, half my guard,
Forth to the rock-seat where he dwells in ward
O'er birds and wonders; rend the stone with crow
And trident; make one wreck of high and low,

21

And toss his bands to all the winds of air!
   Ha, have I found the way to sting thee, there?
The rest, forth through the town!   And seek amain
This girl-faced stranger, that hath wrought such bane
To all Thebes, preying on our maids and wives.
Seek till ye find; and lead him here in gyves,
Till he be judged and stoned, and weep in blood
The day he troubled Pentheus with his God!
[*The guards set forth in two bodies;* PENTHEUS *goes into the
   Castle.*

TEIRESIAS

Hard heart, how little dost thou know what seed
Thou sowest!   Blind before, and now indeed
Most mad!—Come, Cadmus, let us go our way,
And pray for this our persecutor, pray
For this poor city, that the righteous God
Move not in anger.—Take thine ivy rod
And help my steps, as I help thine.   'Twere ill,
If two old men should fall by the roadway.   Still,
Come what come may, our service shall be done
To Bacchios, the All-Father's mystic son.
   O Pentheus, named of sorrow!   Shall he claim
From all thy house fulfilment of his name,
Old Cadmus?—Nay, I speak not from mine art,
But as I see—blind words and a blind heart!
[*The two Old Men go off towards the Mountain.*

CHORUS

Some Maidens
Thou Immaculate on high;
Thou Recording Purity;
Thou that stoopest, Golden Wing,
Earthward, manward, pitying.

22

Hearest thou this angry King?
Hearest thou the rage and scorn
    'Gainst the Lord of Many Voices,
Him of mortal mother born,
    Him in whom man's heart rejoices,
Girt with garlands and with glee,
First in Heaven's sovranty?
    For his kingdom, it is there,
    In the dancing and the prayer,
In the music and the laughter,
    In the vanishing of care,
And of all before and after;
In the Gods' high banquet, when
    Gleams the grape-blood, flashed to heaven;
Yea, and in the feasts of men
Comes his crownèd slumber; then
    Pain is dead and hate forgiven!

Others

Loose thy lips from out the rein;
Lift thy wisdom to disdain;
Whatso law thou canst not see,
Scorning; so the end shall be
Uttermost calamity!
'Tis the life of quiet breath,
    'Tis the simple and the true,
Storm nor earthquake shattereth,
    Nor shall aught the house undo
Where they dwell.   For, far away,
Hidden from the eyes of day,
    Watchers are there in the skies,
    That can see man's life, and prize
Deeds well done by things of clay.
    But the world's Wise are not wise,

23

Claiming more than mortal may.
Life is such a little thing;
  Lo, their present is departed,
And the dreams to which they cling
Come not.   Mad imagining
  Theirs, I ween, and empty-hearted!

Divers Maidens
  Where is the Home for me?
  O Cyprus, set in the sea,
Aphrodite's home In the soft sea-foam,
  Would I could wend to thee;
Where the wings of the Loves are furled,
And faint the heart of the world.

  Aye, unto Paphos' isle,
  Where the rainless meadows smile
With riches rolled From the hundred-fold
  Mouths of the far-off Nile,
Streaming beneath the waves
To the roots of the seaward caves.

  But a better land is there
  Where Olympus cleaves the air,
The high still dell Where the Muses dwell,
  Fairest of all things fair!
Desire is there, and the Crowning of Desire,
And peace to adore thee, thou Spirit of Guiding Fire!

_____

  A God of Heaven is he,
  And born in majesty;
Yet hath he mirth In the joy of the Earth,
  And he loveth constantly
Her who brings increase,
The Feeder of Children, Peace.

24

No grudge hath he of the great;
No scorn of the mean estate;
But to all that liveth His wine he giveth,
Griefless, immaculate;
Only on them that spurn
Joy, may his anger burn.

Love thou the Day and the Night;
Be glad of the Dark and the Light;
And avert thine eyes From the lore of the wise,
That have honour in proud men's sight.
The simple nameless herd of Humanity
Hath deeds and faith that are truth enough for me!

[*As the Chorus ceases, a party of the guards return, leading in
the midst of them* DIONYSUS, *bound. The* SOLDIER *in
command stands forth, as* PENTHEUS, *hearing the tramp of
feet, comes out from the Castle.*

SOLDIER

Our quest is finished, and thy prey, O King,
Caught; for the chase was swift, and this wild thing
Most tame; yet never flinched, nor thought to flee,
But held both hands out unresistingly—
No change, no blanching of the wine-red cheek.
He waited while we came, and bade us wreak
All thy decree; yea, laughed, and made my hest
Easy, till I for very shame confessed
And said: 'O stranger, not of mine own will
I bind thee, but his bidding to fulfil
Who sent me.'

And those prisoned Maids withal
Whom thou didst seize and bind within the wall
Of thy great dungeon, they are fled, O King,
Free in the woods, a-dance and glorying

25

To Bromios.   Of their own impulse fell
To earth, men say, fetter and manacle,
And bars slid back untouched of mortal hand.
Yea, full of many wonders to thy land
Is this man come. . . . Howbeit, it lies with thee!

PENTHEUS

Ye are mad!—Unhand him.   Howso swift he be,
My toils are round him and he shall not fly.
[*The guards loose the arms of* DIONYSUS; PENTHEUS *studies
   him for a while in silence, then speaks jeeringly.* DIONYSUS
   remains gentle and unafraid.
Marry, a fair shape for a woman's eye,
Sir stranger!   And thou seek'st no more, I ween!
Long curls, withal!   That shows thou ne'er hast been
A wrestler!—down both cheeks so softly tossed
And winsome!   And a white skin!   It hath cost
Thee pains, to please thy damsels with this white
And red of cheeks that never face the light!
[DIONYSUS *is silent.*
Speak, sirrah; tell me first thy name and race.

DIONYSUS

No glory is therein, nor yet disgrace.
Thou hast heard of Tmolus, the bright hill of flowers?

PENTHEUS

Surely; the ridge that winds by Sardis' towers.

DIONYSUS

Thence am I; Lydia was my fatherland.

PENTHEUS

And whence these revelations, that thy band
Spreadeth in Hellas?

26

DIONYSUS
Their intent and use
Dionysus oped to me, the Child of Zeus.

PENTHEUS (*brutally*)
Is there a Zeus there, that can still beget
Young Gods?

DIONYSUS
Nay, only He whose seal was set
Here in thy Thebes on Semelê.

PENTHEUS
What way
Descended he upon thee?   In full day
Or vision of night?

DIONYSUS
Most clear he stood, and scanned
My soul, and gave his emblems to mine hand.

PENTHEUS
What like be they, these emblems?

DIONYSUS
That may none
Reveal, nor know, save his Elect alone.

PENTHEUS
And what good bring they to the worshipper?

DIONYSUS
Good beyond price, but not for thee to hear.

27

PENTHEUS

Thou trickster! Thou wouldst prick me on the more
To seek them out!

DIONYSUS
His mysteries abhor
The touch of sin-lovers.

PENTHEUS
And so thine eyes
Saw this God plain; what guise had he?

DIONYSUS
What guise
It liked him. 'Twas not I ordained his shape.

PENTHEUS

Aye, deftly turned again. An idle jape,
And nothing answered!

DIONYSUS
Wise words being brought
To blinded eyes will seem as things of nought.

PENTHEUS

And comest thou first to Thebes, to have thy God
Established?

DIONYSUS
Nay; all Barbary hath trod
His dance ere this.

PENTHEUS
A low blind folk, I ween,
Beside our Hellenes!

28

DIONYSUS
                    Higher and more keen
In this thing, though their ways are not thy way.

PENTHEUS
How is thy worship held, by night or day?

DIONYSUS
Most oft by night; 'tis a majestic thing.
The darkness.

PENTHEUS
                    Ha! with women worshipping?
'Tis craft and rottenness!

DIONYSUS
                         By day no less,
Whoso will seek may find unholiness.

PENTHEUS
Enough!   Thy doom is fixed, for false pretence
Corrupting Thebes.

DIONYSUS
                    Not mine; but thine, for dense
Blindness of heart, and for blaspheming God!

PENTHEUS
A ready knave it is, and brazen-browed,
This mystery-priest!

DIONYSUS
                    Come, say what it shall be,
My doom; what dire thing wilt thou do to me?

29

PENTHEUS

First, shear that delicate curl that dangles there.
[*He beckons to the soldiers, who approach* DIONYSUS.

DIONYSUS

I have vowed it to my God; 'tis holy hair.
[*The soldiers cut off the tress.*

PENTHEUS

Next, yield me up thy staff!

DIONYSUS

     Raise thine own hand
To take it. This is Dionysus' wand.
[PENTHEUS *takes the staff.*

PENTHEUS

Last, I will hold thee prisoned here.

DIONYSUS

      My Lord
God will unloose me, when I speak the word.

PENTHEUS

He may, if e'er again amid his bands
Of saints he hears thy voice!

DIONYSUS

     Even now he stands
Close here, and sees all that I suffer.

PENTHEUS

      What!
Where is he? For mine eyes discern him not.

30

410

DIONYSUS
Where I am!   'Tis thine own impurity
That veils him from thee.

PENTHEUS
                    The dog jeers at me!
At me and Thebes!   Bind him!
[*The soldiers begin to bind him.*

DIONYSUS
                    I charge ye, bind
Me not!   I having vision and ye blind!

PENTHEUS
And I, with better right, say bind the more!
[*The soldiers obey.*

DIONYSUS
Thou knowest not what life thou livest, nor
What deed thou doest, nor what man thou art!

PENTHEUS (*mocking*)
Agâvê's son, and on the father's part
Echîon's, hight Pentheus!

DIONYSUS
                    So let it be,
A name fore-written to calamity!

PENTHEUS
Away, and tie him where the steeds are tied;
Aye, let him lie in the manger!—There abide
And stare into the darkness!—And this rout
Of womankind that clusters thee about,

31

Thy ministers of worship, are my slaves!
It may be I will sell them o'er the waves,
Hither and thither; else they shall be set
To labour at my distaffs, and forget
Their timbrel and their songs of dawning day!

DIONYSUS

I go; for that which may not be, I may
Not suffer! Yet for this thy sin, lo, He
Whom thou deniest cometh after thee
For recompense. Yea, in thy wrong to us,
Thou hast cast Him into thy prison-house!

[DIONYSUS, *without his wand, his hair shorn, and his arms
     tightly bound, is led off by the guards to his dungeon.* PEN-
     THEUS *returns into the Palace.*

CHORUS

Some Maidens

Acheloüs' roaming daughter,
Holy Dircê, virgin water,
Bathed he not of old in thee,
The Babe of God, the Mystery?
When from out the fire immortal
   To himself his God did take him,
   To his own flesh, and bespake him:
" Enter now life's second portal,
Motherless Mystery; lo, I break
Mine own body for thy sake,
   Thou of the Twofold Door, and seal thee
Mine, O Bromios,"—thus he spake—
   " And to this thy land reveal thee."

32

412

All

Still my prayer toward thee quivers,
  Dircê, still to thee I hie me;
Why, O Blessèd among Rivers,
  Wilt thou fly me and deny me?
    By His own joy I vow,
    By the grape upon the bough,
Thou shalt seek Him in the midnight, thou shalt love Him,
  even now!

Other Maidens

Dark and of the dark impassioned
Is this Pentheus' blood; yea, fashioned
Of the Dragon, and his birth
From Echîon, child of Earth.
He is no man, but a wonder;
  Did the Earth-Child not beget him,
  As a red Giant, to set him
Against God, against the Thunder?
He will bind me for his prize,
Me, the Bride of Dionyse;
  And my priest, my friend, is taken
Even now, and buried lies;
  In the dark he lies forsaken!

All

Lo, we race with death, we perish,
  Dionysus, here before thee!
Dost thou mark us not, nor cherish,
  Who implore thee, and adore thee?
    Hither down Olympus' side,
    Come, O Holy One defied,
Be thy golden wand uplifted o'er the tyrant in his pride!

33

A Maiden

Oh, where art thou?   In thine own
Nysa, thou our help alone?
O'er fierce beasts in orient lands
    Doth thy thronging thyrsus wave,
    By the high Corycian Cave,
Or where stern Olympus stands;
In the elm-woods and the oaken,
    There where Orpheus harped of old,
    And the trees awoke and knew him,
    And the wild things gathered to him,
As he sang amid the broken
    Glens his music manifold?
Blessed Land of Piërie,
Dionysus loveth thee;
    He will come to thee with dancing,
Come with joy and mystery;
With the Maenads at his hest
Winding, winding to the West;
    Cross the flood of swiftly glancing
Axios in majesty;
Cross the Lydias, the giver
    Of good gifts and waving green;
Cross that Father-Stream of story,
Through a land of steeds and glory
Rolling, bravest, fairest River
    E'er of mortals seen!

A Voice Within
Io! Io!
Awake, ye damsels; hear my cry,
    Calling my Chosen; hearken ye

A Maiden
Who speaketh?   Oh, what echoes thus?

34

ANOTHER

A Voice, a Voice, that calleth us!

THE VOICE

Be of good cheer!   Lo, it is I,
    The Child of Zeus and Semelê.

A MAIDEN

O Master, Master, it is Thou!

ANOTHER

O Holy Voice, be with us now!

THE VOICE

Spirit of the Chained Earthquake,
Hear my word; awake, awake!
[*An Earthquake suddenly shakes the pillars of the Castle.*

A MAIDEN

Ha! what is coming?   Shall the hall
Of Pentheus racked in ruin fall?

LEADER

Our God is in the house!   Ye maids adore Him!

CHORUS

                    We adore Him all!

THE VOICE

Unveil the Lightning's eye; arouse
The fire that sleeps, against this house!
[*Fire leaps up on the Tomb of Semelê.*

35

A MAIDEN

Ah, saw ye, marked ye there the flame
From Semelê's enhallowed sod
Awakened? Yea, the Death that came
Ablaze from heaven of old, the same
Hot splendour of the shaft of God?

LEADER

Oh, cast ye, cast ye, to the earth! The Lord
Cometh against this house! Oh, cast ye down,
Ye trembling damsels; He, our own adored,
God's Child hath come, and all is overthrown!

[*The Maidens cast themselves upon the ground, their eyes
earthward.* DIONYSUS, *alone and unbound, enters from
the Castle.*

DIONYSUS

Ye Damsels of the Morning Hills, why lie ye thus dismayed?
Ye marked him, then, our Master, and the mighty hand he
laid
On tower and rock, shaking the house of Pentheus?—But
arise,
And cast the trembling from your flesh, and lift untroubled
eyes.

LEADER

O Light in Darkness, is it thou? O Priest is this thy face?
My heart leaps out to greet thee from the deep of loneliness.

DIONYSUS

Fell ye so quick despairing, when beneath the Gate I passed?
Should the gates of Pentheus quell me, or his darkness make
me fast?

36

416

LEADER

Oh, what was left if thou wert gone?   What could I but
  despair?
How hast thou 'scaped the man of sin?   Who freed thee
  from the snare?

DIONYSUS

I had no pain nor peril; 'twas mine own hand set me free.

LEADER

Thine arms were gyvèd!

DIONYSUS

      Nay, no gyve, no touch, was laid on me!
'Twas there I mocked him, in his gyves, and gave him dreams
  for food.
For when he led me down, behold, before the stall there
  stood
A Bull of Offering.   And this King, he bit his lips, and
  straight
Fell on and bound it, hoof and limb, with gasping wrath
  and sweat.
And I sat watching!—Then a Voice; and lo, our Lord
  was come,
And the house shook, and a great flame stood o'er his
  mother's tomb.
And Pentheus hied this way and that, and called his thralls
  amain
For water, lest his roof-tree burn; and all toiled, all in vain.
Then deemed a-sudden I was gone; and left his fire, and sped
Back to the prison portals, and his lifted sword shone red.
But there, methinks, the God had wrought—I speak but
  as I guess—
Some dream-shape in mine image; for he smote at emptiness,

37

Stabbed in the air, and strove in wrath, as though 'twere me
 he slew.

Then 'mid his dreams God smote him yet again!   He
 overthrew

All that high house.   And there in wreck for evermore
 it lies,

That the day of this my bondage may be sore in Pentheus'
 eyes!

And now his sword is fallen, and he lies outworn and wan

Who dared to rise against his God in wrath, being but
 man.

And I uprose and left him, and in all peace took my path

Forth to my Chosen, recking light of Pentheus and his
 wrath.

 But soft, methinks a footstep sounds even now within
 the hall;

'Tis he; how think ye he will stand, and what words speak
 withal?

I will endure him gently, though he come in fury hot.

For still are the ways of Wisdom, and her temper trembleth
 not!

[*Enter* PENTHEUS *in fury.*

PENTHEUS

It is too much!   This Eastern knave hath slipped
His prison, whom I held but now, hard gripped
In bondage.—Ha!   'Tis he!—What, sirrah, how
Show'st thou before my portals?
[*He advances furiously upon him.*

DIONYSUS
     Softly thou!
 And set a quiet carriage to thy rage

38

418

PENTHEUS

How comest thou here?   How didst thou break thy cage?
Speak!

DIONYSUS

Said I not, or didst thou mark not me,
There was One living that should set me free?

PENTHEUS

Who?   Ever wilder are these tales of thine.

DIONYSUS

He who first made for man the clustered vine.

PENTHEUS

I scorn him and his vines!

DIONYSUS

For Dionyse
'Tis well; for in thy scorn his glory lies.

PENTHEUS (*to his guard*)

Go swift to all the towers, and bar withal
Each gate!

DIONYSUS

What, cannot God o'erleap a wall?

PENTHEUS

Oh, wit thou hast, save where thou needest it!

DIONYSUS

Whereso it most imports, there is my wit!—
Nay, peace!   Abide till he who hasteth from

39

The mountain side with news for thee, be come.
We will not fly, but wait on thy command.
[*Enter suddenly and in haste a Messenger from the Mountain.*

MESSENGER

Great Pentheus, Lord of all this Theban land,
I come from high Kithaeron, where the frore
Snow spangles gleam and cease not evermore. . . .

PENTHEUS

And what of import may thy coming bring?

MESSENGER

I have seen the Wild White Women there, O King,
Whose fleet limbs darted arrow-like but now
From Thebes away, and come to tell thee how
They work strange deeds and passing marvel.   Yet
I first would learn thy pleasure.   Shall I set
My whole tale forth, or veil the stranger part?
Yea, Lord, I fear the swiftness of thy heart,
Thine edgèd wrath and more than royal soul.

PENTHEUS

Thy tale shall nothing scathe thee.—Tell the whole.
It skills not to be wroth with honesty.
Nay, if thy news of them be dark, 'tis he
Shall pay it, who bewitched and led them on.

MESSENGER

Our herded kine were moving in the dawn
Up to the peaks, the greyest, coldest time,
When the first rays steal earthward, and the rime
Yields, when I saw three bands of them.   The one
Autonoë led, one Ino, one thine own

40

Mother, Agâvê.   There beneath the trees
Sleeping they lay, like wild things flung at ease
In the forest; one half sinking on a bed
Of deep pine greenery; one with careless head
Amid the fallen oak leaves; all most cold
In purity—not as thy tale was told
Of wine-cups and wild music and the chase
For love amid the forest's loneliness.
Then rose the Queen Agâvê suddenly
Amid her band, and gave the God's wild cry,
"Awake, ye Bacchanals! I hear the sound
Of hornèd kine.   Awake ye! "—Then, all round,
Alert, the warm sleep fallen from their eyes,
A marvel of swift ranks I saw them rise,
Dames young and old, and gentle maids unwed
Among them.   O'er their shoulders first they shed
Their tresses, and caught up the fallen fold
Of mantles where some clasp had loosened hold,
And girt the dappled fawn-skins in with long
Quick snakes that hissed and writhed with quivering tongue.
And one a young fawn held, and one a wild
Wolf cub, and fed them with white milk, and smiled
In love, young mothers with a mother's breast
And babes at home forgotten!   Then they pressed
Wreathed ivy round their brows, and oaken sprays
And flowering bryony.   And one would raise
Her wand and smite the rock, and straight a jet
Of quick bright water came.   Another set
Her thyrsus in the bosomed earth, and there
Was red wine that the God sent up to her,
A darkling fountain.   And if any lips
Sought whiter draughts, with dipping finger-tips
They pressed the sod, and gushing from the ground
Came springs of milk.   And reed-wands ivy-crowned

41

Ran with sweet honey, drop by drop.—O King,
Hadst thou been there, as I, and seen this thing,
With prayer and most high wonder hadst thou gone
To adore this God whom now thou rail'st upon!

Howbeit, the kine-wardens and shepherds straight
Came to one place, amazed, and held debate;
And one being there who walked the streets and scanned
The ways of speech, took lead of them whose hand
Knew but the slow soil and the solemn hill,
And flattering spoke, and asked: " Is it your will,
Masters, we stay the mother of the King.
Agâvê, from her lawless worshipping,
And win us royal thanks? "—And this seemed good
To all; and through the branching underwood
We hid us, cowering in the leaves. And there
Through the appointed hour they made their prayer
And worship of the Wand, with one accord
Of heart and cry—" Iacchos, Bromios, Lord,
God of God born! "—And all the mountain felt,
And worshipped with them; and the wild things knelt
And ramped and gloried, and the wilderness
Was filled with moving voices and dim stress.

Soon, as it chanced, beside my thicket-close
The Queen herself passed dancing, and I rose
And sprang to seize her. But she turned her face
Upon me: " Ho, my rovers of the chase,
My wild White Hounds, we are hunted! Up, each rod
And follow, follow, for our Lord and God! "
Thereat, for fear they tear us, all we fled
Amazed; and on, with hand unweaponèd
They swept toward our herds that browsed the green
Hill grass. Great uddered kine then hadst thou seen
Bellowing in sword-like hands that cleave and tear,
A live steer riven asunder, and the air

42

Tossed with rent ribs or limbs of cloven tread.
And flesh upon the branches, and a red
Rain from the deep green pines. Yea, bulls of pride,
Horns swift to rage, were fronted and aside
Flung stumbling, by those multitudinous hands
Dragged pitilessly. And swifter were the bands
Of garbèd flesh and bone unbound withal
Than on thy royal eyes the lids may fall.

Then on like birds, by their own speed upborne,
They swept toward the plains of waving corn
That lie beside Asôpus' banks, and bring
To Thebes the rich fruit of her harvesting.
On Hysiae and Erythrae that lie nursed
Amid Kithaeron's bowering rocks, they burst
Destroying, as a foeman's army comes.
They caught up little children from their homes,
High on their shoulders, babes unheld, that swayed
And laughed and fell not; all a wreck they made;
Yea, bronze and iron did shatter, and in play
Struck hither and thither, yet no wound had they;
Caught fire from out the hearths, yea, carried hot
Flames in their tresses and were scorchèd not!

The village folk in wrath took spear and sword,
And turned upon the Bacchae. Then, dread Lord,
The wonder was. For spear not barbèd brand
Could scathe nor touch the damsels; but the Wand,
The soft and wreathèd wand their white hands sped,
Blasted those men and quelled them, and they fled
Dizzily. Sure some God was in these things!

And the holy women back to those strange springs
Returned, that God had sent them when the day
Dawned, on the upper heights; and washed away
The stain of battle. And those girdling snakes
Hissed out to lap the waterdrops from cheeks

43

And hair and breast.

            Therefore I counsel thee,
O King, receive this Spirit, whoe'er he be,
To Thebes in glory. Greatness manifold
Is all about him; and the tale is told
That this is he who first to man did give
The grief-assuaging vine. Oh, let him live;
For if he die, then Love herself is slain,
And nothing joyous in the world again!

LEADER

Albeit I tremble, and scarce may speak my thought
To a king's face, yet will I hide it not.
Dionyse is God, no God more true nor higher!

PENTHEUS

It bursts hard by us, like a smothered fire,
This frenzy of Bacchic women! All my land
Is made their mock.—This needs an iron hand!
    Ho, Captain! Quick to the Electran Gate;
Bid gather all my men-at-arms thereat;
Call all that spur the charger, all who know
To wield the orbèd targe or bend the bow;
We march to war!—'Fore God, shall women dare
Such deeds against us? 'Tis too much to bear!

DIONYSUS

Thou mark'st me not, O King, and holdest light
My solemn words; yet, in thine own despite,
I warn thee still. Lift thou not up thy spear
Against a God, but hold thy peace, and fear
His wrath! He will not brook it, if thou fright
His Chosen from the hills of their delight.

44

PENTHEUS

Peace, thou!   And if for once thou hast slipped thy chain,
Give thanks!—Or shall I knot thine arms again?

DIONYSUS

Better to yield him prayer and sacrifice
Than kick against the pricks, since Dionyse
Is God, and thou but mortal.

PENTHEUS

                    That will I!
Yea, sacrifice of women's blood, to cry
His name through all Kithaeron!

DIONYSUS

                              Ye shall fly,
All, and abase your shields of bronzen rim
Before their wands.

PENTHEUS

                    There is no way with him,
This stranger that so dogs us!   Well or ill
I may entreat him, he must babble still!

DIONYSUS

Wait, good my friend!   These crooked matters may
Even yet be straightened.
[PENTHEUS *has started as though to seek his army at the gate.*

PENTHEUS

                    Aye, if I obey
Mine own slaves' will; how else?

DIONYSUS

                              Myself will lead
The damsels hither, without sword or steed.

45

PENTHEUS

How now?—This is some plot against me!

DIONYSUS
                                                    What
Dost fear?   Only to save thee do I plot.

PENTHEUS

It is some compact ye have made, whereby
To dance these hills for ever!

DIONYSUS
                    Verily,
That is my compact, plighted with my Lord!

PENTHEUS (*turning from him*)

Ho, armourers!   Bring forth my shield and sword!—
And thou, be silent!

DIONYSUS

(*after regarding him fixedly, speaks with resignation*)
                    Ah!—Have then thy will!
[*He fixes his eyes upon* PENTHEUS *again, while the armourers
    bring out his armour; then speaks in a tone of command.*
Man, thou wouldst fain behold them on the hill
Praying!

PENTHEUS

(*who during the rest of this scene, with a few exceptions, simply
    speaks the thoughts that* DIONYSUS *puts into him, losing
    power over his own mind*)
                    That would I, though it cost me all
The gold of Thebes!

46

DIONYSUS
                    So much?   Thou art quick to fall
To such great longing.

PENTHEUS
(somewhat bewildered at what he has said)
                    Aye; 'twould grieve me much
To see them flown with wine.

DIONYSUS
                         Yet cravest thou such
A sight as would much grieve thee?

PENTHEUS
                         Yes; I fain
Would watch, ambushed among the pines.

DIONYSUS
                              'Twere vain
To hide.   They soon will track thee out.

PENTHEUS
                         Well said!
'Twere best done openly.

DIONYSUS
                    Wilt thou be led
By me, and try the venture?

PENTHEUS
                    Aye, indeed!
Lead on.   Why should we tarry?

47

DIONYSUS
First we need
A rich and trailing robe of fine-linen
To gird thee.

PENTHEUS
Nay; am I a woman, then,
And man no more?

DIONYSUS
Wouldst have them slay thee dead?
No man may see their mysteries.

PENTHEUS
Well said!—
I marked thy subtle temper long ere now.

DIONYSUS
'Tis Dionyse that prompteth me.

PENTHEUS
And how
Mean'st thou the further plan?

DIONYSUS
First take thy way
Within.   I will array thee.

PENTHEUS
What array?
The woman's?   Nay, I will not.

DIONYSUS
Doth it change
So soon, all thy desire to see this strange
Adoring?

48

PENTHEUS

    Wait! What garb wilt thou bestow
About me?

DIONYSUS

    First a long tress dangling low
Beneath thy shoulders.

PENTHEUS
Aye, and next?

DIONYSUS

               The said
Robe, falling to thy feet; and on thine head
A snood.

PENTHEUS
    And after? Hast thou aught beyond?

DIONYSUS
Surely; the dappled fawn-skin and the wand.

PENTHEUS (*after a struggle with himself*)
Enough! I cannot wear a robe and snood.

DIONYSUS
Wouldst liefer draw the sword and spill men's blood?

PENTHEUS (*again doubting*)
True, that were evil.—Aye; 'tis best to go
First to some place of watch.

DIONYSUS
          Far wiser so,
Than seek by wrath wrath's bitter recompense.

49

PENTHEUS

What of the city streets?   Canst lead me hence
Unseen of any?

DIONYSUS

Lonely and untried
Thy path from hence shall be, and I thy guide!

PENTHEUS

I care for nothing, so these Bacchanals
Triumph not against me!...Forward to my halls
Within!—I will ordain what seemeth best.

DIONYSUS

So be it, O King!   'Tis mine to obey thine hest,
Whate'er it be.

PENTHEUS

(after hesitating once more and waiting)
Well, I will go—perchance
To march and scatter them with serried lance,
Perchance to take thy plan. . . . I know not yet.
[*Exit* PENTHEUS *into the Castle.*

DIONYSUS

Damsels, the lion walketh to the net.
He finds his Bacchae now, and sees and dies,
And pays for all his sin!—O Dionyse,
This is thine hour and thou not far away.
Grant us our vengeance!—First, O Master, stay
The course of reason in him, and instil
A foam of madness.   Let his seeing will,
Which ne'er had stooped to put thy vesture on,
Be darkened, till the deed is lightly done.
Grant likewise that he find through all his streets
Loud scorn, this man of wrath and bitter threats

50

That made Thebes tremble, led in woman's guise.
  I go to fold that robe of sacrifice
On Pentheus, that shall deck him to the dark,
His mother's gift!—So shall he learn and mark
God's true Son, Dionyse, in fulness God,
Most fearful, yet to man most soft of mood.
[*Exit* DIONYSUS, *following* PENTHEUS *into the Castle.*

CHORUS
Some Maidens
Will they ever come to me, ever again,
    The long long dances,
On through the dark till the dawn-stars wane?
Shall I feel the dew on my throat, and the stream
Of wind in my hair?   Shall our white feet gleam
    In the dim expanses?
Oh, feet of a fawn to the greenwood fled,
    Alone in the grass and the loveliness;
Leap of the hunted, no more in dread,
    Beyond the snares and the deadly press:
Yet a voice still in the distance sounds,
A shout, a threat, and a haste of hounds;
O wildly labouring, fiercely fleet,
    Onward yet by river and glen . . .
Is it joy or terror, ye storm-swift feet?
    To the dear lone lands untroubled of men,
Where no voice sounds, and amid the shadowy green
The little things of the woodland live unseen.

What else is Wisdom?   What of man's endeavour
  Or God's high grace, so lovely and so great?
  To stand from fear set free, to breathe and wait;
  To hold a hand uplifted over Hate;
And shall not loveliness be loved for ever?

51

Others

O Strength of God, slow art thou and still,
    Yet failest never!
On them that worship the Ruthless Will,
On them that dream, doth His judgment wait,
Dreams of the proud man, making great
    And greater ever,
Things which are not of God.   In wide
    And devious coverts, hunter-wise,
He coucheth Time's unhasting stride,
    Following, following, him whose eyes
Look not to Heaven.   For all is vain,
The pulse of the heart, the plot of the brain,
That striveth beyond the laws that live.
And is thy Faith so much to give,
Is it so hard a thing to see,
That the Spirit of God, whate'er it be,
The Law that abides and changes not, ages long,
The Eternal and Nature-born—these things be strong?

What else is Wisdom?   What of man's endeavour
    Or God's high grace so lovely and so great?
    To stand from fear set free, to breathe and wait;
    To hold a hand uplifted over Hate;
And shall not Loveliness be loved for ever?

LEADER

    Happy he, on the weary sea,
Who hath fled the tempest and won the haven.
    Happy whoso hath risen, free,
Above his striving.   For strangely graven
    Is the orb of life, that one and another
    In gold and power may outpass his brother.
    And men in their millions float and flow

52

And seethe with a million hopes as leaven;
 And they win their will, or they miss their will,
 And the hopes are dead or are pined for still;
  But whoe'er can know,
  As the long days go,
That To Live is happy, hath found his Heaven!

[*Re-enter* DIONYSUS *from the Castle.*

DIONYSUS

O eye that cravest sights thou must not see,
O heart athirst for that which slakes not! Thee,
Pentheus, I call; forth and be seen, in guise
Of woman, Maenad, saint of Dionyse,
To spy upon His Chosen and thine own
Mother!
[*Enter* PENTHEUS, *clad like a Bacchanal, and strangely excited,*
 a spirit of Bacchic madness overshadowing him.
  Thy shape, methinks, is like to one
Of Cadmus' royal maids!

PENTHEUS
   Yea; and mine eye
Is bright! Yon sun shines twofold in the sky,
Thebes twofold and the Wall of Seven Gates. . . .
And is it a Wild Bull this, that walks and waits
Before me? There are horns upon thy brow!
What art thou, man or beast? For surely now
The Bull is on thee!

DIONYSUS
   He who erst was wrath,
Goes with us now in gentleness. He hath
Unsealed thine eyes to see what thou shouldst see.

53

PENTHEUS

Say; stand I not as Ino stands, or she
Who bore me?

DIONYSUS

When I look on thee, it seems
I see their very selves.—But stay; why streams
That lock abroad, not where I laid it, crossed
Under the coif?

PENTHEUS

I did it, as I tossed
My head in dancing, to and fro, and cried
His holy music!

DIONYSUS (*tending him*)

It shall soon be tied
Aright. 'Tis mine to tend thee. . . . Nay, but stand
With head straight.

PENTHEUS

In the hollow of thy hand
I lay me. Deck me as thou wilt.

DIONYSUS

Thy zone
Is loosened likewise; and the folded gown
Not evenly falling to the feet.

PENTHEUS

'Tis so,
By the right foot. But here, methinks, they flow
In one straight line to the heel.

DIONYSUS (*while tending him*)

And if thou prove
Their madness true, aye, more than true, what love
And thanks hast thou for me?

54

PENTHEUS (*not listening to him*)
                              In my right hand
Is it, or thus, that I should bear the wand,
To be most like to them?

DIONYSUS
                              Up let it swing
In the right hand, timed with the right foot's spring. . . .
'Tis well thy heart is changed.

PENTHEUS (*more wildly*)
                              What strength is this!
Kithaeron's steeps and all that in them is—
How say'st thou?—Could my shoulders lift the whole.

DIONYSUS
Surely they can, if so thou wilt!   Thy soul,
Being once so sick, now stands as it should stand.

PENTHEUS
Shall it be bars of iron?   Or this bare hand
And shoulder to the crags, to wrench them down?

DIONYSUS
Wouldst wreck the Nymphs' wild temples, and the brown
Rocks where Pan pipes at noonday?

PENTHEUS
                              Nay; not I!
Force is not well with women.   I will lie
Hid in the pine-brake.
                    DIONYSUS
                              Even as fits a spy
On holy and fearful things, so shalt thou lie!

55

PENTHEUS (*with a laugh*)
They lie there now, methinks—the wild birds, caught
By love among the leaves, and fluttering not!

DIONYSUS
It may be. That is what thou goest to see,
Aye, and to trap them—so they trap not thee!

PENTHEUS
Forth through the Thebans' town! I am their king,
Aye, their one Man, seeing I dare this thing!

DIONYSUS
Yea, thou shalt bear their burden, thou alone;
Therefore thy trial awaiteth thee.—But on;
With me into thine ambush shalt thou come
Unscathed; then let another bear thee home!

PENTHEUS
The Queen, my mother.

DIONYSUS
                    Marked of every eye.

PENTHEUS

For that I go!

DIONYSUS
Thou shalt be borne on high.

PENTHEUS

That were like pride

DIONYSUS
Thy mother's hands shall share

Thy carrying.

56

PENTHEUS
Nay; I need not such soft care.

DIONYSUS
So soft?

PENTHEUS
Whate'er it be, I have earned it well.
[*Exit* PENTHEUS *towards the Mountain.*

DIONYSUS
Fell, fell art thou; and to a doom so fell
Thou walkest, that thy name from South to North
Shall shine, a sign for ever.—Reach thou forth
Thine arms, Agâvê, now, and ye dark-browed
Cadmeian sisters!   Greet this prince so proud
To the high ordeal, where save God and me,
None walks unscathed!—The rest this day shall see.
[*Exit* DIONYSUS *following* PENTHEUS.

CHORUS
Some Maidens
O hounds raging and blind,
    Up by the mountain road,
Sprites of the maddened mind,
    To the wild Maids of God;
Fill with your rage their eyes,
    Rage at the rage unblest,
Watching in woman's guise,
    The spy upon God's Possessed.

A Bacchanal
Who shall be first, to mark
    Eyes in the rock that spy,
Eyes in the pine-tree dark—
    Is it his mother?—and cry:

57

"Lo, what is this that comes,
  Haunting, troubling still,
Even in our heights, our homes,
  The wild Maids of the Hill?
What flesh bare this child?
  Never on woman's breast
Changeling so evil smiled;
  Man is he not, but Beast!
Lion-shape of the wild,
  Gorgon-breed of the waste!"

All the Chorus
Hither, for doom and deed!
  Hither with lifted sword,
  Justice, Wrath of the Lord,
Come in our visible need!
Smite till the throat shall bleed,
Smite till the heart shall bleed,
Him the tyrannous, lawless, Godless, Echîon's earthborn seed!

Other Maidens
Tyrannously hath he trod;
  Marched him, in Law's despite,
Against thy Light, O God,
  Yea, and thy Mother's Light;
Girded him, falsely bold,
  Blinded in craft, to quell
And by man's violence hold
  Things unconquerable.

A Bacchanal
A strait pitiless mind
  Is death unto godliness;
And to feel in human kind
  Life, and a pain the less.

58

Knowledge, we are not foes!
  I seek thee diligently;
But the world with a great wind blows,
  Shining, and not from thee;
Blowing to beautiful things,
  On, amid dark and light,
Till Life, through the trammellings
  Of Laws that are not the Right,
Breaks, clean and pure, and sings
  Glorying to God in the height!

All the Chorus
Hither for doom and deed!
  Hither with lifted sword,
  Justice, Wrath of the Lord,
Come in our visible need!
Smite till the throat shall bleed,
Smite till the heart shall bleed,
Him the tyrannous, lawless, Godless, Echîon's earthborn
  seed!

LEADER
Appear, appear, whatso thy shape or name,
  O Mountain Bull, Snake of the Hundred Heads,
    Lion of Burning Flame!
O God, Beast, Mystery, come!   Thy mystic maids
Are hunted!—Blast their hunter with thy breath,
    Cast o'er his head thy snare;
And laugh aloud and drag him to his death,
  Who stalks thy herded madness in its lair!

[*Enter hastily a* MESSENGER *from the Mountain, pale and
  distraught.*

MESSENGER
Woe to the house once blest in Hellas!   Woe
To thee, old King Sidonian, who didst sow

59

The dragon-seed on Ares' bloody lea!
Alas, even thy slaves must weep for thee.

LEADER

News from the mountain?—Speak!   How hath it sped?

MESSENGER

Pentheus, my king, Echîon's son, is dead!

LEADER

All hail, God of the Voice,
Manifest ever more!

MESSENGER

What say'st thou?—And how strange thy tone, as though
In joy at this my master's overthrow!

LEADER

With fierce joy I rejoice,
Child of a savage shore;
For the chains of my prison are broken, and the dread where
I cowered of yore!

MESSENGER

And deem'st thou Thebes so beggared, so forlorn
Of manhood, as to sit beneath thy scorn?

LEADER

Thebes hath o'er me no sway!
None save Him I obey,
Dionysus, Child of the Highest, Him I obey and adore!

MESSENGER

One can forgive thee.—Yet 'tis no fair thing,
Maids, to rejoice in a man's suffering.

60

LEADER

Speak of the mountain side!
Tell us the doom he died,
The sinner smitten to death, even where his sin was sore!

MESSENGER

We climbed beyond the utmost habitings
Of Theban shepherds, passed Asôpus' springs,
And struck into the land of rock on dim
Kithaeron—Pentheus, and, attending him,
I, and the Stranger who should guide our way.
Then first in a green dell we stopped, and lay,
Lips dumb and feet unmoving, warily
Watching, to be unseen and yet to see.

A narrow glen it was, by crags o'ertowered,
Torn through by tossing waters, and there lowered
A shadow of great pines over it.   And there
The Maenad maidens sate; in toil they were,
Busily glad.   Some with an ivy chain
Tricked a worn wand to toss its locks again;
Some, wild in joyance, like young steeds set free,
Made answering songs of mystic melody.

But my poor master saw not the great band
Before him.   "Stranger," cried he, "where we stand
Mine eyes can reach not these false saints of thine.
Mount we the bank, or some high-shouldered pine,
And I shall see their follies clear!"   At that
There came a marvel.   For the Stranger straight
Touched a great pine-tree's high and heavenward crown,
And lower, lower, lower, urged it down
To the herbless floor.   Round like a bending bow,
Or slow wheel's rim a joiner forces to,
So in those hands that tough and mountain stem
Bowed slow—oh, strength not mortal dwelt in them!—

61

To the very earth. And there he set the King.
And slowly, lest it cast him in its spring,
Let back the young and straining tree, till high
It towered again amid the towering sky;
And Pentheus in the branches! Well, I ween,
He saw the Maenads then, and well was seen!
For scarce was he aloft, when suddenly
There was no Stranger any more with me,
But out of Heaven a Voice—oh, what voice else?—
'Twas He that called! " Behold, O damosels,
I bring ye him who turneth to despite
Both me and ye, and darkeneth my great Light.
'Tis yours to avenge! " So spake he, and there came
'Twixt earth and sky a pillar of high flame.
And silence took the air, and no leaf stirred
In all the forest dell. Thou hadst not heard
In that vast silence any wild thing's cry.
And up they sprang; but with bewildered eye,
Agaze and listening, scarce yet hearing true.
Then came the Voice again. And when they knew
Their God's clear call, old Cadmus' royal brood,
Up, like wild pigeons startled in a wood,
On flying feet they came, his mother blind,
Agâvê, and her sisters, and behind
All the wild crowd, more deeply maddened then,
Through the angry rocks and torrent-tossing glen,
Until they spied him in the dark pine-tree:
Then climbed a crag hard by and furiously
Some sought to stone him, some their wands would fling
Lance-wise aloft, in cruel targeting.
But none could strike. The height o'ertopped their rage,
And there he clung, unscathed, as in a cage
Caught. And of all their strife no end was found.
Then, "Hither," cried Agâvê; " stand we round

62

And grip the stem, my Wild Ones, till we take
This climbing cat-o'-the-mount!   He shall not make
A tale of God's high dances!"   Out then shone
Arm upon arm, past count, and closed upon
The pine, and gripped; and the ground gave, and down
It reeled.   And that high sitter from the crown
Of the green pine-top, with a shrieking cry
Fell, as his mind grew clear, and there hard by
Was horror visible.   'Twas his mother stood
O'er him, first priestess of those rites of blood.
He tore the coif, and from his head away
Flung it, that she might know him, and not slay
To her own misery.   He touched the wild
Cheek, crying: " Mother, it is I, thy child,
Thy Pentheus, born thee in Echîon's hall!
Have mercy, Mother!   Let it not befall
Through sin of mine, that thou shouldst slay thy son!"
    But she, with lips a-foam and eyes that run
Like leaping fire, with thoughts that ne'er should be
On earth, possessed by Bacchios utterly,
Stays not nor hears.   Round his left arm she put
Both hands, set hard against his side her foot,
Drew . . . and the shoulder severed!—Not by might
Of arm, but easily, as the God made light
Her hand's essay.   And at the other side
Was Ino rending; and the torn flesh cried,
And on Autonoë pressed, and all the crowd
Of ravening arms.   Yea, all the air was loud
With groans that faded into sobbing breath,
Dim shrieks, and joy, and triumph-cries of death.
And here was borne a severed arm, and there
A hunter's booted foot; white bones lay bare
With rending; and swift hands ensanguinèd
Tossed as in sport the flesh of Pentheus dead.

63

443

His body lies afar.   The precipice
Hath part, and parts in many an interstice
Lurk of the tangled woodland—no light quest
To find.   And, ah, the head!   Of all the rest,
His mother hath it, pierced upon a wand,
As one might pierce a lion's, and through the land,
Leaving her sisters in their dancing place,
Bears it on high.   Yea, to these walls her face
Was set, exulting in her deed of blood,
Calling upon her Bromios, her God,
Her Comrade, Fellow-Render of the Prey,
Her All-Victorious, to whom this day
She bears in triumph . . . her own broken heart!

For me, after that sight, I will depart
Before Agâvê comes.—Oh, to fulfil
God's laws, and have no thought beyond His will,
Is man's best treasure.   Aye, and wisdom true,
Methinks, for things of dust to cleave unto!
[*The* MESSENGER *departs into the Castle.*

CHORUS

Some Maidens
Weave ye the dance, and call
Praise to God!
Bless ye the Tyrant's fall!
Down is trod
Pentheus, the Dragon's Seed!
Wore he the woman's weed?
Clasped he his death indeed,
Clasped the rod?

A Bacchanal
Yea, the wild ivy lapt him, and the doomed
Wild Bull of Sacrifice before him loomed.

64

Others

Ye who did Bromios scorn,
    Praise Him the more,
Bacchanals, Cadmus-born;
    Praise with sore
Agony, yea, with tears!
Great are the gifts he bears!
Hands that a mother rears
    Red with gore!

LEADER

But stay, Agâvê cometh! And her eyes
Make fire around her, reeling! Ho, the prize
Cometh! All hail, O Rout of Dionyse!
[*Enter from the Mountain* AGAVE, *mad, and to all seeming*
wondrously happy, bearing the head of PENTHEUS *in her*
hand. The CHORUS MAIDENS *stand horror-struck at the*
sight: the LEADER, *also horror-struck, strives to accept it*
and rejoice in it as the God's deed.

AGAVE

Ye from the lands of Morn!

LEADER

Call me not; I give praise!

AGAVE

Lo, from the trunk new-shorn
Hither a Mountain Thorn
Bear we! O Asia-born
    Bacchanals, bless this chase!

LEADER

I see. Yea; I see.
Have I not welcomed thee?

65

AGAVE (*very calmly and peacefully*)
He was young in the wildwood:
  Without nets I caught him!
  Nay; look without fear on
    The Lion; I have ta'en him!

LEADER
Where in the wildwood?
  Whence have ye brought him?

AGAVE
Kithaeron. . . .

LEADER
           Kithaeron?
AGAVE
The Mountain hath slain him!

LEADER
Who first came nigh him?

AGAVE
I, I, 'tis confessèd!
And they named me there by him
  Agâvê the Blessèd!

LEADER
Who was next in the band on him?

AGAVE
The daughters. . . .

LEADER
          The daughters?

66

AGAVE

Of Cadmus laid hand on him.
    But the swift hand that slaughters
Is mine; mine is the praise!
Bless ye this day of days!

[*The* LEADER *tries to speak, but is not able;* AGAVE *begins gently stroking the head.*

AGAVE

Gather ye now to the feast!

LEADER

Feast!—O miserable!

AGAVE

See, it falls to his breast,
Curling and gently tressed,
The hair of the Wild Bull's crest—
    The young steer of the fell!

LEADER

Most like a beast of the wild
That head, those locks defiled.

AGAVE (*lifting up the head, more excitedly*)
He wakened his Mad Ones,
    A Chase-God, a wise God!
        He sprang them to seize this!
        He preys where his band preys.

LEADER (*brooding, with horror*)
In the trail of thy Mad Ones
    Thou tearest thy prize, God!

67

447

AGAVE
Dost praise it?

LEADER
I praise this?

AGAVE
Ah, soon shall the land praise!

LEADER
And Pentheus, O Mother
Thy child?

AGAVE
He shall cry on
My name as none other,
Bless the spoils of the Lion!

LEADER
Aye, strange is thy treasure!

AGAVE
And strange was the taking!

LEADER
Thou art glad?

AGAVE
Beyond measure;
Yea, glad in the breaking
Of dawn upon all this land,
By the prize, the prize of my hand!

68

448 ————————————————

LEADER

Show then to all the land, unhappy one,
The trophy of this deed that thou hast done!

AGAVE

Ho, all ye men that round the citadel
And shining towers of ancient Thêbê dwell,
Come!   Look upon this prize, this lion's spoil,
That we have taken—yea, with our own toil,
We, Cadmus' daughters!   Not with leathern-set
Thessalian javelins, not with hunter's net,
Only white arms and swift hands' bladed fall.
Why make ye much adô, and boast withal
Your armourers' engines?   See, these palms were bare
That caught the angry beast, and held, and tare
The limbs of him! . . . Father! . . . Go, bring to me
My father! . . . Aye, and Pentheus, where is he,
My son?   He shall set up a ladder-stair
Against this house, and in the triglyphs there
Nail me this lion's head, that gloriously
I bring ye, having slain him—I, even I!
[*She goes through the crowd towards the Castle, showing the
head and looking for a place to hang it.   Enter from the
Mountain* CADMUS, *with attendants, bearing the body of*
PENTHEUS *on a bier.*

CADMUS

On, with your awful burden.   Follow me,
Thralls, to his house, whose body grievously
With many a weary search at last in dim
Kithaeron's glens I found, torn limb from limb,
And through the interweaving forest weed
Scattered.—Men told me of my daughters' deed,

69

When I was just returned within these walls,
With grey Teiresias, from the Bacchanals.
And back I hied me to the hills again
To seek my murdered son.   There saw I plain
Actaeon's mother, ranging where he died,
Autonoë; and Ino by her side,
Wandering ghastly in the pine-copses.
    Agâvê was not there.   The rumour is
She cometh fleet-foot hither.—Ah!   'Tis true;
A sight I scarce can bend mine eyes unto.

AGAVE
(turning from the Palace and seeing him)

My father, a great boast is thine this hour.
Thou hast begotten daughters, high in power
And valiant above all mankind—yea, all
Valiant, though none like me!   I have let fall
The shuttle by the loom, and raised my hand
For higher things, to slay from out thy land
Wild beasts!   See, in mine arms I bear the prize,
That nailed above these portals it may rise
To show what things thy daughters did!   Do thou
Take it, and call a feast.   Proud art thou now
And highly favoured in our valiancy!

CADMUS

O depth of grief, how can I fathom thee
Or look upon thee!—Poor, poor, bloodstained hand!
Poor sisters!—A fair sacrifice to stand
Before God's altars, daughter; yea, and call
Me and my citizens to feast withal!
    Nay, let me weep—for thine affliction most,
Then for mine own.   All, all of us are lost,
Not wrongfully, yet is it hard, from one
Who might have loved—our Bromios, our own!

70

AGAVE

How crabbèd and how scowling in the eyes
Is man's old age!—Would that my son likewise
Were happy of his hunting, in my way,
When with his warrior bands he will essay
The wild beast!—Nay, his valiance is to fight
With God's will!   Father, thou shouldst set him right. . . .
Will no one bring him hither, that mine eyes
May look on his, and show him this my prize!

CADMUS

Alas, if ever ye can know again
The truth of what ye did, what depth of pain
That truth shall bring!   Or were it best to wait
Darkened for evermore, and deem your state
Not misery, though ye know no happiness?

AGAVE

What seest thou here to chide, or not to bless?

CADMUS (*after hesitation, resolving himself*)
Raise me thine eyes to yon blue dome of air!

AGAVE

'Tis done.   What dost thou bid me seek for there?

CADMUS

Is it the same, or changèd in thy sight?

AGAVE

More shining than before, more heavenly bright!

CADMUS

And that wild tremor, is it with thee still?

71

AGAVE (*troubled*)
I know not what thou sayest; but my will
Clears, and some change cometh, I know not how.

CADMUS
Canst hearken then, being changed, and answer, now?

AGAVE
I have forgotten something; else I could.

CADMUS
What husband led thee of old from mine abode?

AGAVE
Echîon, whom men named the Child of Earth.

CADMUS
And what child in Echîon's house had birth?

AGAVE
Pentheus, of my love and his father's bred.

CADMUS
Thou bearest in thine arms an head—what head?

AGAVE
(*beginning to tremble, and not looking at what she carries*)
A lion's—so they all said in the chase.

CADMUS
Turn to it now—'tis no long toil—and gaze.

AGAVE
Ah!   What is this?   What am I carrying here?

72

CADMUS

Look once upon it full, till all be clear!

AGAVE

I see . . . most deadly pain!   Oh, woe is me!

CADMUS

Wears it the likeness of a lion to thee?

AGAVE

No; 'tis the head—O God!—of Pentheus, this!

CADMUS

Blood-drenched ere thou wouldst know him!   Aye, 'tis his.

AGAVE

Who slew him?—How came I to hold this thing?

CADMUS

O cruel Truth, is this thine home-coming?

AGAVE

Answer!   My heart is hanging on thy breath!

CADMUS

'Twas thou.—Thou and thy sisters wrought his death.

AGAVE

In what place was it?   His own house, or where?

CADMUS

Where the dogs tore Actaeon, even there.

AGAVE

Why went he to Kithaeron?   What sought he?

Y   73

453

CADMUS

To mock the God and thine own ecstasy.

AGAVE

But how should we be on the hills this day?

CADMUS

Being mad!   A spirit drove all the land that way.

AGAVE

'Tis Dionyse hath done it.   Now I see.

CADMUS

Ye wronged Him.   Ye denied his deity.

AGAVE (*turning from him*)

Show me the body of the son I love!

CADMUS (*leading her to the bier*)

'Tis here, my child.   Hard was the quest thereof.

AGAVE

Laid in due state?
[*As there is no answer, she lifts the veil of the bier and sees.*
Oh, if I wrought a sin,
'Twas mine!   What portion had my child therein?

CADMUS

He made him like to you, adoring not
The God; who therefore to one bane hath brought
You and this body, wrecking all our line,
And me.   Aye, no man-child was ever mine;
And now this first-fruit of the flesh of thee,
Sad woman, foully here and frightfully

74

Lies murdered!   Whom the house looked up unto,
[*Kneeling by the body.*
O Child, my daughter's child! who heldest true
My castle walls; and to the folk a name
Of fear thou wast; and no man sought to shame
My grey beard, when they knew that thou wast there,
Else had they swift reward!—And now I fare
Forth in dishonour, outcast, I, the great
Cadmus, who sowed the seed-rows of this state
Of Thebes, and reaped the harvest wonderful.
O my belovèd, though thy heart is dull
In death, O still belovèd, and alway
Belovèd!   Never more, then, shalt thou lay
Thine hand to this white beard, and speak to me
Thy "Mother's Father"; ask "Who wrongeth thee?
Who stints thine honour, or with malice stirs
Thine heart?   Speak, and I smite thine injurers!"
But now—woe, woe, to me and thee also,
Woe to thy mother and her sisters, woe
Alway!   Oh, whoso walketh not in dread
Of Gods, let him but look on this man dead!

LEADER

Lo, I weep with thee.   'Twas but due reward
God sent on Pentheus; but for thee . . . 'Tis hard.

AGAVE

My father, thou canst see the change in me,

*   *   *   *   *

*   *   *   *   *

[*A page or more has been here torn out of the MS. from which all our copies of "The Bacchae" are derived. It evidently contained a speech of Agâvê (followed presumably by some words of the Chorus), and an appearance of* DIONYSUS

75

*upon a cloud. He must have pronounced judgment upon the
Thebans in general, and especially upon the daughters of
CADMUS, have justified his own action, and declared his determination to establish his godhead. Where the MS. begins
again, we find him addressing CADMUS.]*

*　　　*　　　*　　　*　　　*

DIONYSUS

*　　　*　　　*　　　*　　　*
*　　　*　　　*　　　*　　　*

And tell of Time, what gifts for thee he bears,
What griefs and wonders in the winding years.
For thou must change and be a Serpent Thing
Strange, and beside thee she whom thou didst bring
Of old to be thy bride from Heaven afar,
Harmonia, daughter of the Lord of War.
Yea, and a chariot of kine—so spake
The word of Zeus—thee and thy Queen shall take
Through many lands, Lord of a wild array
Of orient spears.　And many towns shall they
Destroy beneath thee, that vast horde, until
They touch Apollo's dwelling, and fulfil
Their doom, back driven on stormy ways and steep.
Thee only and thy spouse shall Ares keep,
And save alive to the Islands of the Blest.
　Thus speaketh Dionysus, Son confessed
Of no man but of Zeus!—Ah, had ye seen
Truth in the hour ye would not, all had been
Well with ye, and the Child of God your friend!

AGAVE
Dionysus, we beseech thee.　We have sinned.

DIONYSUS
Too late!　When there was time, ye knew me not.

76

AGAVE

We have confessed.   Yet is thine hand too hot.

DIONYSUS

Ye mocked me, being God; this is your wage.

AGAVE

Should God be like a proud man in his rage?

DIONYSUS

'Tis as my sire, Zeus, willed it long ago.

AGAVE (*turning from him almost with disdain*)

Old Man, the word is spoken; we must go.

DIONYSUS

And seeing ye must, what is it that ye wait?

CADMUS

Child, we are come into a deadly strait,
All; thou, poor sufferer, and thy sisters twain,
And my sad self.   Far off to barbarous men,
A grey-haired wanderer, I must take my road.
And then the oracle, the doom of God,
That I must lead a raging horde far-flown
To prey on Hellas; lead my spouse, mine own
Harmonia, Ares' child, discorporate
And haunting forms, dragon and dragon-mate,
Against the tombs and altar-stones of Greece,
Lance upon lance behind us; and not cease
From toils, like other men, nor dream, nor past
The foam of Acheron find my peace at last.

AGAVE

Father!   And I must wander far from thee!

CADMUS

O Child, why wilt thou reach thine arms to me,
As yearns the milk-white swan, when old swans die?

AGAVE

Where shall I turn me else?   No home have I.

CADMUS

I know not; I can help thee not.

AGAVE

Farewell, O home, O ancient tower!
Lo, I am outcast from my bower,
And leave ye for a worser lot.

CADMUS

Go forth, go forth to misery,
The way Actaeon's father went!

AGAVE

Father, for thee my tears are spent.

CADMUS

Nay, Child, 'tis I must weep for thee;
For thee and for thy sisters twain.

AGAVE

On all this house, in bitter wise,
Our Lord and Master, Dionyse,
Hath poured the utter dregs of pain.

DIONYSUS

In bitter wise, for bitter was the shame
Ye did me, when Thebes honoured not my name.

78

AGAVE

Then lead me where my sisters be;
      Together let our tears be shed,
Our ways be wandered; where no red
Kithaeron waits to gaze on me;
Nor I gaze back; no thyrsus stem,
      Nor song, nor memory in the air.
      Oh, other Bacchanals be there,
Not I, not I, to dream of them!

[AGAVE *with her group of attendants goes out on the side away
  from the Mountain.* DIONYSUS *rises upon the Cloud and
  disappears.*

CHORUS

There be many shapes of mystery.
And many things God makes to be,
      Past hope or fear.
And the end men looked for cometh not,
And a path is there where no man thought.
      So hath it fallen here.   [*Exeunt.*

79

NOTES ON THE BACCHAE

INTRODUCTORY NOTE

THE *Bacchae*, being from one point of view a religious drama, a kind of "mystery play," is highly traditional in form and substance, and repeats a canonical Dionysiac legend, often previously treated; for example, in the *Edoni* of Aeschylus. It is full of allusions both to the myth and to the religion of Dionysus.

1. The Myth, as implied by Euripides. Semelê, daughter of Cadmus, being loved by Zeus, asked her divine lover to appear to her once in his full glory; he came, a blaze of miraculous lightning, in the ecstasy of which Semelê died, giving premature birth to a son. Zeus, to save this child's life and make him truly God as well as Man, tore open his own flesh and therein fostered the child till in due time, by a miraculous and mysterious Second Birth, the child of Semelê came to full life as God.

2. The Religion of Dionysus is hard to formulate or even describe, both because of its composite origins and because of its condition of constant vitality, fluctuation, and development.

(*a*) The first datum, apparently, is the introduction from Thrace of the characteristic God of the wild northern mountains, a God of Intoxication, of Inspiration, a giver of superhuman or immortal life. His worship is superposed upon that of divers native Tree or Vegetation Gods, already

worshipped in Greece. He becomes specially associated
with the Vine. Originally a god of the common folk,
despised and unauthorised, he is eventually so strong as to
be adopted into the Olympian hierarchy as the " youngest "
of the Gods, son of Zeus. His " Olympian " name, so to
speak, is Dionysus, but in his worship he is addressed by
numbers of names, more or less mystic and secret—Bromios,
Bacchios or Baccheus, Iacchos, Eleuthereus, Zagreus,
Sabazios, etc. Some of these may be the names of old
spirits whom he has displaced; some are his own Thracian or
Asiatic names. Together with his many names, he has many
shapes, especially appearing as a Bull, the type of strength,
and a Serpent, which sloughs its skin and renews its life.

(*b*) This religion, very primitive and barbarous, but
possessing a strong hold over the emotions of the common
people, was seized upon and transfigured by the great wave
of religious reform, known under the name of Orphism,
which swept over Greece and South Italy in the sixth
century B.C., and influenced the teachings of such philosophers as Pythagoras, Aristeas, Empedocles, and the many
writers on purification and the world after death. Orphism
may very possibly represent an ancient Cretan religion in
clash or fusion with one from Thrace. At any rate, it was
grafted straight upon the Dionysus-worship, and, without
rationalising, spiritualised and reformed it. Ascetic, mystical, ritualistic, and emotional, Orphism easily excited both
enthusiasm and ridicule. It lent itself both to inspired
saintliness and to imposture. In doctrine it laid especial
stress upon sin and the sacerdotal purification of sin; on the
eternal reward due beyond the grave to the pure and the
impure, the pure living in an eternal ecstasy—" perpetual
intoxication," as Plato satirically calls it—the impure toiling
through long ages to wash out their stains. It recast in
various ways the myth of Dionysus, and especially the story

81

———————————————————————————— 461

of his Second Birth. All true worshippers become in a mystical sense one with the God; they are born again and are "Bacchoi." Dionysus being the God within, the perfectly pure soul is possessed by the God wholly, and becomes nothing but the God.

Based on very primitive rites and feelings, on the religion of men who made their gods in the image of snakes and bulls and fawns, because they hardly felt any difference of kind between themselves and the animals, the worship of Dionysus kept always this feeling of kinship with wild things. The beautiful side of this feeling is vividly conspicuous in *The Bacchae*. And the horrible side is not in the least concealed.

A curious relic of primitive superstition and cruelty remained firmly imbedded in Orphism—a doctrine irrational and unintelligible, and for that very reason wrapped in the deepest and most sacred mystery: a belief in the sacrifice of Dionysus himself, and the purification of man by his blood.

In its agricultural form this rite was harmless enough. Dionysus was the grape and its juice his blood. Osiris was the wheat; the sowing of the grain meant the tearing (Sparagmos) and scattering of his body. But it seems that the savage Thracians, in the fury of their worship on the mountains, when they were possessed by the God and became "wild beasts," actually tore with their teeth and hands any hares, goats, fawns, or the like that they came across. There survives a constant tradition of inspired Bacchanals in their miraculous strength tearing even bulls asunder—a feat, happily, beyond the bounds of human possibility. The wild beast that tore was, of course, the savage God himself. And by one of those curious confusions of thought, which seem so inconceivable to us and so absolutely natural and obvious to primitive men, the beast torn was also the God. The mystic congregations of later times, in their most holy gatherings, solemnly partook of the blood of a bull, which was, by a mystery, the blood of Dionysus-Zagreus himself, the "Bull of God," slain in sacrifice for the purification of man. And the Maenads of poetry and myth, among more beautiful proofs of their superhuman or infra-human character, have always to tear the surrogate of their god in pieces and taste of his blood. It is noteworthy, and throws much light on the spirit of Orphism, that apart from this sacramental tasting of the blood, the Orphic worshipper held it an abomination to eat the flesh of animals at all. The same religious fervour and zeal for purity which made him reject the pollution of animal food, made him at the same time cling to a ceremonial which would utterly disgust the ordinary hardened flesh-eater. It fascinated him just because it was so incredibly primitive and uncanny; because it was a mystery which transcended reason.

It will be observed that Euripides, though certainly familiar with Orphism—which he mentions in *The Hippolytus* and treated at length in *The Cretans*—has in *The Bacchae* gone back behind Orphism to the more primitive stuff from which it was made. He has little reference to any specially Orphic doctrine; not a word, for instance, about the immortality of the soul. And his idealisation or spiritualisation of Dionysus-worship proceeds along the lines of his own thought, not on those already fixed by the Orphic teachers.

P. 8, l. 17, *Asia all, that by the salt sea lies*, etc., *i.e.* the coasts of Asia Minor inhabited by Greeks, Ionia, Aeolis, and Doris.

P. 8, l. 27, *From Dian seed.*—Dian = belonging to Zeus. The name Dionysus seemed to be derived from Διός, the genitive of "Zeus."

P. 9, l. 50, *Should this Theban town essay with wrath and battle*, etc.—This suggestion of a possibility which is never realised or approached is a method often used by the Greek poets for reconciling variant forms of a traditional story. There are traces of a version in which Pentheus led an army.

Pp. 10–14, ll. 64–169.—This first song of the Chorus covers a great deal of Bacchic doctrine and myth. The first strophe, " Oh blessèd he in all wise," etc., describes the bliss of Bacchic purity; the antistrophe gives the two births of Dionysus, from Semelê and from the body of Zeus, mentioning his mystic epiphanies as Bull and as Serpent. The next strophe is an appeal to Thebes, the birthplace or " nurse " of the God's mother, Semelê; the antistrophe, an appeal to the cavern in Crete, the birthplace of Zeus, the God's father, and the original home of the mystic Timbrel. The Epode, or closing song, is full, not of doctrine, but of the pure poetry of the worship.

Pp. 14–22, ll. 170–369, *Teiresias and Cadmus.*—Teiresias seems to be not a spokesman of the poet's own views—far from it—but a type of the more cultured sort of Dionysiac priest, not very enlightened, but ready to abate some of the extreme dogmas of his creed if he may keep the rest. Cadmus, quite a different character, takes a very human and earthly point of view: the God is probably a true God; but even if he is false, there is no great harm done, and the worship will bring renown to Thebes and the royal family. It is noteworthy how full of pity Cadmus is—the sympathetic kindliness of the sons of this world as contrasted with the pitilessness of gods and their devotees. See especially the last scenes of the play. Even his final outburst of despair at not dying like other men (p. 80), shows the same sympathetic humanity.

84

NOTES

Pp. 17 ff., ll. 215–262.—Pentheus, though his case against the new worship is so good, and he might so easily have been made into a fine martyr, like Hippolytus, is left harsh and unpleasant, and very close in type to the ordinary "tyrant" of Greek tragedy (cf. pp. 22, 46). It is also noteworthy, I think, that he is, as it were, out of tone with the other characters. He belongs to a different atmosphere, like, to take a recent instance, Golaud in *Pelléas et Mélisande*.

P. 18, l. 263, *Injurious King*, etc.—It is a mark of the highly traditional style of this play that it allows the Chorus Leader to make remarks which are not "asides," but are yet not heard or noticed by anybody.

P. 18, l. 264, *Sower of the Giants' Sod.*—Cadmus, by divine guidance, slew a dragon and sowed the teeth of it like seed in the "Field of Ares." From the teeth rose a harvest of Earth-born, or "Giant" warriors, of whom Echîon was one.

P. 19, l. 287, *Learn the truth of it, cleared from the false.* —This timid essay in rationalism reminds one of similar efforts in Pindar (e.g. *Ol.* i). It is the product of a religious and unspeculative mind, not feeling difficulties itself, but troubled by other people's questions and objections. (See above on Teiresias.)

P. 19, l. 292, *The world-encircling fire.*—This fire, or ether, was the ordinary material of which phantoms or apparitions were made.

Pp. 21–22, ll. 330–369.—These three speeches are very clearly contrasted. Cadmus, thoroughly human, thinking of sympathy and expediency, and vividly remembering the fate of his other grandson, Actaeon; Pentheus, angry and "tyrannical"; Teiresias speaking like a Christian priest of the Middle Ages, almost like Tennyson's Becket.

85

P. 22, l. 370.—The goddess Ὁσία, " Purity," seems to be one of the many abstractions which were half personified by philosophy and by Orphism. It is possible that the word is really adjectival, " Immaculate One," and originally an epithet of some more definite goddess, e.g. as Miss Harrison suggests, of Nemesis.

In this and other choruses it is very uncertain how the lines should be distributed between the whole chorus, the two semi-choruses, and the various individual choreutae.

P. 26, l. 453, *Marry, a fair shape.*—In Aeschylus' *Edoni* also Dionysus is of almost feminine beauty.

P. 27, l. 471, *These emblems.*—There were generally associated with mysteries, or special forms of worship, certain relics or sacred implements, without which the rites could not be performed. Cf. Hdt. vii. 153, where Telines of Gela stole the sacred implements or emblems of the nether gods, so that no worship could be performed, and the town was, as it were, excommunicated.

P. 30, ll. 493 ff., *The soldiers cut off the tress.*—The stage directions here are difficult. It is conceivable that none of Pentheus' threats are carried out at all; that the God mysteriously paralyses the hand that is lifted to take his rod without Pentheus himself knowing it. But I think it more likely that the humiliation of Dionysus is made, as far as externals go, complete, and that it is not till later that he begins to show his superhuman powers.

P. 31, l. 508, *So let it be.*—The name Pentheus suggests 'mourner,' from *penthos*, ' mourning.'

P. 32, l. 519, *Acheloüs' roaming daughter.*—Acheloüs was the Father of all Rivers.

P. 34, l. 556, *In thine own Nysa.*—An unknown divine

86

mountain, supposed to account for the second part of the name Dionysus.

P. 34, l. 571, *Cross the Lydias*, etc.—These are rivers of Thrace which Dionysus must cross in his passage from the East, the Lydias, the Axios, and some other, perhaps the Haliacmon, which is called "the father-stream of story."

P. 35, l. 579, *A Voice, a Voice.*—Bromios, the God of Many Voices—for, whatever the real derivation, the fifth-century Greeks certainly associated the name with βρέμω, 'to roar'—manifests himself as a voice here and below (p. 62).

Pp. 36–38, ll. 604–641, *Ye Damsels of the Morning Hills*, etc.—This scene in longer metre always strikes me as a little unlike the style of Euripides, and inferior. The earthquake and the accompanying incidents are part of the canonical legend and have to be brought in. Cf. the *Edoni*.

P. 44, ll. 781 ff., *Call all that spur the charger*, etc.—The typical ' Ercles vein ' of the tragic tyrant.

Pp. 46–50, ll. 810 ff.—This scene of the ' hypnotising ' —if one may use the word—of Pentheus probably depends much on the action, which, however, I have not ventured to prescribe. Pentheus seems to struggle against the process all through, to be amazed at himself for consenting, while constantly finding fresh reasons for doing so.

P. 48, l. 822, *Am I a woman, then.*—The robe and coif were, in the original legend, marks of the Thracian dress worn by the Thracian followers of Dionysus, and notably by Orpheus. The tradition became fixed that Pentheus wore such a robe and coif; and to the Greeks of Euripides' time such a dress seemed to be a woman's. Hence this turn of the story.

87

EURIPIDES

P. 51, ll. 877–881.—The refrain of this chorus about the fawn is difficult to interpret. I have practically interpolated the third line ("To stand from fear set free, to breathe and wait"), in order (1) to show the connection of ideas; (2) to make clearer the meaning (as I understand it) of the two Orphic formulæ, "What is beautiful is beloved for ever," and "A hand uplifted over the head of Hate." If I am wrong, the refrain is probably a mere cry for revenge, in the tone of the refrain, "Hither for doom and deed," on p. 58. It is one of the many passages where there is a sharp antagonism between the two spirits of the Chorus, first, as furious Bacchanals, and, secondly, as exponents of the idealised Bacchic religion of Euripides, which is so strongly expressed in the rest of this wonderful lyric.

P. 53, l. 920, *Is it a Wild Bull this?*—Pentheus, in his Bacchic possession, sees fitfully the mystic shapes of the God beneath the human disguise. This second-sight, the exaltation of spirit, and the feeling of supernatural strength come to Pentheus as they came to the two Old Men. But to them the change came peacefully and for good; to Pentheus it comes by force, stormily and for evil, because his will is against the God.

P. 57, l. 976, *O hounds raging and blind.*—i.e. Spirits of Madness. This lyric prepares us for what follows, especially for Agâvê's delusion, which otherwise might have been hard to understand. I have tried to keep the peculiar metre of the original, the dochmiac, with a few simple licences. The scheme is based on ∪́ ∪́∪́ or ∪́‿ ∪́∪́, the latter being much commoner.

Pp. 58–59, ll. 997–1011.—The greater part of this chorus is generally abandoned as unintelligible and corrupt. The last ten lines ("Knowledge, we are not foes," etc.) will, I

88

think, make sense if we accept a very slight conjecture of my own. The four lines before that ("A strait pitiless mind," etc.) are an almost literal translation of the MS. reading, which, however, is incorrect in metre, and therefore cannot be exactly what Euripides wrote.

P. 60, l. 1036, *And deem'st thou Thebes so beggared.*— The couplet is incomplete in the MS. But the sense needed is obvious.

P. 63, l. 1120, *Let it not befall through sin of mine*, etc. —This note of unselfish feeling, of pity and humanity, becomes increasingly marked in all the victims of Dionysus towards the end of the play, and contrasts the more vividly with the God's pitilessness. Cadmus is always gentle, and always thinking of the sufferings of others; and, indeed, so is Agâvê, after her return to reason, though with more resentment against the oppressor.

Pp. 65–69, ll. 1165–1200.—This marvellous scene defies comment. But I may be excused for remarking (1) that the psychological change of the chorus is, to my mind, proved by the words of the original, and does not in the least depend on my interpolated stage directions; (2) the extraordinary exultation of Agâvê is part of her Bacchic possession. It is not to be supposed that, if she had really killed a lion, such joy would be the natural thing.

P. 67, *after* l. 1183, *The Leader tries to speak*, etc.—It is also possible that by some error of a scribe two lines have been omitted in the MS. But I think the explanation given in the text more probable and more dramatic.

P. 68, l. 1195, *And Pentheus, O Mother?*—The Leader mentions Pentheus, I suppose, in order deliberately to test Agâvê's delusion, to see if she is indeed utterly unconscious of the truth.

EURIPIDES

P. 71, l. 1267, *More shining than before*, etc.—The sight of the pure heaven brings back light to her mind—that is clear. But does she mean that the sky is brighter because of her madness which still remains, or that it is brighter now, after having been darkened in her madness?

P. 75, l. 1313, *And now I fare forth in dishonour.*—He has not yet been sentenced to exile, though he might well judge that after such pollution all his family would be banished.

P. 76, l. 1330, *For thou must change and be a Serpent Thing*, etc.—A prophecy like this is a very common occurrence in the last scenes of Euripides' tragedies. " The subject of the play is really a long chain of events. The poet fixes on some portion of it—the action of one day, generally speaking—and treats it as a piece of vivid concrete life, led up to by a merely narrative introduction (the Prologue), and melting away into a merely narrative close. The method is to our taste undramatic, but it is explicable enough. It falls in with the tendency of Greek art to finish, not with a climax, but with a lessening of strain " (*Greek Literature*, p. 267).

The prophecy was that Cadmus and Harmonia should be changed into serpents and should lead a host of barbarian invaders—identified with an Illyrian tribe, the Encheleis—against Hellas; they should prosper until they laid hands on the treasures of Delphi, and then be destroyed. Herodotus says that the Persians were influenced by this prophecy when they refrained from attacking Delphi (Hdt. ix. 42).